San Anselmo Public Library
110 Tunstead Avenue
San Anselmo, CA 94960

SAN ANSELMO LIBRARY

3 1111 02221 2953

DISCARDED

D1550801

CLIMBI
CALIFORNIA'S
FOURTEENERS

Climbing California's
FOURTEENERS

The Route Guide to
the Fifteen Highest Peaks

by Stephen F. Porcella and Cameron M. Burns

THE
MOUNTAINEERS

To Sandy Porcella and Ann Robertson

Published by
The Mountaineers
1001 SW Klickitat Way, Suite 201
Seattle, WA 98134

© 1998 by Stephen F. Porcella and Cameron M. Burns

All rights reserved

First printing 1998, second printing 1999

No part of this book may be reproduced in any form, or by any electronic, mechanical, or other means, without permission in writing from the publisher.

Published simultaneously in Great Britain by Cordee, 3a DeMontfort Street, Leicester, England, LE1 7HD

Manufactured in the United States of America

Edited by Kris Fulsaas
Maps by Gray Mouse Graphics
Cover design by Watson Graphics
Book design by Alice C. Merrill
Layout by Jacqulyn Weber

Cover photograph: *Cameron Burns on the Diamond Arête, Mount Russell* (Photo by Steve Porcella) Backcover inset: Photo by Steve Porcella
Frontispiece: *Dave Wilson on Left Wing Extremist, Mount Whitney* (Photo © Galen Rowell/ Mountain Light) ▪

Library of Congress Cataloging-in-Publication Data
Porcella, Stephen
        Climbing California's fourteeners: the route guide to the fifteen
highest peaks / by Stephen F. Porcella and Cameron M. Burns. — 1st
ed.
            p.   cm.
        Includes bibliographical references and index.
        ISBN 0-89886-555-7
        1. Mountaineering—California—Guidebooks. 2. California—
Guidebooks. I. Burns, Cameron. II. Title.
GV199.42.C22P67 1998
917.9404'53—dc21   97-46406
                                                                                          CIP

 Printed on recycled paper

contents

CALIFORNIA'S FOURTEENERS

preface

Our involvement with California's high mountains formally began in 1989, when we spent four and a half months in the Sierra Nevada. For us it was the opportunity of a lifetime, a chance to totally immerse ourselves in a range that we had visited regularly for more than twenty years.

We knew of the writings and guidebooks printed on Colorado's 14,000-foot peaks. We always felt that "our" Pacific mountains were as big, if not bigger, than those in Colorado, and to us they were the best in the country. There came a time when we knew that a book would eventually be written about California's highest summits and we wanted, more than anything else, for it to do justice to these mountains and the people who climbed them. We thought that, from our previous experience in the range and by setting lofty goals, we could fulfill this tall order.

We started out by attempting to climb every route on every peak. In the end we managed to do about sixty-five different routes on these mountains, eleven of which were new technical routes. This amounted to a little over a third of all of the new and old routes known on these peaks. Walking horizontally, for a change of pace, we completely circumnavigated all but three of the mountains. It is important to realize that we had a heck of a lot of fun.

In between bouts of climbing, during a three-year period following 1989, we spent a total of two months in the Sierra Club Library and the University of California Berkeley's Bancroft Library, digging, hunting, and searching for every tidbit of information on these big mountains. In addition, whenever we had time, we put up flyers at trailheads, camps, and bulletin boards requesting information on these peaks.

The culmination of our efforts produced a manuscript that was 400-plus pages long containing 150-plus photos. No one would publish it. Besides the weight and bulk of such a beast, there was just too much history to hold anyone's attention except ours. The book was too big because we wanted to include everyone's unique story. After five years of sitting on the beast, we finally agreed with The Mountaineers to go through the painful process of editing it down.

Information for these routes came to us in all shapes, sizes, and styles. To the best of our ability, we have tried to sift through what is real and what is not. In the process we found mistakes of all sorts, some that extended back more than a hundred years and that were passed on in subsequent guidebooks like a bad family trait. We confirmed and corrected many of these chronic errors by going out and actually checking those routes on those mountains.

It has not been possible to show or truthfully describe where some routes go. Mostly this has been because we were unable to contact the original first ascensionists or because information in the historical record is limited. In these cases, either the route has not been shown in the photo or, in rare cases, the route has been omitted. C'est la vie.

We have drawn lines on our photos because in some circumstances a line can be worth more than a thousand words about a route. In addition, many people actually prefer a line on a photo to written information. This guidebook gives the reader a choice. You can use the photos together with the written information to make sure that you do not waste time and that you get on the right route. However, if you want to maintain a wilderness experience, you can skip the written information and go with just the line on the photo.

Most important, perhaps, the line on the photo tells you quickly what has not been done. Although many of the biggest, most-direct routes on these peaks have been climbed, there are still countless new routes to do. Throughout our travels we found many walls, gullies, and spaces between those lines on the photos that contained cracks, fissures, and other weaknesses. For those seeking a new route, and a wilderness experience in a pristine country, the possibilities on these mountains are endless.

Trash, Feces, and Karma

Given our own unending awe during our miracle of discovery, in both the Sierra Nevada and the White Mountains, and on Mount Shasta, we were always shocked by the fact that many climbers and hikers still try to stash as much of their unwanted litter as they possibly can. We found plastic packaging wedged between boulders around campsites, litter thrown along the sides of trails, and, worst of all, human excrement and tissue paper placed under rocks next to potable water sources. On routes way up in the sky, we have found climbing tape wedged into cracks next to belay stations, cigarette butts smashed into fissures, and chewing gum pasted to quartzite crystals. Yuck!

During one trip to the Palisade Glacier, we were so stunned that anyone could defile such a pristine area that we began taking photographs for use in this book of the trash and feces left by other groups. We soon ran out of film, but, not to be deterred, we began picking up whatever we could find, loading it in our packs, and carrying it out to the trailhead with us. Most depressing was, when we came back a month later, we found the entire place trashed again.

This brings us to karma.

People, young and old, those just born and those yet to be born, deserve to have California's high mountains left as clean for them as they were left for us.

Anything else is shortchanging the future, upsetting the balance, and destroying the mountains and the environment that brings so much joy, happiness, and peace to everyone. Those who carry out their trash and their feces are doing the Sierra Nevada and the universe a great deed, and to them goes all of the good karma they deserve.

We hope that you enjoy the high peaks of California as much as we have. Mount Shasta, the White Mountains, and the Sierra Nevada are incredibly beautiful places. The adventures you live out among these mountains will form memories and experiences that will last a lifetime.

Be safe, keep the mountains clean and pristine, and good climbing!

Steve Porcella and Cam Burns
May 1997

Acknowledgments

This book could not have been done without the extraordinary help of a number of individuals. First, we thank Kerry and Mary Burns and Robert and Yvonne Porcella for all of their help, encouragement, and support over the years when we worked on this endeavor. We thank Galen Rowell for being very helpful with crucial route information and for providing spectacular photographs. Not only is Galen an excellent climber, photographer, and writer, but he is also a really cool guy. We are grateful for the assistance of Glen Dawson, who took and provided many spectacular photos of the first great climbers and routes done on these peaks. A special thanks to Valerie Cohen, daughter of Ruth Mendenhall, who provided the writings and photographs detailing Ruth and John Mendenhall's ascents on these big mountains. The incredible self-portrait photographs taken by Orlando Bartholomew during his solo winter traverse of the Sierra Nevada were contributed generously by Gene Rose, author and historian of Orlando Bartholomew's winter feat, and Phil Bartholomew, Bart's son. Our idol, David Brower, provided photos, stories, and crucial route information on historic ascents, and he entertained us when we smelled our worst and served us incredible waffles. An unbelievable thank-you goes to Warren Harding for his written contributions and anecdotes and for proving that the legends were all true. If you have never met Dick Beach, you should. He is a great guy and we thank him for the talks, the stories, the written and verbal information, and the photos. Any kid would be lucky to be taught by Dick Beach. Alan Bartlett was extremely helpful in providing detailed route information. Alan also contributed writings for which we are extremely grateful. We thank Doug Robinson for his captivating advice, encouragement, and kind compliments. Dave Trydahl and the people at the White Mountain Research Station opened their doors to two dirtier than dirt climbers who knocked on them. We thank Dave for all of the written information on the station, the photographs, and the hospitality. A special thanks to Craig McCollum for the use of all of his high-quality darkroom equipment. We thank Mike Graber for providing important information on Mount Sill, and Bill Roberts of the Bancroft Library for doing some last-minute file diving. John Fisher provided unique historical information on the traversing of the crest. We thank Gary Hetrick for sharing his knowledge of computers and darkroom physics. Mike Chessler was crucial in providing helpful information and very good advice. Mike Carville was helpful with the new route information on Keeler Needle, while Gerry Adams provided a very detailed description of the first big traverse of the Palisade Crest. Much thanks to Charley Shimanski for opening the AAC library to us. We thank Lito Tejada-Flores for his coolness and his information on Mount Williamson. Robin Ingraham, Jr., was extremely helpful and generous in providing very important information and historical photos. Jules Eichorn was a kick to be around and we began to miss him the moment he left town. Thanks to Dave Bohn for permission to use Norma Clyde's words to describe first ascent route conditions.

We thank the late, great H. Adams Carter for motivating and spurring us on to higher realms. Smoke Blanchard we met in the memories of those who knew him. Saving the best for last, we thank Sandra Elliott Porcella for all of her kind and generous help.

Many other people contributed to the fulfillment of this book in ways big and small. Some of these people climb mountains made of rock or snow and some climb mountains made of the mind or of the hands. We acknowledge all of them for their help, friendliness, generosity, and kindness. Thanks to Lesley Gaunt of the Mount Whitney Ranger Station; Howard Grice, John Louth, and Keith Waterfall—all of the White Mountain Ranger Station; Mike, Penny, Jessica, Natalie, and Kate Sandy; Bob and Sylvia Robertson; Leif Voeltz of the 5th Season; David Alt; Walt Borneman; the "Neecer" Waterbury; James Wilson of Wilson's East Side Sports; Andy Stone; Luke Laeser; Marc Jensen; Marian Helling; Keith Osborne; Steve Roper; Vittoria Lee Porcella; Royal Robbins; Angelo Burtoni Lorenzo Porcella; Ethan, Iris, and Walden Putterman; John Caratti; Daniel Waterhead "let's climb something really heinous" McCollum; a special thanks to John Swanson; thanks also to Ralph Judd; Bob Belland; Tom Schwan; Patti Rosa; Brian "Big B" Stevenson; Bob Evans; Kit Tilly; Jim Bono; Dan "the Man" Hogan; Cris Grant; Big John Carlson; Mike Chaussee; Tom Deunsing; Martina and Jos Van Putten; Jeanne Wilson; Merry Schrumpf; "mad dog" Karstens; Jean and Sabrina DeLataillade; Jon Butler; Jesse Harvey; Mike and Claire Schillaci; Paul "The Beaver" McBride; Burton and Betsy Elliott of Elliott's Trans-Sierra Flight Service; Susan, Sally, and Steve Elliott; Culley White; Kevin Ball of the White Mountain Research Station; Don Porcella; Greg, Madhu, Sarina, and Robbie Porcella; Dan "I'm freezing my ass off" Rothenburg; Dennis Junt; Grey Thompson; Peter Croft; Bruce Chesebro; Puppy-Doug Bryant; Tom Wilkie; Brian Cooper; Eric Bjornstad; Doug Scott; Adrian Burgess; Dave Wilson; Ligon; R. J. Secor; Bill Oliver; John Moynier; Claude Fiddler; Pete Lowry; Pete Dolan; Don Hampton; everyone at the Sierra Club Library; Dave Zendher; Kevin Sugar; Gary Powell; Suresh Subramani; Dave Scheven; Don Craig; Dave Ingal; Eric Ishigo; Frank Crowley; Mike McDermott; Tim, Suzanne, Nick, Vince, Eric, Mike, Mimi, and Elie Byrd; Charlie Fowler; Bruce Anderson; Mike Merenda; Tim Churchill; Paul Klink; Jon "Eck!" Eck; Guilliermo Pinot; Rick, Nancy, Susan, Aerial, and Elise Torre; Craig Kenyon; Rod Sutherland; Hal Herring; Elmo; Hobbes; Scott Allen; and, of course, Gillian Burns.

Caution

This book is not intended to instruct the reader in the techniques of modern rock climbing or mountaineering. Both activities are hazardous, and it is the responsibility of the individual to learn and understand the proper techniques for safe participation in those activities. The individual also assumes all risks, damages, or injury that may result from improper use of this guidebook. Although we have given some information about rock-climbing techniques, this guidebook is not meant as a substitute for personal instruction by a qualified person. Route descriptions detail a specific line up the mountain. Many variations exist and it is up to the individual climbing party to make the best choices for their own safety.

Norman Clyde on Devils Crag, setting his sights on the Palisades to the east (Photo by David Brower)

introduction

In 1776, while war raged on America's eastern seaboard and a nation was being born, Pedro Font, a Franciscan missionary attached to the Anza expedition, was sent north to explore *alta California*. Reaching the current site of San Francisco, Font climbed a nearby hill and, looking east, gazed upon a broad plain, behind which stood a massive range of mountains, "*una gran sierra nevada.*" Font placed the "Sierra Nevada" range on his crude map of California and, ever since, European explorers, adventurers, and wanderers of all manner have sought out the high mountains of the Golden State for direction, resources, and, perhaps most important of all, wilderness experience and physical health.

Of course, it's highly probable that the white man's exploits among the high mountains of California have eclipsed the likelihood that some of the summits were reached by indigenous peoples who came many centuries before Señor Font.

Spanish missionaries were followed, in course, by trappers, miners, shepherds, and settlers, eager to seek out furs, minerals, and a new life.

It wasn't until the California Geological Survey came onto the scene that recorded, well-planned, exploratory mountaineering was introduced. The organization's impressive list of first ascents and explorations throughout the state in a small way inspired common folk to pursue climbing mountains as a leisure activity or, in some cases, a competitive activity complete with the award of recognition.

The 14,000-foot peaks in California, which are the subject of this book, are another subject altogether from those in Colorado or Washington. In most cases, the California peaks are steep, sheer-walled spires, many of which require technical, Class 5 climbing skills to reach the summit. In addition, most of these peaks are also much less accessible than Colorado's 14,000-foot mountains, meaning their summits are less frequently trodden and their surrounds are generally pristine wilderness. What they lack in number they more than adequately make up in providing numerous precipitous walls, spectacular summit monoliths, and incredibly great relief vistas.

11

Besides the sheer technical demands of California's high mountains, each peak has a character, an allure all its own. There's the shimmering white east face of Mount Whitney, with its long, committing technical routes illuminated by crimson, early morning sunlight; the wild, complex twin-summitted spire of Split Mountain with its fluted arêtes composed of red, yellow, gray, and black rock; the brooding hulk of the North Palisade, with its superb alpine routes; the surreal high-altitude desert summit of White Mountain; and the glaciated volcanic mass of Mount Shasta. The list goes on and the superlatives are endless.

Many people have come to the Sierra Nevada to explore and to climb. Some of these individuals are John Muir, Clarence King, David Brower, and Joseph N. Le Conte. These people were originally climbers who later became famous for their exploits other than those endured on these high peaks. Throughout the research for this book, one individual stood apart from all the rest: Norman Clyde. Clyde's legacy began and ended in the Sierra Nevada. There are many books and texts that discuss his remarkable personality, his literary exploits, or even the incredible mass of his mammoth packs. This book is not the time or place to discuss these things. Instead, we mention that it was on these big peaks that Clyde left his mark.

On these mountains and others throughout the range, Clyde amassed a list of adventurous first ascents that borders on legendary status today. The routes, the first ascents, or in some cases the first descents on these high mountains, many times solo, are to this day still looked upon with awe and trepidation. Clyde pushed human endurance and climbing skill to a level that many advanced mountaineers and climbers still cannot match today. Interestingly, you will never find a quote or passage of Clyde's that alludes to any type of fear, loneliness, or self-doubt during his vagabond climbing life. Rather, he was solid and purposeful, and he was as much a part of these mountains as they were of him. Norman Clyde and this range of rock and light were and perhaps still are one and the same.

When reading Clyde's personal accounts of his travels through the Sierra, we were struck by the impressive natural state of the range back then. Alas, times change and, while it may be good for the collective human consciousness for more people to hike and climb, it is not always the best for preserving the natural state of wild places. The following are some guidelines for keeping the mountains clean and wild.

Wilderness Ethics

The preservation of the natural mountain environment, for the experience and enjoyment of future generations, is the responsibility of all who visit the high places. The accumulation of human feces and trash is the single greatest problem in the Sierra Nevada today.

Keep the Sierra Nevada Pristine

Dispose of human feces as follows. If you are in the Mount Whitney basin, use the composting toilets. If you are off the trail in a large forest, bury it 6–8 inches deep. If you are above timberline in a popular area, pack it out (more on this below). If above timberline and far, far away from people, spread it out as thinly as possible on a rock facing the sun. If you are on a glacier (for example, Palisade Glacier), use a crevasse. *If you use toilet paper, always pack it out.*

Those who carry out their feces from the popular routes are great mountaineers in the truest sense and deserve all the good karma they get. Small paper lunch bags (to poop in), filled with some lime or kitty litter, and a strong, polyvinyl plastic bag (to store and carry the paper bags out) is a system that works wonders. Leave the bag open while camping so that the excrement can dry to a lightweight, less odorous form.

Eight Commandments to Keep the Mountains Clean

1. Carry out more trash than you carry in, even if it is not yours.
2. Never camp, or leave human feces, urine, toothpaste, or soap, within 200 feet of a water source.
3. Leave the area as you found it. Keep any fires small and build them only in existing fire rings and only where safe and legally permitted. When done with your fire ring, take it apart and return the area to its natural state. Leave flowers, rocks, and other natural features undisturbed. Don't create tent ditches.
4. Don't place bolts on established routes or summits.
5. Don't make ducks or cairns. These can mislead people.
6. Use neutral-colored rappel slings. Bright colors are unsightly.
7. Stay on the trails. Cutting across switchbacks causes irreparable erosion that wears our mountains down faster.
8. Always fill out a wilderness permit with the local land management agency, such as the U.S. Forest Service, National Park Service, and Bureau of Land Management.

Safety Considerations

In the world of mountaineering, the mountaineer's single most important consideration is safety. The life of a climber, yours and your companions', should always be your number-one priority. Every aspect of your climb should revolve around safety, for among California's 14,000-foot peaks there is no room for error. On many of these high peaks, climbers young and old, experienced and inexperienced, have died. No route, no climb, no mountain is worth the life of a human being.

Modern equipment, from good footwear to specific rock- and ice-climbing equipment, allows almost anyone with ambition the means with which to climb difficult routes. However, common sense and experience also are necessary for safe and enjoyable climbing. In addition, knowing how to read the weather, knowing rope-handling skills, knowing first aid in high-mountain environments, dealing with potential rock- and icefall, and knowing how to perform self-rescue are equally important. In the following subsections, we discuss each of these topics, how they relate to California's highest peaks, and why they are important for safe and enjoyable climbing.

Using a Rope and Protection

On many of the 14,000-foot summits in the Sierra Nevada, the easiest route can be quite difficult due to steepness, exposure, or the presence of ice. For these reasons we suggest the use of a rope for the ascent and descent of some of these peaks. The first step in using a rope to safeguard an ascent is to know proper rope-handling techniques. These techniques run the gamut from lead climbing on a rope, setting an anchor and belaying a partner, and rappelling. There are many books on this subject but, unfortunately, books cannot substitute for actually getting out and practicing these important techniques. We strongly encourage all beginners or aspiring climbers to practice on the little cliffs and crags near their homes before setting out on these big peaks. Being on a high California peak with an approaching storm or accident in progress is no place to realize that your rope skills are lacking. Currently, there are many qualified guide schools that teach courses on rope-handling technique. Unless you are proficient and experienced on Class 4 and 5 rock, we strongly suggest that you take such a course before attempting some of the more difficult peaks. Check with your local mountaineering shop or outdoor club for listings of mountaineering and climbing schools and the courses that are available.

In addition to rope training, the art of placing and removing protection, or "pro," as it is commonly called, is the second most important aspect of climbing. The rock in the Sierra Nevada is generally very good (compared to most other places in the United States). We found that a set of wires or stoppers, along with a set of camming devices and/or hexes, a bunch of lightweight carabiners (enough for all pieces and webbing) and lots of 1-inch tubular webbing—ten to twelve 5-foot pieces—individually tied with a water knot and thrown over the shoulder, are sufficient for almost all of the routes in this book. The ten to twelve pieces of tied tubular webbing are very important because they allow you the possibility of untying so as to put them around a horn, tree branch, or notch for rappelling. Sewn slings and tapped quick draws do not allow this extremely important flexibility. If possible, you should never trust old or dated webbing for rappelling. With some of the more extreme technical routes, specific gear is needed, but a list of that equipment is provided in those route descriptions.

Your Athletic Ability, Experience, and Judgment

Once you know proper rope techniques and the art of placing pro, the next step is to know your own limits and, most importantly, those of the people in your party. Know when to back down. In numerous incidents on the high peaks, an experienced climber refused to acknowledge slower and less-experienced climbers in the group. In almost every incident, someone was hurt or killed.

Make sure that your ability and that of your partners are somewhat equally matched on the harder routes on these mountains. If any of you have difficulty, can one of you lead the way to safety? In addition, know how to communicate with your partner in potentially adverse conditions. If the leader is 150 feet out from you, in a snowstorm, high winds, or darkness, do you have a system of com-

munication? It can be as simple as five hard, consecutive pulls on the rope to sig-
nify off belay/you are on belay. Perhaps most important is to have a climbing system down, a way that both of you deal with rope management, equipment, haul
bags, jumaring, etc. Make sure you and your partner have the same style of climbing, that you do things and think about things in a similar fashion. For example,
on a long route with darkness coming on, if you are good with leading cracks
and placing natural gear (camming devices, stoppers, hexes, etc.), yet you are tired
and need a break, will your partner, who is good at leading 5.12+ bolted sport
routes, be able to lead the next two 5.10 crack pitches that will get you off the
mountain? One thousand feet off the deck is no place to learn that the two of
you have totally different styles of climbing.

Knowing when to back down off of a route is often the most important at-
tribute one can have in the mountains. Knowing when to stop can often mean
the difference between returning to a warm sleeping bag or, at the very least, spending a hypothermic night on a peak. If you find yourself trying to decide whether
you should continue climbing or retreat, just remember that it is better to stay on
the conservative side. The mountain will always be there for another day when
the weather might be more favorable, or when your abilities and experience have
improved.

Last, it is important to understand that your limits and judgment may be
impaired by altitude, weather conditions, rock conditions, and fatigue. These im-
pairments can be subtle in their presentation, but devastating in their influence.
Listen to and watch your partners and yourself. Common sense and conservative
decisions are the keys to safety and thrilling success on these mountains. Currently, there are many qualified guide schools that can instruct and give pointers
on these cognitive aspects of being safe in the mountains.

Clothing and Outdoor Gear

We strongly argue against the use of cotton of any type except for one T-shirt
for extremely hot weather. Obviously, a good layering system involving
polypropylene and/or wool is essential, especially at high altitude. We recommend
medium-weight polypropylene long underwear, a double or triple layer of socks
(no cotton!), sturdy boots or shoes, a wool or polyester pullover, and a light but
waterproof jacket. A hat and pair of gloves aren't essential, but they can become
very important if the weather turns cold or wet. Wear a helmet on technical climbing routes. Besides protecting your head from falls, rockfall, or impacts, it keeps
you warm.

If you're planning to camp or bivouac in the mountains, a good sleeping bag
can mean the difference between agony and ecstasy. Consult with your local
mountain shop about bags temperature-rated for the season and location of your
climb. We have found 0-degree-Fahrenheit bags to be the minimum for "under
the stars" comfort during the summer. In winter a bag rated at -20 to -30 degrees
Fahrenheit should be taken for these mountains. Both down-filled and poly-
fiber-filled bags work well on California's fourteeners.

Self-portrait of Orlando Bartholomew during his 1928 winter traverse of the Sierra Nevada; the west face of Split Mountain and the Horseshoe Arête in the background (Photo courtesy of Phil Bartholomew)

The Ten Essentials

Be prepared for emergencies of any kind by always packing the Ten Essentials—even on a day trip.

1. **Extra clothing**—wool or polypro in case what you're wearing gets soaked or you get cold.
2. **Extra food**—bring enough food for another day's meals.
3. **Sunglasses**—protect your eyes from the sun's UV exposure and glare.
4. **Pocket knife**—this basic instrument has a multitude of uses in the backcountry.
5. **Flashlight**—bring extra batteries and an extra bulb.
6. **Matches** or lighter—pack these in a waterproof container.
7. **Firestarter**—this helps in wet weather when wood isn't dry enough for matches alone to start a fire.
8. **First-aid kit**—tailor its contents to your trip, and know how to use it.

9. **Map**—bring a detailed topographical map of the area. Covering the map with clear packing tape will waterproof it and make it last forever.
10. **Compass**—know how to use it!

Hypothermia and Altitude Sickness

These two ailments are probably indirectly responsible for more accidents in the mountains than anything else. Hypothermia can occur almost anywhere under any conditions. Altitude sickness affects people differently and can sometimes affect a person at elevations as low as 8,000 feet.

There is not enough space in this guidebook to thoroughly discuss hypothermia and altitude sickness and their treatments. Inform yourself about these important topics; read other books or take a wilderness first-aid course. Know how altitude sickness and hypothermia can occur, and how they should be treated. Know that both can be insidious in their presentation, affecting judgment and stamina long before you are aware. Do not go into the mountains without this crucial information. Odds are that if you climb all of California's fourteeners, you will experience one or both of these conditions at some point in time. Written material on these two very important topics can be found at your local mountain shop or library.

Weather

Check the weather reports before you leave. Know how to read cloud types and shapes, what they mean, and what they portend. Electrical storms are vey common on all of California's high peaks, and numerous people have been struck by lightning on them. If you see a few dark clouds appearing early in the morning, it might be wise to wait and see what happens, or even reschedule your climb for another day. Lightning strikes occur in the bottoms of valleys, on small ridges, and near summits. There is good information in various instructional mountaineering books on what to do in case you are caught in an electrical storm while on the summit of a peak. Know this information well.

Because of the altitude of these high mountains, a sudden rain shower or onset of high winds can trigger a sudden drop in temperature. Always take enough clothing to prevent hypothermia.

A foot of snow in July. If you have never heard about this in the Sierra Nevada, we are here to tell you that it happens, and if you are unprepared you will be miserable. In the winter it can be much worse, with snow levels from a single storm ranging from 1 to 12 feet. The best prevention is to be prepared and to check the long-range forecasts. One of the benefits of the range being in California is that the Pacific provides a vast, blank canvas upon which storms can be tracked and monitored. Before you start a big trip, know what is happening in the Pacific. If there is a massive storm coming down from the Aleutians or churning up from Baja, you might want to postpone your trip, or pack extra gear. When you are on a route, most storms in the Sierra will give a little bit of warning (provided you are not on the blindside of the mountain!). Be aware, however, that no matter where you are, storms can develop and be upon you literally within minutes on White Mountain or Shasta.

Rock- and Icefall

On many of the routes in this guidebook, rock- and icefall are minimal, but they are not *completely* unlikely. There is no way to prevent danger from ice- and rockfall other than to avoid areas where it is frequent. In general, a couloir containing darkly stained snow or ice usually indicates present rock- or icefall. It is best to avoid such an area even if it is, for example, the U-Notch on North Palisade. This is perhaps the most important reason for wearing a helmet.

Bears

Bears are a real problem at Whitney Portal (see chapter 3, Mount Whitney) and at Anvil Camp (see chapter 5, Mount Williamson) and are starting to populate Cottonwood Lakes Basin as well (see chapter 1, Mount Langley). They have not been seen in the North Fork of Lone Pine Creek, yet. In order to keep them from being attracted to new areas, tie up your food whenever possible and do not leave any food-related items (dirty dishes, food wrappers, etc.) out. Anything that contains food remnants or odors, even toothpaste, should be hung out of reach.

Rescue

When you plan a trip into the backcountry, realize that you are on your own. Although there is search and rescue available, plan as though it is not. Because of the ruggedness and isolation of the Sierra Nevada, it takes a great deal of time to reach and evacuate people with serious injuries. Seriously injured people can— and often do—die of exposure due to the time required for rescue. Remember, it is especially important to take all necessary precautions to prevent an accident in the backcountry.

To initiate a search, the party must be missing for a minimum of 24 hours and a member of the immediate family (next of kin) must request a search. Rescues are coordinated by the Sheriff's Office, which determines the involvement of other agencies such as the China Lake Mountain Rescue Group.

For the Sierra Nevada, Mount Shasta, and White Mountain, in the event that a rescue is needed, get to a phone and dial 911.

For the Sierra Nevada and White Mountain, two other phone numbers to use are: Sheriff's Office in Lone Pine, (619) 876-5606; Sheriff's Office in Independence, (619) 878-2441, 24-hour dispatch line.

For Mount Shasta rescues, the Siskiyou County Sheriff's Department is responsible. It can be reached by dialing 911 or (916) 926-2552.

Wilderness Regulations

Simply put, wilderness permits for overnight camping are required year-round for hiking or climbing on all of the 14,000-foot peaks in the Sierra Nevada. The following is the most up-to-date information available as of this writing.

Sierra Nevada

The regulation of wilderness permits is a constantly changing phenomenon sensitive to the amount of traffic frequenting the high Sierra. Wilderness permits for overnight camping are required year-round. If you are not carrying your permit, a ranger can and probably will issue a citation. Permits are generally not required for day use (non-overnight trips) except in the Mount Whitney Zone (see section below).

During the heavy use period of summer, all of the best access trails to the 14,000-foot peaks are subject to quotas, except for Red Lake Trail (see chapter 7, Split Mountain). A set number of people are allowed to enter the wilderness each day, limiting the number of people allowed to camp overnight in the wilderness area. Quotas help protect the wilderness resource and provide a quality backcountry experience for everyone. Because the quota is based on entry date and entry trail, hikers may enter only on the entry date and trail specified on their permit. For all areas except the Mount Whitney Zone, the quota time period extends from the last Friday in June through September 15.

The Mount Whitney Zone

The Mount Whitney Zone's boundaries are, to the east, just above Lone Pine Lake; to the west, at the outlet of Timberline Lake; to the north, along the Sequoia National Park–Inyo National Forest boundary to Mount Russell (on the west side of the boundary line); and to the south, along the crest from trail crest to Arc Pass. The Mount Whitney Zone is jointly managed by Inyo National Forest and Sequoia–Kings Canyon National Parks. For climbers attempting routes on any of the east faces above Iceberg Lake, accessed via the North Fork of Lone Pine Creek, the zone starts at the notch of the Mountaineer's Route and at the crest of the technical routes.

The Mount Whitney Zone has a "destination" quota. This destination quota means that a Zone Stamp is required for day hikers, backpackers, and climbers who enter this area, regardless of their entry point. In other words, if you are a climber about to top out on an east-face route somewhere on Whitney, with rack, haul bag, and whatever, you had better have your Zone Stamp on your wilderness permit. A ranger could be standing there, on the Whitney Portal Trail, ready to cite you if you don't have one. This zone quota is in effect from May 22 through October 15.

All persons in the Mount Whitney Zone are required to have a special Zone Stamp on their permit to enter or exit the Mount Whitney Zone. This stamp can be issued at any point that is issuing the Mount Whitney Zone permit.

For day hikes in the Mount Whitney Zone, permits are required. Day hike permits are valid only for the date printed on the permit. Hikers wishing to start *before* midnight (using a full moon as a light source) need an overnight permit to access the trail.

Obtaining a Permit

Web sites: For the most current information available on wilderness permits and regulations, visit the following web sites. For the Sierra Nevada, much of the following updated information is available at the Inyo National Forest On-Line Information Source (www.r5.pswfs.gov/inyo/index.htm). For wilderness permits, there's a sub-site (www.r5.pswfs.gov/inyo/vvc/permits.htm).

National parks: For trips originating in Yosemite or Sequoia–Kings Canyon National Parks, obtain a permit from the appropriate park office. The permit covers wilderness travel into adjacent national forest wildernesses for the duration of the trip. If a permit is issued for entry on the national forest, it is valid for travel in the national park *as long as it is noted on the permit.*

Permits outside the quota period: Permits outside the quota period for trails outside the Mount Whitney Zone are available on a self-issue basis at Inyo National Forest ranger stations from September 16 through the last Thursday in June. Permits outside the quota period for the Mount Whitney Zone are available on a self-issue basis from October 16 through May 21 at Inyo National Forest ranger stations.

Obtaining permits without a reservation: Permits that have not been reserved through the Inyo National Forest Wilderness Reservation Service (see section below) may be obtained on a first-come, first-served basis starting the day before entry. These permits can be picked up at any Inyo National Forest ranger station. Demand for permits is high on Fridays, Saturdays, and holidays.

Maximum group size is fifteen persons. Certain organized groups and educational institutions may require an Outfitter/Guide special-use permit. Call a Forest Service ranger station for more information.

The entrance stations at Rock Creek and Bishop Creek are closed. Permits for Big Pine Creek are not available at the Upper Sage Flat campground. Please pick up permits at a ranger station.

Inyo National Forest Wilderness Reservation Service (INFWRS): A private contractor, Inyo National Forest Wilderness Reservation Service, now takes reservations and issues reserved permits. A reservation application may be obtained or downloaded via the Internet at the web site mentioned above. Overnight use on quota trails throughout the Inyo National Forest is 100 percent reservable through this service. Reservations are accepted from six months in advance up to two days before entry on the trail. Permits for non-quota trails are available at any Inyo National Forest ranger station, or through the reservation service for convenience.

Inyo National Forest Wilderness Reservation Service is located in the Big Pine Chamber of Commerce (126 South Main Street North, Highway 395). The mailing address is P.O. Box 430, Big Pine, CA 93513; phone (760) 938-1136; fax & TTY (760) 938-1137; toll-free phone (888) 374-3773. Hours are 8:00 A.M. to 4:30 P.M., Monday to Friday in winter, seven days a week in summer.

Fees for the reservation service (there is no charge for wilderness permits) are: Overnight permits for all trails, $3.00 per person. Mount Whitney Zone Stamp (on overnight permits), $1.00 per person in addition. Mount Whitney day hike permit, $2.00 per person. Payment is accepted by credit card (Visa, MasterCard, American Express, Discover Card, and EuroVisa), check, or money order. Make checks payable to INFWRS.

A trip itinerary will be requested when a reservation is made. All permits reserved through INFWRS will be mailed directly to the party leader. If requested, or if the reservation is made within a week of entry, the permit can be sent to the ranger station chosen by the reserver. Reserved permits for the following day will be put in an outside pickup box for the convenience of reservation holders who arrive after office hours.

When reserving a wilderness permit, we recommend using the phone to call in reservations. This enables the reserver to immediately know the status of the request, and the reservation agent can make alternate suggestions. If you are writing or faxing a request, list at least two alternate starting dates and/or trails, in order of preference. Chances of obtaining a reservation are greater if party size is kept small and starting dates are other than Friday, Saturday, or holiday weekends. Include your phone number in case there are questions regarding your reservation request.

Please notify Inyo National Forest Wilderness Reservation Service as soon as possible with cancellations or reduction in party size in order to help other wilderness users obtain permits. INFWRS offers a refund policy for cancellations. The reserved permit must be returned before a refund can be processed.

Status of trails: The following list of approach trails gives information regarding their reservation status, quota, level of use, and restrictions.

Cottonwood Lakes Trail is reservable. The quota is 60 people per day. Use is heavy and no fires are allowed. Only 12 of the 60 people accessing the Cottonwood Lakes Trail each day may enter the Mount Whitney Zone.

George Creek Trail has no quota. Use is light. No dogs are allowed in the area (Bighorn Sheep Zoological Area). Cross-country travel and entry into the area is limited (open April 15–May 15 and December 15–January 1).

Mount Whitney Trail (overnight) quota is 50 people per day. Use is heavy. The quota period is May 22–October 15. No camping is permitted at Mirror Lake or Trailside Meadow. No fires are permitted. Toilets are located at Outpost and Trail Camps.

Mount Whitney Trail (day hikes) quota is 150 people and use is heavy. The quota period is May 22–October 15. No fires are allowed. Toilets are located at Outpost and Trail Camps.

North Fork Lone Pine Creek Trail is reservable. The quota is 15 people per day and use is moderate. The quota period is May 22–October 15. No fires are allowed. Cross-country travel is prevalent; this is primarily a drainage that provides access to climbing routes on Mount Whitney (Class 3–5).

Shepherd Pass Trail is reservable. The quota is 15 people per day and use is moderate. No fires are allowed at Anvil Camp. No dogs are allowed (Bighorn Sheep Zoological Area). Cross-country travel and entry into Mount Williamson area are limited. Open only December 15–July 15.

North Fork Big Pine Trail is reservable. The quota is 24 people per day and use is heavy. Campfires are prohibited.

South Fork Big Pine Trail is reservable. The quota is 12 people per day and use is moderate. Campfires are prohibited.

Bishop Pass Trail is reservable. The quota is 36 people per day and use is heavy. Campfires are prohibited in the Bishop Pass area. Refer to the Sequoia–Kings Canyon National Parks regulations for park travel.

Red Lake Trail has no quota and use is moderate.

White Mountain

As of this writing, no wilderness permits are required for hiking to the summit of White Mountain, nor is any registration process in effect. However, if you plan on using a stove to cook on, you need to get a campfire permit from a suitable ranger station. There is basically no wood anywhere near the summit of White Mountain, but the permit is required even if you are only using a stove in this area.

Mount Shasta

Wilderness permits are required for Mount Shasta. Currently there is no charge or quota for these permits. Overnight permits may be obtained at Mount Shasta Ranger Station, 204 West Alma Street, Mount Shasta City, CA 96067; (916) 926-4511. Hours are 8:00 A.M. to 4:30 P.M., Monday to Friday.

Day use permits may be obtained at the Mount Shasta Ranger Station during normal working hours or after hours, or at the Bunny Flat Trailhead. Overnight wilderness permits cannot be obtained at the Bunny Flat Trailhead. Call the Mount Shasta Ranger Station before you arrive in the town of Mount Shasta in order to receive the most current information available on wilderness permits.

A Mount Shasta recreational Parking Daily Pass is required for North Gate, Brewer Creek, and Clear Creek Trailheads. The cost of this pass is $5.00 per vehicle per day.

A Mount Shasta Summit Pass is required for each person climbing the mountain. The pass is good for three days from the time of purchase and costs $15.00 per person. Season parking passes and summit passes are also available.

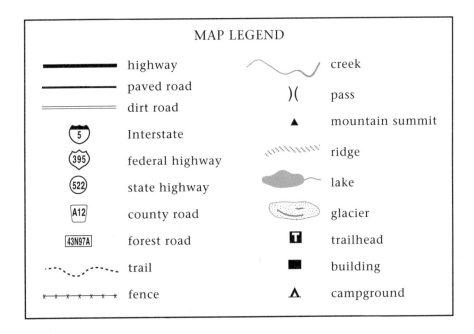

MAP LEGEND

highway		creek	
paved road		pass	
dirt road			
Interstate		mountain summit	
federal highway		ridge	
state highway		lake	
county road		glacier	
forest road		trailhead	
trail		building	
fence		campground	

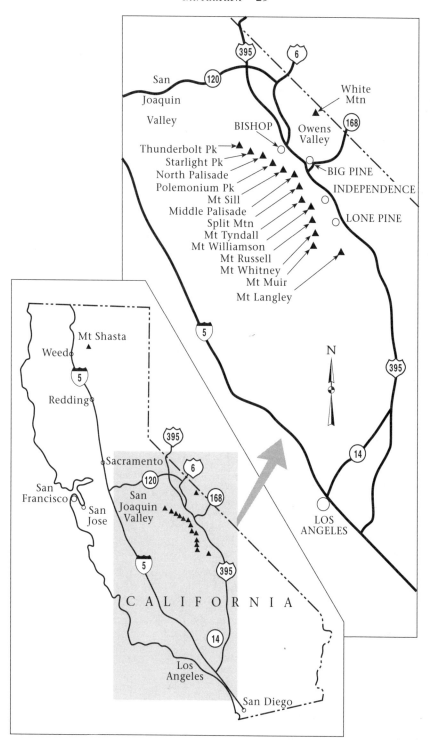

395

6

San
Joaquin
Valley

120

White
Mtn

BISHOP

Owens
Valley

168

Thunderbolt Pk
Starlight Pk
North Palisade
Polemonium Pk
Mt Sill
Middle Palisade
Split Mtn
Mt Tyndall
Mt Williamson
Mt Russell
Mt Whitney
Mt Muir
Mt Langley

BIG PINE
INDEPENDENCE

LONE PINE

5

N

395

14

LOS
ANGELES

Mt Shasta
Weed
5
Redding

Sacramento
395
6
120
168
San
Joaquin
Valley
San
Francisco
San
Jose
5
395

C A L I F O R N I A

14

Los
Angeles

San Diego

Access to California's 14,000-foot Peaks

Nearly all of California's 14,000-foot peaks are located within a 100-mile radius of the town of Bishop, California. Bishop lies directly east of San Jose, and directly north of Los Angeles on the eastern side of the Sierra Nevada. It can be reached by Highway 395 from the north or south. The other towns mentioned in this guidebook, Big Pine, Independence, and Lone Pine, lie south of Bishop, 15 miles, 40 miles, and 58 miles, respectively. Route descriptions for the 14,000-foot peaks of the Sierra Nevada begin at these towns.

To get to Bishop from the north (San Francsico, Merced, and Sacramento), drive east toward Yosemite and get on Highway 120. After crossing Tioga Pass, turn south (right) onto Highway 395. Tioga Pass is subject to winter closure and may not open until late spring.

From the south (Los Angeles and San Diego), the quickest way to get to Bishop is via Interstate 5 north to Highway 14 north. Continue on Highway 14 until it merges with Highway 395 near Inyokern. You will pass through Lone Pine, Independence, and Big Pine on the way up Highway 395 to Bishop.

White Mountain Peak is reached by driving east from the town of Big Pine on Highway 168. The description in this guidebook for White Mountain Peak begins at Big Pine.

Mount Shasta lies in the northern portion of the state and is best reached by driving north on Interstate 5 from most cities in California. The route description for getting to the base of the peak begins at the town of Mount Shasta, which is 59 miles north of Redding on Interstate 5.

How to Use This Book

Each of the fifteen chapters in this book covers one of the fifteen 14,000-foot peaks of California. The sequence of chapters is from south to north. Each chapter begins with information that details historical exploration of the peak, including the naming of the peak, mountain geography, and the first ascent, and subsequent new routes or lines of ascent follow. Numerous historical photos have been included in this book to provide more information on particular routes and the people who climbed them. In some instances these photos can provide quite a bit of information.

Then the various approaches are given for reaching the different routes on the different faces and aspects of the peak. Most of the detailed information on approaches to these mountains is targeted to the east side of the Sierra Nevada. We have mentioned how to get to these mountains from the west, but we did not include extensive descriptions, trailhead approaches, and maps for this direction of approach. The reason we did not provide information on most western, southern, and northern approaches is simple. All of the 14,000-foot peaks in the Sierra Nevada are closest to, and most easily reached from, the east side of the range. We don't want to discourage people from approaching these mountains from the west, north, or south; however, be forewarned that in many cases approach hikes of 20 miles or more may be required as compared to the relatively short approach from the east. **The information that is provided on the west-**

ern, northern, and southern approaches assumes the reader has some knowledge of the John Muir Trail, the High Sierra Trail, and the Scenic Trail. If you are intent upon approaching these peaks from these alternative directions, consult the appropriate topographical maps listed below to gain more information on the various trailheads and trails used to accomplish this. Regardless of the direction of approach, once you are in the vicinity of these mountains, the route descriptions are equal in quantity and quality of information regardless of the face or side of the mountain that one wants to climb.

Accompanying these approach descriptions are mileage logs and maps that provide more information on getting there. These maps were drawn from old Forest Service maps that showed many of the dirt roads necessary for reaching these trailheads and are very accurate with regards to proportion and comparison to the mileage logs. The mileage logs were constructed by driving the approach roads and noting the mileage distances for important landmarks. In many cases we drove

The west face of Middle Palisade (Photo by Ansel Adams. © 1997 by the Trustees of the Ansel Adams Publishing Rights Trust. All rights reserved)

these roads three or four times over three years in order to make certain they were accurate. Alas, geography is an ever-changing medium. Thus, while the mileage logs are the most accurate at the time of this publication, be aware that the washout of a single road from a previously severe winter can drastically change the approach to some of these trailheads.

The maps and approach descriptions provided are not meant to replace USGS topographical maps available on quadrangles that contain these peaks. Rather, this information is intended as a supplement to those maps where information is presented in a more clear and correct fashion. We recommend using the new 1:24,000-scale maps where 1 inch equals 2,000 feet when attempting to climb one of these mountains. The 1:62,500-scale maps, where 1 inch equals 1 mile, are just as useful but they may lack some of the intricate detail present on the newer maps. This detail can become relevant if you are attempting a new route or if you are looking for the intended route of descent in relation to your route of ascent.

Other maps we suggest for use on these mountains are the Trails Illustrated reissues of the USGS 1:111,850 maps where 1 inch equals 1⅛ mile. While these maps lack the details of the 1:24,000 maps, they contain more area than either of the two previously described maps, and therefore can be carried as one map containing information for several peaks. This becomes especially important when planning a trip where you are hoping to do several 14,000-foot peaks or adjacent peaks.

Last with regards to maps, the Forest Service publishes and provides maps that show roads, trails, creeks, lakes, etc.—everything but topographical lines. We found it extremely useful to get one of these maps when checking in with the appropriate ranger station for use during the drive to the trailhead.

Following the approach information are the routes themselves. All of the routes are numbered consecutively for each chapter, and they are presented in a circumnavigational sequence beginning with the most highly traveled approach to each peak. For example, the sequence of the routes for Mount Russell starts on the southwest face and moves counterclockwise around the mountain to end with the northwest face. The first route described for each peak is the most popular, the easiest route of ascent, or the most common route for descent.

Ratings for the climbs are listed in the route heading, and these are defined later in this section. Within the route descriptions, the best approach as well as alternative approaches are mentioned. First ascent information is described when available. At the end of each route description, the safest line of descent is provided in brief.

At the end of each chapter is a list of references. To our knowledge this is the only guidebook published to date on the Sierra Nevada where historical information is referenced. If you are intrigued by some of the history that we have presented in this book and you wish to delve further, contact the Sierra Club Library in San Francisco or the American Alpine Club in Golden, Colorado. Use the references we have provided to narrow your search. If by chance we have overlooked anything or mis-referenced anything, please contact us via The Mountaineers Books. While we humans are prone to mistakes, we want to make every effort to keep the record straight and tell it the way it really happened.

How Climbs Are Rated

This book provides information that allows people to climb routes that are no more difficult than a couple of thousand feet of stairs, with a little bit less oxygen than normal (unless you are acclimatized), to sustained, grade V routes involving free climbing, hard nailing, haul bags, and port-a-ledges. The next few sections are a summary of what the climbing grades mean in this book.

Free Climbing Classification

Free climbing is done when you climb the rock using only your hands and feet to move upward. Free climbing class ratings are listed using the Class 1–5 rating system adopted by the Sierra Club in 1937.

There are several very important things to remember when interpreting free climbing ratings. Climbing ratings are very subjective and depend upon when they were assigned, who assigned them, and what criteria that person used to give that particular rating. For example, Norman Clyde was a hone-master, a guy who lived for climbing and climbed to live. This exclusive lifestyle allows you to get pretty good and very comfortable on difficult terrain. Routes first done by Norman Clyde are usually more difficult than the original Class 3–4 ratings that he assigned to them. Equally important is the understanding that back in those days the rating system was limited to the range of Class 1–5. People could climb pretty hard back in the old days; however, their system of measurement was more limited than it is today. For example, a route done in 1964 and rated 5.6 will be much more difficult than a 5.6 route first done in 1994. Another point to note is that upper-level, decimal Class ratings that are near to each other may feel the same. For example, a 5.10d route may be equal in intensity to a 5.11a route. This is especially true if the 5.10d was put up in 1978 while the 5.11a was done in 1988.

A big benefit of this book is that we have climbed most of these routes listed for these big peaks. We have reassessed the old grades and in some cases modified them to be more accurate with regards to modern-day classification of climbing ratings and difficulties. To climb and thrash on a route whose Class assignment is much lower than the actual difficulty is to be sandbagged. A general, safe guideline to avoid sandbagging on these big peaks, especially with old Norman Clyde routes, is to climb those routes whose ratings are lower than what you are proficient at. After you get used to the area and you learn the history, who first climbed and rated which routes, go for the harder stuff.

Class 1—Hiking. Almost any footwear is appropriate, from tennis shoes to boots. Class 1 usually means that a trail may or may not be present, the hands are not required in any way for upward movement, and climbing can be likened to a gentle stairway. Examples include White Mountain Peak via the South Face or Mount Whitney via the Mount Whitney Portal Trail.

Class 2—Hiking over rough terrain. Again, the footwear is the same as for Class 1, and the hands may be used to steady oneself for movement around or over obstacles. A trail may or may not be present. Examples include hiking up talus (rocky terrain) or a sandy slope where the sand may shift a bit when weighted. Class 2 climbing can be likened to a normal stairway without a railing. Examples include Split Mountain via the North Ridge.

Class 3—Scrambling over rock or talus where handholds and footholds are used for balance and upward movement. Footwear recommendations are the same as for Class 1 and 2, but climbing shoes with sticky rubber make progress much easier. A rope should be available for inexperienced hikers or climbers. The terrain is steep and if one were to slip and fall, moderate to serious injury (depending on how you land) may result. Class 3 climbing can be likened to a steep, narrow-step stairway (no railing) that rises 40 feet or higher. Examples include the East Face of Middle Palisade, and the Mountaineers Route on Mount Whitney.

Class 4—Very steep, but not completely vertical terrain, usually not requiring strength of grip, but comprised of severe exposure. Severe exposure often means having hundreds of feet of "air" below you, so that feelings of vertigo may simmer in your mind. Sticky rubber climbing shoes make Class 4 climbing appear more secure and not as difficult. A rope should be used for safety unless one is proficient in this type of terrain. Knowledge of belays, anchors, and rappels is a prerequisite for a Class 4 route. A fall could be fatal. Class 4 climbing can be likened to climbing a nearly vertical ladder 50 to 70 feet high. Examples include Polemonium Peak and the Northwest Chute on Starlight Peak.

Class 5—Very steep to dead vertical or slightly overhanging rock. Sticky rubber climbing shoes are strongly recommended. Strenuous and sometimes difficult or technical climbing moves are required for upward progress. Knowledge of types of hand grips or finger and hand jamming techniques for crack climbing is necessary. Exposure can be extreme and a rope is often considered essential. Climbing gear should be available for immediate use to protect the leader in case he or she falls. An unprotected, ropeless fall is usually fatal while on Class 5 terrain. Class 5 climbing could be likened to a vertical or slightly overhanging ladder hundreds of feet high where the rungs are unevenly spaced, making for unusual reaches and moves. Examples include the U-Notch Chimney pitch on North Palisade and the Horseshoe Arête on Split Mountain.

Class 5 subdivisions—Class 5 climbs are further divided using the Yosemite Decimal System. Class 5 is subdivided into 14 categories (as of this writing) of climbing difficulty that are written as 5.0 to 5.14. From Class 5.10 to 5.14, the climbing may be further subdivided by difficulty with the letter designations a, b, c, and d, such as 5.10b or 5.12c. These letter grades are minor increases in difficulty that are not so large as to warrant a full grade increase (i.e., 5.10 to 5.11).

Water Ice Climbing Classification

Ice climbing has its own system of classification based upon free-climbing frozen water with ice axes and crampons. An assortment of tubular metal screws and pitons placed into the ice are used to protect the leader. Ice climbs are classified using the Water Ice Classification System, abbreviated WI, and ranging from WI 1 to WI 5.

WI 1—40- to 50-degree ice. Water Ice 1 designates moderate snow slopes and ice fields where crampons are required, and the ice ax is not required for balance or upward movement but for safety and purchase.

WI 2—50- to 65-degree ice. Consists of snow or ice that is steep enough to warrant self-belay with an ice ax while moving upward. The ax is used for balance and purchase.

WI 3—65- to 80-degree ice.

WI 4—80- to 90-degree ice.

WI 5—90- to 100-degree ice. Long, continuous sections of 90-degree ice requiring powerful moves, endurance, and good technique. Placing protection without stances is the norm.

Aid Climbing Classification

Some of the climbing routes on these high peaks involve what is known as aid climbing. Aid climbing is defined as anytime you use hardware rather than hands or feet to climb the rock. Aid ratings are listed as A0 to A6. To date, there are no A5 or A6 routes on California's 14,000-foot peaks.

Aid climbing involves placing gear or protection in cracks or on small protrusions on the rock face, pulling on those pieces once they are secure, and moving upward. In other words, with aid climbing the climber is no longer climbing the rock with just hands and feet. Instead, he or she is now climbing by pulling on or stepping onto the gear he or she has fixed temporarily to the rock. Aid climbing is broken down into seven ratings, and the gradations are dependent upon the number and tenuousness of pieces that could potentially pull out from the force generated by a falling body.

A0—A0 is the lowest aid rating and is applied to routes in which a climber has rested his weight on the rope (and therefore the gear in the rock). A0 usually involves rappelling off of fixed gear. By definition, no upward progress is accomplished using aid techniques on a route rated A0.

A1—Usually involves camming devices and stopper placements where if you were to fall, your most recent piece would most likely hold you and not pull out. The climbing usually consists of high-quality rock and cracks that take pitons or camming devices well. A1 is also commonly used for describing a rappel down into or across a notch that involves placing a 1-inch tubular webbing runner around or over a solid block.

A2—Involves gear placements that are more tenuous than those seen in A1 but are still strong enough such that if you fell, maybe only one or two of your most recent pieces would pop out before a good placement would stop your fall. Potential fall distances typically range between 5 and 15 feet.

A3—Sections of a pitch, or rope length of climbing, have really good gear placements, while others are very tenuous. A3 usually means that at some point in the climb, four to six pieces of gear could pull out of the rock in the advent of a fall, thus creating a total falling distance of 30 to 40 feet. The fall would be stopped by more solid gear placed below the dicey or tenuous section.

A4—The potential exists for falling and pulling out half a rope length (70–80 feet) of gear. The classic A4 pitch involves climbing on relatively good gear placements for 50 to 70 feet from the belay to a really solid placement, such as a bolt, and then climbing the remaining portion of the route (70–80 feet) on really marginal placements. Thus, if you were to fall near the top of the pitch, you would pull out all of the gear until you came to the bolt, therefore producing a 140-foot fall. Typically, A4 climbing involves A5-type climbing, but there is one spot somewhere in the pitch where the gear is solid enough to stop a leader from falling all the way back to the belay.

A5—If you fall, you fall all the way back to the anchor at the belay, in the process pulling out all of the gear you placed. A5 climbing is very serious and takes nerves of steel. Imagine placing and climbing on marginal pieces for 150 feet, such that at any moment, if you were to fall, nothing would stop your earthly plunge until the rope went tight at the belay. This would produce a total fall length of 300 feet. It gets really exciting those last few feet before you reach the next solid belay station.

A6—A rare designation that means A5 climbing, but the belay is so weak it would not hold if the leader fell. Yes, you guessed it; if the leader falls, everybody plummets.

Grade Classification

Grade classification refers to the length of time it takes a reasonably fit party (that can handle the Class of climbing) to finish the climb. Grades range from I to VII, indicated with roman numerals. No Grade VI or Grade VII routes exist on the 14,000-foot peaks at this time. It is possible that if someone does an extreme, superthin, aid climbing nail-up on one of the peak's big walls a Grade VI may someday come into being.

Grade I—A short route usually involving only one or two pitches of climbing, where a pitch is one rope length (usually 150–160 feet) and the climbing takes 2 to 3 hours to complete.

Grade II—Usually two to three pitches of climbing where the climbing can take 3 to 4 hours to complete.

Grade III—Can be four to six pitches of variable difficulty such that the climb takes most average climbers 4 to 6 hours to complete.

Grade IV—Typically involves a full day of climbing. The route can be two to three pitches of very difficult or tedious climbing such as A4 or A5, or it can be eight to twelve pitches of moderate free climbing. Whatever the terrain, Grade IVs typically take a full day of climbing, from dawn to just before sunset or dusk, to finish.

Grade V—Often the route of choice for aspiring hard men and women. The Grade V designation usually means that most average climbers who can handle the difficulties of the route will need to bivy overnight at least once somewhere on the route. Alternatively, if the difficulties are at the beginning, the climbers can climb the first two or three pitches, fix ropes to anchors, rappel, sleep at the base of the rock, and the next morning jumar, or climb the ropes, to reach their high point from the day before. Once at their high point, now early in the morning, the climbers can continue the route to complete it that day. In other words, it still takes two days to climb the route. If a climbing team is in good shape and the difficulties of the route are below their abilities, then it is possible and quite exciting to do the route in one long day.

Grade VI—Typically takes four to ten days for a party of average ability to complete. Examples are present all over El Capitan in Yosemite Valley.

Grade VII—May take two to three weeks to complete.

How Ratings Are Shown in This Book

Climbing classifications are listed for each route after the route title. First, the Grade of the climb appears, in roman numerals, followed by the free climbing Class, and then, if aid is required, the aid designation. For example, the Hairline Route on Mount Whitney is currently listed at Grade V, Class 5.10, Aid 3. In this book, this is listed after the route title as V, 5.10, A3.

Routes rated at Class 5 or lower are given a non-decimal Class rating, preceded by the word "Class." For example, the Starlight Buttress Route rating is listed after the route title as Class 4. The reason Grade classifications are not given for most Class 5 or lower routes is that these easier climbing grades are very subjective.

Chapter 1
Mount Langley

For a moment a sense of doubt came over me lest I had been mistaken.

Clarence King, reflecting on whether he had made the first ascent of
the true Mount Whitney, *Mountaineering in the Sierra Nevada*, 1872

Mount Langley, the southernmost
14,000-foot peak in the Sierra Nevada, has more in common with California's
desert mountains than with its high Sierran relatives to the north. The 14,027-
foot mountain, although its summit is granite, is covered with a dry layer of
white granitic sand and gravel and vegetation is almost nonexistent. The term
"high desert" is never more appropriate than when it is used to describe Mount
Langley.

It has been said that Mount Langley is an uninteresting peak, with little or
no mountaineering possibilities. The statement could not be further from the truth.
Mount Langley, perhaps more than any other peak in the Sierra Nevada, offers
the ambitious mountaineer some of the biggest untouched high-altitude walls in
the range. The south face of Langley, rising above the Cottonwood Lakes, presents an impressive 700-foot wall, over a half mile wide. The northern side of the
mountain, with an even greater relief, offers an incredible selection of sharp arêtes,
buttresses, and knife-blade ridges.

The story of Mount Langley, like the story of many other Californian peaks,
is inextricably linked to the story of Mount Whitney.

On July 6, 1864, two members of the illustrious California Geological Survey, Clarence King and Richard Cotter, stood on top of Mount Tyndall. King
thought he had just climbed the highest mountain in the state. On the summit,
however, it became obvious that there were several peaks higher than the one
upon which he stood. King wrote, in *Mountaineering in the Sierra Nevada,* in 1872:

The north face of Mount Langley (Photo by Steve Porcella)

"To our surprise, upon sweeping the horizon with my level, there appeared two peaks equal in height with us, and two rising even higher. That which looked highest of all was a cleanly cut helmet of granite upon the same ridge with Mount Tyndall, lying about 6 miles south, and fronting the desert with a bold square bluff which rises to the crest of the peak, where a white fold of snow trims it gracefully.

"Mount Whitney, as we afterward called it in honor of our chief, is probably the highest land within the United States. Its summit looked glorious, but inaccessible."

King and Cotter rejoined William Brewer and the survey party on the western flank of the Sierra. Brewer was especially glad to see the return of his companions. As King wrote in *Mountaineering in the Sierra Nevada,* Brewer later admitted, "King, you have relieved me of a dreadful task. For the last three days I have been composing a letter to your family, but somehow I did not get it beyond 'It becomes my painful duty to inform you.'"

Although Clarence King had failed to climb the highest peak to the south, the newly named Mount Whitney that they sighted from the summit of Mount Tyndall, he now had an incurable form of summit fever. King asked for permission for another attempt on Whitney. Brewer consented to the plan, gave King a hundred dollars for supplies, and told him the Survey would expect him at Galen Clark's Ranch on August 1. King had two weeks to try to climb the mountain. He left Visalia on July 14, with two soldiers, a pack horse, and enough food for fourteen days.

By this time, King had already decided that the mountain was inaccessible from the north or northwest. The route that the party now tried would approach the high peaks from the southwest.

After several days of following the newly created Hockett Trail, King's expedition joined an Indian trail that took them onto the plateau east of Kern Canyon. Then, turning east, the group passed to the north of a mountain that King named Sheep Rock. Sheep Rock is present-day Mount Langley, and it was so named by King because of the numerous flocks of bighorn sheep on its flanks. The small expedition worked its way through a pass south of the Whitney massif, a tedious climb according to the official Survey report.

Professor Whitney, state geologist, later wrote in a report of the Geological Survey published in 1865: "Mr King worked for three days before he could reach the base of the mountain whose summit he was endeavoring to attain." King's choice of route was poor and his attempt was stymied by a formidable wall 300 to 400 feet tall. Concluding the ascent was impossible, King retreated to Visalia.

Failing for the second time to climb his nemesis, Clarence King left California and returned to the east. In 1867, King was named U.S. Geologist in charge of the Geological Exploration of the Fortieth Parallel under Brigadier General A. A. Humphreys, the U.S. Chief of Engineers. Although he was only twenty-four, King now held a position of considerable rank.

In 1871, while he was organizing a survey of the continental divide, King found time to attempt Mount Whitney a third time. After purchasing supplies in

San Francisco, King was supposed to head to Wyoming, where his summer's work awaited him. Instead, he took a stagecoach to Lone Pine. Although he gave General Humphreys several scientific reasons for his diversion to Lone Pine, they could not disguise the obvious reasons for King's visit to the southern Sierra: he wanted to climb Mount Whitney. He arrived by stagecoach in Lone Pine on June 18, 1871.

On June 21, with a French mountaineer, Paul Pinson, who was visiting in the Lone Pine area at the time, King started for the mountain.

While they were climbing "Mount Whitney" (really Mount Langley), King and Pinson were engulfed in a thick cloudbank. When they reached the summit, on June 22, the cloud cleared for a moment, allowing them views to the west, southwest, and north. Through the swirling clouds, King caught sight of a peak that he thought to be Mount Brewer. He also saw what he believed to be the path he and Cotter once traveled. And, for a few short moments, "Mount Tyndall" pushed itself through the thick clouds.

Left to right: Mount Whitney, Mount Russell, and Mount Williamson from the summit of Mount Langley (Photo by Orlando Bartholomew)

It is obvious that King, being 6 miles further south than he had anticipated, was looking upon the peaks of the Whitney region, and the mountain he called "Tyndall" was really Mount Whitney. Once again King had made an enormous error. Instead of climbing the real Mount Whitney, King summited the mountain he had named Sheep Rock only five years earlier.

King's account of his ascent of Mount Langley, which he titled "Mount Whitney," appears in his classic account *Mountaineering in the Sierra Nevada.* It is a fascinating story because in it King described his confusion at his previous observations concerning the topography of the mountain, and, at the time of the book's writing in 1872, he still hadn't learned that his ascent of "Mount Whitney" was really a climb of Mount Langley.

King returned to his work with the Geological Survey thinking that he had finally conquered the real Mount Whitney. Certainly he had climbed the mountain that Owens Valley residents were calling Mount Whitney, but it wasn't the mountain he had named from the summit of Mount Tyndall in 1864.

In the August 10, 1872, edition of the *Inyo Independent,* a brief news article announced that Inyo County Sheriff Mr. Mulkey, accompanied by W. T. Grant and George Foster, had taken his wife and daughter to the summit of "Mount Whitney" (Mount Langley) on July 19. Mrs. Mulkey and her daughter claimed to have made the first female ascent of the mountain, the first female ascent of a 14,000-foot peak in the Sierra Nevada.

According to Grant's report in the August 17, 1872, edition of the *Inyo Independent,* the group rode "to within 3 feet of the monument erected by Clarence King to commemorate his triumph in making the perilous (?) ascent." The existence of the question mark in the newspaper article shows that the Mulkey party didn't consider the climb anything difficult.

A week later, the *Inyo Independent* gave credit to Sheriff Mulkey for finding an easy, suitable path up the mountain, one that even the weakest of mules could ascend. The newspaper went as far as to publish a thorough description of the route, one of the earliest climbing guides printed in California. The route description in the *Inyo Independent* concluded: "There are three monuments of rock on the peak, the oldest of which was laid by William Bellows in '64, who was probably the first white man to reach the apex."

One of the more interesting stories about Mount Langley is the story of the arrow shaft and the summit cairn that Clarence King found when he climbed the peak in 1871. In *Mountaineering in the Sierra Nevada,* he described what he and Pinson found on the top of Mount Whitney (Langley): "Close beside us a small mound of rock was piled upon the peak, and solidly built into it an arrow shaft, pointing due west."

It is noteworthy that Clarence King wrote of seeing a summit cairn during his 1871 ascent. This is significant for several reasons. One is that there is no evidence that Indians ever built summit cairns in the Sierra Nevada. Two, if a white man built this cairn, that would mean that someone else had summited this peak before King, yet he did not entertain this possibility. Three, the Mulkey party described seeing three summit cairns on Mount Langley during their climb in 1872.

The north face of Mount Langley from the summit of Mount Whitney (Photo by Steve Porcella)

It is highly likely that William Bellows built one in 1864, as the *Inyo Independent* reported him doing, while the second cairn can be attributed to King and Pinson, who engraved their names "upon a half dollar, and placed it in a hollow of the crest." The existence of a third cairn in 1872 implies that either another party ascended Mount Langley between June 1871 and July 1872, or else Clarence King failed to see the second cairn during the storm he experienced on the summit.

It seems probable that the arrow shaft was placed there either by Bellows or someone in his party, because it pointed due west, not an uncommon route for descent of Mount Langley. Bellows may have been trying to show future climbers an easy route down the tall peak that avoided getting close to the precipitous north face.

It is important to note that in all likelihood, long before the advent of the white man, Indians used New Army Pass as a trade route to reach Indian communities west of the crest. Historically a large herd of bighorn sheep congregated on the slopes of Langley, so it is very probable, given Langley's easy west slope, that Indians hiked to the summit to spot and hunt game.

The first winter ascent of Mount Langley contains none of the complex history of the first ascent. This feat, remarkable for its time, was accomplished solo by Orlando Bartholomew on January 4, 1928, during his winter traverse of the Sierra Nevada. Two hundred feet below the top of the mountain, Bart rested and was surprised to see a giant Sierra hare, which leapt from under the rocks on which he stood and bounded over the summit. Interestingly, twenty-six years later, Warren Harding also would report seeing a giant Sierra hare on the summit of Williamson during a winter ascent of its east ridge.

Mount Langley was named after Samuel Pierpont Langley, the director of the Allegheny Observatory in Pittsburgh, who led the first atmospheric studies from the summit of Mount Whitney.

Climbing Routes on Mount Langley

Routes are presented in a counterclockwise fashion starting with route 1.

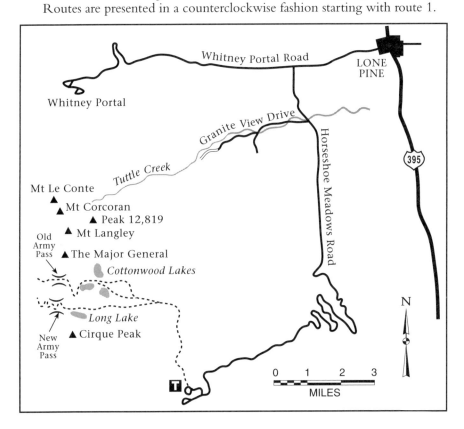

Eastern Approach via Cottonwood Lakes

Use this approach for routes 1 and 2.

The easiest, safest, and most popular way to achieve Mount Langley's summit is via Cottonwood Lakes and Old Army Pass, which can be done in one very long day from the Cottonwood Lakes Trailhead. Although the round trip is about 21 miles, the amount of elevation gain from Cottonwood Lakes to the summit is only 4,000 feet. A more leisurely ascent can be made with a camp at Cottonwood Lakes, which are halfway to the peak. Begin the drive to the Cottonwood Lakes Trailhead from the town of Lone Pine.

Mileage Log

0	Corner of Highway 395 and Whitney Portal Road in Lone Pine. Go west on Whitney Portal Road.
3.1	Turn left (south) on Horseshoe Meadows Road.
21.3	A sign reads, "TRAIL PASS, COTTONWOOD PASS (arrow forward), NEW ARMY PASS, COTTONWOOD LAKES (arrow right)." Turn right (north). (Note: It is important that you turn right here. If you continue straight,

you will reach the Cottonwood Pass Trailhead, which is not the correct trailhead. Many hikers have lost hours trying to correct this mistake.)
21.9   Arrive at Cottonwood Lakes Trailhead parking lot. The trailhead is marked by a signed interpretive display.

The Cottonwood Lakes Trail leaves the trailhead parking area at its northwest end. Follow it all the way to the Cottonwood Lakes. From the first lake, Mount Langley becomes obvious; it is the large peak to the north. Although the summit is not visible at this point, the expansive granite cliff of the south face is in plain view. The summit is just beyond the mountain's visible high point.

Eastern Approach via Tuttle Creek

The North Face Route (route 3) may require a very different approach to the eastern slopes of the mountain. The approach to this route is extremely steep and difficult. It is comprised of an interminable hike up loose gravel and sand, and is recommended to only the heartiest of mountain men and women. The following mileage log begins in downtown Lone Pine. This approach can be used for route 3.

Mileage Log

0   Corner of Highway 395 and Whitney Portal Road in Lone Pine. Go west on Whitney Portal Road.
3.1   Turn left (south) on Horseshoe Meadows Road.
5.1   Turn right (west) onto Granite View Drive (dirt).
7.5   The road forks. Follow the right (north) branch.
9.5   A small turnaround/parking area is reached. This is the best place to park passenger cars.
9.9   Another parking area, smaller than the first, is reached. Four-wheel-drive vehicles can be parked here.

Above the second turnout, the road quickly becomes a hiking trail. After about 1 mile of a high-quality foot trail, an old, abandoned religious shelter is reached. From this point on, there are only very faint discontinuous foot trails leading up Tuttle Creek (which heads south above the shelter) to the base of the North Face of Mount Langley. This approach is primarily cross-country with no trail.

Route 1, Cottonwood Lakes to Army Pass, Class 1–2

Use the Eastern Approach via Cottonwood Lakes.

The upper portion of this climb, near the summit plateau, was probably the route ascended by Sheriff and Mrs. Mulkey, their daughter, W. T. Grant, and George Foster on August 10, 1872.

From Cottonwood Lakes, it is very important that you do not confuse Old Army Pass with New Army Pass. New Army Pass is reached by taking a trail to Long Lake and High Lake. Old Army Pass is directly west of the three large lakes in the Cottonwood Lakes basin, and is a rough and unmaintained trail. If you are not already on a trail (there are many in this basin) that leads to Old Army Pass, hike cross-country toward the large southwestern Cottonwood Lake. Once at the

The south face of Mount Langley (Photo by Cameron Burns)

lake, follow its northern shoreline and pick up a trail that leads up and over the pass.

After the pass has been gained, the remainder of the climb is a fairly straight-forward march up steep gravel to the north. Continue hiking until the summit plateau is reached, then head east, to the summit itself. The best way to know when to head east is when the dramatic north face is reached; the vista and the geographical expanse are nothing less than awe-inspiring. At this point, head east.

The easiest descent of Mount Langley is made by returning down the Cottonwood Lakes Trail via Old Army Pass.

Route 2, East–Southeast Ridge, Class 3

Use the Eastern Approach via Cottonwood Lakes.

It isn't known who made the first ascent of this steep route, which is a quick descent route for climbs on Mount Langley's massive south face.

From the southernmost of Cottonwood Lakes, continue directly north, toward the south face of Mount Langley. After reaching the northernmost lake, negotiate the boulder field toward the south face itself. A steep chute soon appears to the right (east) of the face. This chute, a healthy talus slog, allows quick access to the East-Southeast Ridge, just west of Peak 12,819. After crossing the ridge, the easier ground on the eastern slope of the mountain can be followed to the summit.

The last few hundred feet of the route negotiate a Class 3 buttress near the top of the mountain.

Use the same route for the descent or use route 1 for descent.

Route 3, North Face, Class 3

Use either approach.

The first ascent of the massive north face was made by Nelson P. Nies and Howard S. Gates in August 1937.

High in the Tuttle Creek Canyon, just to the north of the north face of Mount Langley a bench south of the creek will be obvious. Hike to the top of the bench and angle towards a large chute/chimney which is blocked at its top. Climb out of the chimney, then traverse left (southeast), then right (southwest) to a point on the ridge west of the summit. Follow the ridge left (east) to the top of the peak.

Descend by either route 1, Cottonwood Lakes to Army Pass, or route 2, East-Southeast Ridge.

The north face of Mount Langley (Photo by Steve Porcella)

The southeast face of Mount Langley (Photo by Steve Porcella)

References

Inyo Independent. August 17, 1872.

King, Clarence. *Mountaineering in the Sierra Nevada.* 1872. Reprint, Lincoln, Neb.: Bison Books, University of Nebraska Press, 1970.

Rose, Eugene. *High Winter Odyssey: The First Solo Winter Assault of Mount Whitney and the Muir Trail Area.* Berkeley, Calif.: Howell–North Books, 1974.

Hervey H. Voge, ed. *A Climber's Guide to the High Sierra.* San Francisco, Calif.: Sierra Club, 1954.

Whitney, Josiah D. *Geology: Report of Progress and Synopsis of Field Work from 1860–1864.* Vol. 1. Philadelphia: Geological Survey of California, 1865.

Chapter 2
Mount Muir

One can't help but feel that a more worthy mountain could have been chosen to carry the name of one of the Sierra's greatest figures.

Steve Roper, *A Climber's Guide to the High Sierra*, 1976

Mount Muir, elevation 14,015 feet, is less a mountain than an inconspicuous bump on the Sierra Crest south of Mount Whitney. However, one can't help but be impressed with the escarpment of the east face of this peak, or that of the aiguilles (needles or spires) that lie on the ridge leading to Pinnacle Ridge and beyond to Mount Whitney. The east face of Mount Muir offers a pleasant, less populated alternative to the east face of Whitney. In addition, the spectacular aiguilles offer climbing that is as committing and exposed as that found anywhere on the east face of Keeler or Crooks Peak.

The only mountaineering of historical interest on Mount Muir occurred during the summer of 1935 when John Mendenhall, one of the Sierra Nevada's early prolific mountaineers, came to the mountain that year. It was one of his earliest visits to the Whitney area, an area where he would eventually pioneer four new routes. In September, Mendenhall and Nelson Nies climbed the untouched east face of Mount Muir, succeeding on a route they would later call the East Buttress.

Two months later, William Rice and Arthur Johnson climbed the east face proper, lying just south of the east buttress. Although these ascents are the only noteworthy pieces of mountaineering history, it is likely that Mount Muir will one day see more activity on its low-angled southeastern face.

In 1979 Werner Landry and Kenny Cook were the first to explore the unclimbed east-facing walls of the aiguilles to the north of Mount Muir. They climbed the east buttress of Aiguille Extra, the largest aiguille in this region.

Mount Muir from the southeast, with Mount Whitney and Mount Russell in the background (Photo by Steve Porcella)

45

Landry and Cook were followed shortly thereafter by Mike Strassman and Scott Ayers, who climbed three new routes on the aiguilles immediately south of Aiguille Extra including one new route on the south face of Pinnacle Ridge.

Climbing Routes on Mount Muir

The quickest and easiest way to climb Mount Muir is via the Whitney Portal Trail that passes within a few feet of Mount Muir's summit on its way to Mount Whitney. In fact, if you're planning on climbing Mount Whitney, making the short detour to Mount Muir's summit will only delay your climb by a few minutes. Routes on Mount Muir are presented in a counterclockwise fashion starting with route 1.

Eastern Approach via Mount Whitney Trail

Reaching the base of Mount Muir is one of the more straightforward approach hikes in the Sierra Nevada. The following mileage log is used for reaching Whitney Portal. Use this approach for routes 1–13.

Mileage Log

0	Corner of Highway 395 and Whitney Portal Road in Lone Pine. Go west on Whitney Portal Road.
13	Arrive at Whitney Portal.

After parking at Whitney Portal, follow the Mount Whitney Trail for approximately 8 miles. After 8 miles, an extensive bivouac area called Trail Camp is reached. Located there are many campsites, and a toilet facility.

From the Trail Camp area, Mount Muir lies directly west and should be obvious. It is the high point lying just north of Whitney Pass, where the Mount Whitney Trail crosses the Sierra Crest. To reach the base of the eastern escarpment of Mount Muir from Trail Camp, a talus hike is required.

Route 1, Mount Whitney Trail, Class 3

Use the Eastern Approach via Mount Whitney Trail.

As mentioned earlier, the easiest route up Mount Muir is via the Mount Whitney Trail, the same trail that gets one to Trail Camp (see route 2, East Buttress).

To reach the western slope of Mount Muir from Trail Camp, simply continue up the Mount Whitney Trail. West of the Sierra Crest, also known as Trail Crest, the John Muir Trail joins with the Mount Whitney Trail. Continue on the Mount Whitney Trail (also known as the Whitney Portal Trail) approximately 500 yards past the intersection, toward Mount Whitney. Mount Muir is to the right (east). A short scramble leads to the summit of the mountain. There are many variations to this short section of Class 3 rock.

Return to the Mount Whitney Trail and hike back down to Trail Camp.

Route 2, East Buttress, Class 4

Use the Eastern Approach via Mount Whitney Trail.

This high-quality route ascends the obvious rib on the east face of Mount Muir. It was first climbed by John Mendenhall and Nelson Nies on September 11, 1935.

The northeast face of Mount Muir with the Mount Whitney Trail in the distance
(Photo by Cameron Burns)

Hike from Trail Camp to the base of the east face of Mount Muir. From the base of the east face, climb the right-hand side of the rib for several hundred feet. Approximately halfway up the rib, traverse left into a broken chimney system that leads up and right. The crest of the rib itself is regained between two gendarmes. Continue up, staying just left of the rib, in a steep gully system, until the summit ridge is gained.

To descend, hike west to the Mount Whitney Trail and follow the trail down.

Route 3, East Face, Class 4

Use the Eastern Approach via Mount Whitney Trail.

This route, first climbed by Arthur Johnson and William Rice on September 1, 1935, is a variation of the East Buttress Route (route 2).

Hike from Trail Camp to the base of the east face of Mount Muir. From the base of the east face, climb the east rib for several pitches until some relatively difficult slab climbing is encountered. Traverse down and to the left to gain an obvious chute. Climb the chute, at the top of which is a 70-foot squeeze chimney. From here, climb up and right to join the East Buttress Route (route 2) near the summit.

To descend, hike west to the Mount Whitney Trail and follow it down.

Climbing Routes on Pinnacle Ridge, Third Needle, and the Aiguilles

Numerous needle or spirelike formations, known as aiguilles, lie on the ridge joining Mount Whitney and Mount Muir. Also joining this ridge is Pinnacle Ridge, a long serrated cockscomb that separates the Mount Whitney basin from the basin containing Trail Camp. The approach for climbing these formations is the same as that used for reaching the east face of Mount Muir, except you hike north as far as is necessary to obtain the base of your objective route.

Pinnacle Ridge is the long, knife-edged ridge that extends eastward off of Third Needle (see chapter 3, Mount Whitney) and connects with Thor Peak to the east. This ridge divides the North Fork of Lone Pine Creek from Lone Pine Creek.

Aiguille Extra is the first, most prominent tower on the Mount Muir–Mount Whitney ridge immediately south of where Pinnacle Ridge joins with Third Needle. This aiguille is in some respects as spectacular a formation as Keeler Needle to the north. (The needles are described in chapter 3, Mount Whitney.)

Aiguille du Paquoir is a relatively benign tower immediately south of the more spectacular Aiguille Extra. Aiguille Junior lies immediately south of Aiguille du Paquoir, but it is slightly taller than Aiguille du Paquoir. S'brutal lies immediately south of Aiguille Junior.

Route 4, Third Needle, Southeast Buttress, Class 5

Use the Eastern Approach via Mount Whitney Trail for Mount Muir.

First climbed by John Mendenhall, Ruby Wacker, and John Altseimer on September 5, 1948, this route begins on the southern side of Pinnacle Ridge where it abuts Third Needle.

North of the Mount Whitney Trail, the southern side of the east buttress of Third Needle is climbed for about half its height (about 500 feet). The short aid pitch, lying on the east face of the buttress, is followed by a traverse higher up. This traverse puts one on the northeast flank of Third Needle itself, where a rotten chimney is the most obvious feature. Climb the chimney and continue up and right toward the Crooks Peak–Third Needle notch.

Descend via route 1, Mount Whitney Trail.

Route 5, Third Needle, Mendenhall East Face Route (Southeast Face, Right Side), Class 5

Use the Eastern Approach via Mount Whitney Trail for Mount Muir.

This route was first climbed by John and Ruth Mendenhall on September 3, 1939. This was the first route to ascend the east face of Third Needle.

From Trail Camp, hike north to the junction of Pinnacle Ridge and Third Needle; climb the first gully south of this junction. After five pitches of easy climbing, a steep headwall is reached. The remaining portion of the route is best described by Ruth Dyer Mendenhall in a letter to her mother, September 5, 1939:

"There was one very difficult traverse, harder than anything on the Peewee Route [on Mount Whitney], as ticklish I think as anything I have done. There was a really fearsome overhang blocking the vertical chimney above us. So deep

John Mendenhall leading that "ticklish" traverse on the first ascent of the east face of the Third Needle (Photo by Ruth Mendenhall)

in the hollow were we that right below the overhang rose a huge pyramid of snow and ice, cold and shaded, and water dripped hollowly. The only way to get out was a traverse along the northern wall to a ridge. John got up on some virtually invisible footholds, leaving the pack, and hammered in a piton. I sat in the chilly shade and belayed him. The traverse was delicate. His feet kept slipping, slipping and the holds were rounded and practically nonexistent. He inched over, drove in another piton, pulled up a couple of feet of rope and held [it] in his teeth so as not to destroy his precarious balance while he clipped the carabiner over

The east face of Mount Muir; from left to right: Mount Muir, S'brutal, Aiguille Jr., Aiguille du Paquoir, and Aiguille Extra (Photo by Steve Porcella)

the rope and through the eye of the piton. Then he oozed over the top of the ridge, and while he stood there I took his picture."

The remaining portion of the route is Class 4 to the ridge.

Descend via route 1, Mount Whitney Trail.

Route 6, Third Needle, East Face, Left Side, III, 5.3

Use the Eastern Approach via Mount Whitney Trail for Mount Muir.

This route, first climbed by Mike Heath and Bill Sumner in August 1966, deviates from route 5, Third Needle, Mendenhall East Face Route (southeast Face, Right Side), at the headwall.

Climb the chimney, then, from its head, continue up and left until an enormous ledge is reached. Enter an obvious curving chimney above and follow it to the top.

Descend via route 1, Mount Whitney Trail.

Route 7, Pinnacle Ridge Traverse, Class 4–5

Use the Eastern Approach via Mount Whitney Trail for Mount Muir.

This traverse, first performed by Nelson Nies and John Mendenhall (date unknown), involves primarily Class 4–5 climbing.

From the east face of Mount Muir, hike northeast to Pinnacle Ridge. Numerous entrance points onto the ridge will be seen on its southeastern escarpment. However, it is not known if the first ascensionists stayed exactly on the top of the ridge, because some of the gendarmes feel more difficult than Class 4–5. The route ends on top of Third Needle.

To descend, hike west to reach the Mount Whitney Trail and follow the trail back down to Trail Camp.

Route 7a, Pinnacle Ridge Traverse, North Approach, Class 4–5

Use the Eastern Approach via North Fork of Lone Pine Creek, in chapter 3, Mount Whitney.

Pinnacle Ridge may be climbed from the Mount Whitney basin. The start of the climb is basically the same as route 7, Pinnacle Ridge Traverse, in that one looks for an entrance point on the ridge near its eastern terminus. Then traverse the ridge west to Third Needle.

Descend via route 8, Mountaineers Route, in chapter 3, Mount Whitney.

Route 8, Pinnacle Ridge, So Many Aiguilles, So Little Time, III, 5.10+

Use the Eastern Approach via Mount Whitney Trail for Mount Muir.

This route on Pinnacle Ridge was first climbed by Mike Strassman and Scott Ayers sometime between 1985 and 1987.

From Trail Camp, hike north to Pinnacle Ridge. It is not completely clear where this route lies on the south face of Pinnacle Ridge. This route has been described as climbing cracks in the center of a whitish face for six pitches.

The descent may be accomplished several ways. One can descend into the Mount Whitney basin on the less steep north-facing side of the ridge, or one can rappel the route back into the Trail Camp basin. Other options for descent may exist.

Route 9, Aiguille Extra, East Face, V, 5.8, A3

Use the Eastern Approach via Mount Whitney Trail for Mount Muir.

Aiguille Extra was first climbed by Mike Heath and Bill Sumner in June 1971.

From the east face of Mount Muir, hike north across talus and rock shelves until you get near to the junction of Pinnacle Ridge with the ridge joining Mounts Muir and Whitney. Aguille Extra is very obvious. The upper part of the east face of Aiguille Extra contains a long, prominent open book. The East Face Route begins directly below this formation. On a platform 40 feet above the talus or snow, climb four long pitches of mixed free and aid climbing. A series of ledges are soon gained from which the route continues up into the spectacular open book.

To descend, hike west until the Mount Whitney Trail is reached, and follow the trail back down to Trail Camp.

Route 10, Aiguille Extra, East Buttress, V, 5.10, A2

Use the Eastern Approach via Mount Whitney Trail for Mount Muir.

This route was first climbed by Werner R. Landry and Kenny Cook in 1979.

From the east face of Mount Muir, hike north across talus and rock shelves to near the junction of Pinnacle Ridge with the ridge joining Mounts Muir and Whitney. It is not completely clear where this route lies. However, the following first ascensionists' description is provided for those attempting this route.

From a right or north approach to the base of the rock, Class 4 climbing up the eastern prow of the buttress is performed. The actual roped climbing begins with a pitch of loose rock (5.6) and leads to a good crack at the base and to the right of a chimney. The crack (5.9) leads to a good ledge. From this ledge, a thin crack is climbed (5.9) and then the leader must tension traverse (A2) into an off-width crack. From here the climbing goes left (5.7) through a slot below a ledge system and up a short 5.10 region of climbing. Class 3 climbing to the left leads to a large ledge at the base of a headwall. The pitch off the ledge begins with a large block on the left forming a perfect hand-crack for 25 feet (5.10). At the end of this pitch the route moves up a crumbly layback transitioning to small footholds, then traversing right for 30 feet to a good hand-crack (5.8) that ends atop large blocks. The last pitch leads from a corner (ice-covered at the time) to the right and involves a few aid moves up an overhanging wall to finish with 5.4 climbing to a pedestal just below the summit.

A full free rack with an assortment of pins is needed for this climb.

For the descent, head west to the Mount Whitney Trail and follow it back down to Trail Camp.

Route 11, Aiguille du Paquoir, East Face, IV, 5.9

Use the Eastern Approach via Mount Whitney Trail for Mount Muir.

The first tower south of Aiguille Extra, Aiguille du Paquoir was first climbed by Mike Strassman and Scott Ayers sometime between 1985 and 1987.

From the east face of Mount Muir, hike north across talus and rock shelves toward the junction of Pinnacle Ridge with the ridge joining Mounts Muir and Whitney. It is not known where this route lies on the formation, but it ascends corners for eleven pitches to the summit.

To descend, hike to the Mount Whitney Trail and follow it back down to Trail Camp.

Route 12, Aiguille Junior, East Face, IV, 5.10

Use the Eastern Approach via Mount Whitney Trail for Mount Muir.

The first tower immediately south of Aiguille du Paquoir, and slightly taller, Aiguille Junior was first climbed by Mike Strassman and Scott Ayers sometime between 1985 and 1987.

From the east face of Mount Muir, hike north across talus and rock shelves toward the junction of Pinnacle Ridge with the ridge joining Mounts Muir and Whitney. This route starts up the right buttress and climbs eight pitches before traversing to the left (south) edge of the tower. Two pitches up this left edge finish the route.

To descend, hike to the Mount Whitney Trail and follow it back down to Trail Camp.

Route 13, S'brutal, East Face, III, 5.9

Use the Eastern Approach via Mount Whitney Trail for Mount Muir.

Lying immediately south of Aiguille Junior, S'brutal was first climbed by Mike

Strassman and Scott Ayers sometime between 1985 and 1987.

From the east face of Mount Muir, hike north across talus and rock shelves toward the junction of Pinnacle Ridge with the ridge joining Mounts Muir and Whitney. The route ascends the east-facing prow for eight pitches. The first three pitches stay left of the prow.

To descend, hike to the Mount Whitney Trail and follow it back down to Trail Camp.

References

Mendenhall, Ruth Dyer. Personal correspondence, 1939. Salt Lake City, Utah.

Roper, Steve. *A Climber's Guide to the High Sierra*. San Francisco: Sierra Club Books, 1976.

Chapter
Mount Whitney

The highest mountain in the United States is in this county. The highest
mountain in the world is in the moon.

Inyo Independent, May 3, 1873

The top of Mount Whitney, eleva-
tion 14,495 feet, is the single most sought after summit in North America. Thousands of hikers, climbers, and curious trekkers of all ages achieve Whitney's lofty
summit every year. Once considered part of the Mount Whitney complex, three
spires have now gained individual attention for their striking profiles and long,
committing climbing routes. These spires lie just to the south of the summit of
Mount Whitney and comprise the ridge that joins with Mount Muir. They are
Keeler Needle, Day Needle—later renamed Crooks Peak—and Third Needle. The
east faces of Keeler Needle and Crooks Peak are exposed and can be easily viewed
from the Owens Valley. In contrast, Third Needle is actually the culmination of
the joining of Pinnacle Ridge to the Mount Muir–Mount Whitney ridge (Third
Needle is covered in chapter 2, Mount Muir, along with Pinnacle Ridge and the
aiguilles).

To the Paiute Indians of the Owens Valley, Mount Whitney was known as
Too-man-go-yah, roughly translated as "very old man." The Indians believed that
the spirit responsible for the destiny of their people lived inside the mountain,
and from his high perch he observed the Indians and noted their behavior.

To Clarence King of the California Geological Survey, the first ascent of
Too-man-go-yah would represent the ultimate mountaineering achievement.

There are very few peaks in North America whose first ascent has been the
subject of more literature, publicity, disagreement, and controversy than Mount
Whitney.

Norman Clyde belaying on the east face of Mount Whitney (Photo courtesy of Dick Beach)

On July 27, 1873, W. A. Goodyear, a civil engineer, climbed Mount Langley with M. W. Belshaw, and discovered the silver half-dollar on which King's and Pinson's names were etched. Goodyear and Belshaw took observations and discovered the real Mount Whitney to be 300 to 400 feet taller and to the northwest of the mountain on which they stood. It was obvious that Clarence King had mistaken Mount Langley for Mount Whitney and that he had mistaken the true Mount Whitney for Mount Tyndall. Goodyear, whose academic training was nearly identical to King's and who had a dislike for King's showmanship and tendency toward hyperbole, especially when it came to climbing descriptions, saw an opportunity to slam King's reputation. An employee of the State Geological Survey, Goodyear immediately reported King's mistake to the California Academy of Sciences on August 4, 1873.

From Goodyear's report, Clarence King learned of his second, but most important mountaineering mistake. His first mistake was climbing Tyndall thinking it was Whitney, but this was never published. He had published his ascent of Mount Langley as a first ascent of Mount Whitney. At the news of Goodyear's report, King quickly headed for the Pacific coast to correct the situation. King, who was now seen as a prodigious blunderer, was given many sharp pokes by residents of the southern Sierra, and especially by the local newspaper editors.

Unfortunately for King, the locals of Inyo County, having already read the Goodyear report, were making attempts of their own upon the summit of Whitney.

Charles Begole, Albert Johnson, and John Lucas, or the "Fishermen," as they called themselves, had left Lone Pine in order to escape the intense summer heat of the Owens Valley. They had planned nothing more than two weeks of fishing, drinking, and enjoying the cool air of the high country. As the *Inyo Independent* reported on September 13, 1873: "On the 17th of August, these gentlemen were on the summit of Mount Whitney [really Mount Langley]. The other peak was evidently the highest, and they resolved to go to its top. The next day they started, and passing over two deep canyons, spending the entire day in labor, they finally succeeded in reaching its highest point, and have the honor of being first to stand on the greatest elevation in the United States."

As with most mountaineering achievements, it didn't take long for the critics to be heard. In the September 20 edition of the *Independent,* a letter to the editor read:

"Abe Leyda, William Crapo, W. L. Hunter, and myself are the only persons that ever were on the summit of the present Mount Whitney. Mr. [Charles] Rabe took the altitude and found it to be over 15,000 feet, several hundred feet higher than Clarence King's Mount Whitney.

"Yours, T. McDonough."

Unfortunately for McDonough, Charles Rabe later admitted in a report published in the *Independent* on October 11, 1873, to carving his name on a half-dollar and leaving it "among the rocks of the monument."

That Rabe had suggested a monument was soon pointed out by the Fishermen. Lucas, Johnson, and Begole claimed to have erected the monument on August

18, then added in the *Inyo Independent* on October 20, 1873, that "Had any white man ever been upon the spot, we would have discovered some marks or tracks, but we examined the locality throughout and found nothing."

On November 1, 1873, William Crapo claimed that he had climbed the mountain once before, on August 15. He tried to prove this by a written report of his ascent being present in San Francisco ten days before the Fishermen made their climb. Unfortunately for William Crapo, no records of his alleged August 15 ascent were ever found in San Francisco or anywhere else.

Twenty years later, William Crapo's character again appeared in a news item, but this time under less favorable circumstances. On January 5, 1893, the *Inyo Register* reports that Crapo had been charged with murdering the postmaster at Cerro Gordo. Apparently the murder was the result of a minor election dispute.

While the claims and counterclaims of liar and scoundrel were being printed into the history of Inyo County, one of California's most influential conservationists was quietly exploring the Whitney area, observing the wilderness, and climbing the high peaks.

It was October 21 when John Muir ascended the disputed Fishermen's Peak. He climbed by a new route on the northeast side of the mountain, and he climbed alone. The climb Muir made, up the now well-traveled Mountaineers Route, was significant because it showed future climbers that the east side of Whitney was not impossible, and that climbing could take place there.

The first ascent of Mount Whitney by a woman was accomplished by the ebullient Mrs. Anna Mills on the third day of August 1878. In an article in the *Mount Whitney Club Journal* in 1902, she wrote:

"I can candidly say that I have never seen, nor do I expect to see, a picture so varied, so sublime, so awe-inspiring, as that seen from the summit of Mount Whitney on the third day of August 1878."

The debate as to the best name for the newly discovered high peak was fought almost as fiercely as the battle for who the first ascensionists were. Names such as Dome of Inyo, Fowler's Peak (after a Senator Fowler), and Fishermen's Peak were proposed and fought for. Finally, from arguments made by William Brewer, who had been Clarence King's supervisor, the name Mount Whitney was established.

DURING THE LAST TWO DECADES of the nineteenth century, a second wave of curious individuals began to seek Whitney's high point. This group was not interested in the hoopla surrounding climbs made on the mountain, but, more importantly, how the peak could aid the advancement of science.

In 1880, Samuel Pierpont Langley, the director of the Allegheny Observatory in Pittsburgh, Professor W. C. Day of Johns Hopkins University, and J. E. Keeler and Captain Michaelis of the U.S. Signal Service led an expedition to the summit of Whitney. Langley had received advice from Clarence King in choosing a site for his solar heat experiments. King, who was at that time directing the Survey West of the One Hundredth Meridian, suggested the summit of Whitney. Information from Langley's bolometer observations concluded that the solar constant was about three calories, while Professor Day determined that the carbonic acid content of the atmosphere was greater at low altitude than at high altitude. The two prominent spires to the south of Whitney were later named after J. E. Keeler and W. C. Day, respectively.

In the early 1900s, one man independently realized Mount Whitney's importance to the world, and he undertook steps to make the mountain more accessible.

Gustafe F. Marsh was an English miner who had emigrated to the United States in 1889 at the age of twenty. He had worked as a miner in Colorado and California, and was a devoted follower of Isaak Walton. He was also an avid fisherman and visited the Lone Pine area during several fishing trips around the Owens Valley. The Whitney Trail was constructed by Gustafe F. Marsh and the soldiers of the Mount Whitney Military Reservation, and was primarily financed by the people of the Owens Valley. The first trail was completed on the evening of July 18, 1904. By the end of spring 1905, the Whitney Trail was already in a state of disrepair and needed attention. The town of Lone Pine raised more money and, again, Marsh supervised the repairs to the trail.

Over the next twenty-two years, scientific research conducted on the summit of Mount Whitney determined that Mars has no water in its atmosphere and that cosmic rays strike the earth everywhere with equal intensity regardless of topography. It was during this time of research that a summit shelter was built. Financed by a considerable donation from the Smithsonian Institution's Hodgkin's Fund and a grant from a William H. Crocker, in less than thirty days G. F. Marsh built the observatory for the scientific teams stationed on the summit.

By 1926, Mount Whitney was becoming such a popular destination for tourists of all kinds that a plan was hatched to build a tramway to the summit. Apparently this tramway was to offer the nonathletic thrill seeker the same opportunities that his or her mountaineering brethren were already enjoying. An article describing the construction of the tramway was printed in *Popular Mechanics*. The proposed project was compared to the tram in Chamonix Valley, France, which goes to the top of the Aiguille du Midi. Sixty-three supporting towers, from 40 to 90 feet, along with cables and pylons, were described. Power was to be furnished by one of the Los Angeles power stations. Fortunately, this idea never came to fruition.

The next great would-be engineering feat to be proposed for the mountain occurred in 1951 when a group of Southern California television experts explored the summit as a possible site for a television antenna. Fortunately, the distance of the mountain from populated areas made it of little value to the television industry.

THE FIRST WINTER ASCENT of Mount Whitney was accomplished solo, shortly after the first winter ascent of Mount Langley, on January 10, 1929, by Orlando Bartholomew. Bart, as he was known, skied to the base of the western chutes on Whitney, and then replaced skis with ice creepers, which were simple, inexpensive crampons. Bart climbed up into the chutes, his skis dragging by a rope tied around his waist while he struggled in the ice and snow. Climbing the chute, Bart ran into an insurmountable headwall. Rather than retreat, he carefully crossed from one gully to another, avoiding steep dead ends in the icy gullies. After escaping several dead-ending chutes, Bart had to admit that he was lost. He glanced up at yet another headwall and decided to exit the gully to the south, toward Mount Muir. He had reattached his skis, but when he climbed up a dangerous gully, knocking loose a small avalanche that fell for hundreds of feet, the ice creepers went back on. Bart realized he'd need his skis as climbing aids. Poking the back ends of the skis into the hardened snow, Bart used them much like a ladder rung, gaining a foot or two every time he planted the skis. Finally, as Bart surmounted the 13,000-foot level, the snow thinned and there was nothing but rock and ice.

Eventually, at the 13,600-foot level, Bart stumbled upon the Whitney Trail, the main route from Ibex Park (now called Whitney Portal). Bart now scrambled along the crest of the divide, eager to reach the summit quickly so that he might have plenty of time for the descent. In his diary, published in *High Odyssey* by Eugene Rose in 1974, he wrote:

"Though the scramble northward along the crest of the ridge required less sustained effort, there was still much treacherous country to cross. The footing might be at one moment a narrow ledge of ice-covered granite, the next a wind-glazed drift. Impatient as I was to reach the summit, it seemed all obstacles known to mountaineers had been amassed to thwart progress. By the time Whitney's broad shoulder had been reached, the sun was alarmingly low."

Two weeks at high altitude had given Bart great acclimatization, and with his skis flung across one shoulder, he moved quickly up the southern flank of the mountain. Within an hour he was standing upon the summit.

THE FIRST ASCENT of the east face of Mount Whitney was attempted only nineteen months later. Four experienced mountaineers, Jules Eichorn, Glen Dawson, Robert L. M. Underhill, and Norman Clyde, brought together by Francis Farquhar, made the attempt. The attempt was successful and this intrepid ascent is described in this chapter's East Face Route (route 10).

Although the climb had not been particularly difficult, the ascent of Whitney's east face was significant for two major reasons. One, the climb heralded a new standard of technical competence in Californian rock climbing, and two, it turned the Californian climbing community's attention toward more challenging routes on the big established peaks.

As Glen Dawson wrote in the 1932 *Sierra Club Bulletin:* "More and more we are becoming interested in new routes and traverses rather than ascents of peaks by easy routes."

The eastern escarpment that radiates to the north and more prominently to the south of Mount Whitney is perhaps one of the largest continuous walls in the Sierra Nevada. This wall is divided by Pinnacle Ridge, which runs directly west from Third Needle. To the south of Third Needle or Pinnacle Ridge, there are

Left to right: Glen Dawson, Francis Farquhar, Robert Underhill, and Jules Eichorn (Photo by Norman Clyde)

John and Ruth Mendenhall (Photo courtesy of Valerie P. Cohen)

numerous arêtes and walls that rise as smaller versions of Keeler Needle and Crooks Peak. Many of these aiguilles, as they have been designated, present solid grade 3 and 4 routes.

John Mendenhall was already well known for his strength and endurance in the mountains. In his 1930 first ascent of the northeast gully on Laurel Mountain,

Mendenhall is credited as being the first American to make conscious use of a belay. Later, Mendenhall would become known for keeping pace with difficult free climbing during the fifties as well as his contributions to mountaineering. During the thirties and forties, Mendenhall became the single most prolific climber of the Mount Whitney area. Between 1939 and '48, he explored the eastern escarpment by climbing four new routes on the eastern faces of Third Needle, Mount Muir, and Mount Whitney.

IN THE LATE 1950S, climbers from Yosemite Valley came to the high Sierra to attempt the large blank-faced spire known as Keeler Needle, just south of the summit of Mount Whitney. In 1959, Warren Harding had completed the first ascent of the largest monolith in North America, Yosemite's El Capitan. He was working as a busboy at the Awahnee, the world-famous lodge in Yosemite Valley, when he met Rob McKnight and Desert Frank, who were also working at the lodge. From a 1990 interview with Harding, Desert Frank's unique nickname was explained simply: "You know, I never did get that guy's last name."

Harding had also become good friends with Glen Denny, who had just started climbing. According to Harding, he and Denny headed up to the high country to have a look at Keeler Needle. Keeler had seen a few attempts and was at that time considered another wall to be done. Having climbed Whitney before, Harding was familiar with the area.

Harding invited McKnight and Desert Frank to join his small expedition to the high Sierra. In the interview in 1990 he recounted, "Glen and I just invited them along. They were good wine drinkers, and we all got along. It didn't matter that they didn't know much about climbing. Rob had climbed a little bit, not much, but I don't think Desert had ever climbed. Actually it's really to their credit that they were able to get up this thing."

McKnight and Desert Frank kept up with Harding and Denny for the entire four days. Harding led every pitch of the first ascent of Keeler Needle, but was not impressed by its difficulty. In 1990 Harding related: "You hack away at El Cap for forty-seven days, and you're pretty much ready for anything."

In 1972 Galen Rowell, Warren Harding, and Tim Auger made the first winter ascent of Keeler Needle, and in 1973 Jeff Lowe and John Weiland pushed a new aid route up the northeast corner and east face of Keeler Needle. Another route that lies more on the north face of Keeler Needle was climbed in September 1973 by Chuck Pratt and Ken Cook.

In 1976 Chris Vandiver became interested in free climbing the Harding Route on Keeler Needle, and he questioned Rowell as to the feasibility of such a project. Joined by Gordon Wiltsie, these three climbers made two attempts on the route before they were successful.

Claude Fiddler, a prolific Sierra Nevada climber, pointed out to Rowell that the northeast ridge of Whitney, a spectacular winding arête that rises from the Whitney-Russell col to the notch of the Mountaineers Route, was unclimbed. In 1982 Fiddler, Rowell, and Vern Clevenger started up this route under questionable skies and completed the first ascent of this spectacular ridge.

Left to right: Third Needle, Crooks Peak, and Keeler Needle (Photo by Steve Porcella)

Four years later Galen Rowell returned in the winter with Ron Kauk and Michael Graber to do the first winter ascent of the Direct East Face Route on Mount Whitney.

New route activity resumed on Mount Whitney in 1988 with the ascent of The Hairline in 1987 (V, 5.10, A3). This aid route, climbed by Alex Smaus and Bernie Binder, was the first route to take on the large open face that lies to the right (north) of the Direct East Face Route.

Three years later, Galen Rowell and Kike Arnal attempted a new route on the east face of Whitney that lies on the vertical expanse of rock to the left (south) of the Direct East Face Route. Stymied by an overhanging off-width halfway up the route and lacking off-width gear to protect it, Rowell returned the following year with Dave Wilson and together they finished the Left Wing Extremist Route.

That same year, 1991, saw the addition of a new start on Keeler Needle. Mike Carville, Kevin Steele, and Kevin Brown added ten free pitches to the east wall of Keeler Needle before joining up with the Harding Route. Contained within these ten pitches is some of the hardest high-altitude free climbing in the Sierra Nevada.

Warren Harding during the first winter ascent of Keeler Needle (Photo © Galen Rowell/ Mountain Light)

The spire known among climbers and hikers as Day Needle was renamed Crooks Peak in 1995 after Hulda Crooks, also known as Grandma Whitney, for her numerous and inspiring ascents of Mount Whitney from age sixty-six to ninety-one. In 1991, a variation on the last pitches of the Beckey route on Crooks Peak was put up by Porcella and Burns.

Climbing Routes on Mount Whitney

The quickest and easiest way to climb Mount Whitney is via the Mount Whitney Trail, approached from the east. This is also the easiest way of climbing

Mount Muir, and both summits can be climbed in one day from Whitney Portal. Due to the high number of people attempting Mount Whitney, wilderness permits for the Mount Whitney Trail can be extremely hard to come by. Day use permits are available at the trailhead, but these do not allow for overnight camping. Multiday use or overnight camping permits must be applied for in advance. The quota period for overnight use of the Mount Whitney Trail and the North Fork of Lone Pine Creek Trail is from May 22 to October 15. The North Fork of Lone Pine Creek Trail is the most useful trail for quick access to all routes except route 1, Mount Whitney Trail.

From the north, Mount Whitney can be approached by hiking south on the John Muir Trail. At Crab Tree Meadows the John Muir Trail can be followed east until it connects with the Mount Whitney Trail. From the south, Mount Whitney can be approached on either the Pacific Crest National Scenic Trail or the High Sierra Trail, both of which must connect with the John Muir Trail in order to reach Mount Whitney. Because these northern and southern approaches, not to mention potential western approaches, are so far away from Mount Whitney, we have focused on the much shorter approaches from the east. Routes are presented in a clockwise fashion starting with route 1.

Eastern Approach to Whitney Portal

The following mileage log describes the drive from Lone Pine to Whitney Portal. From Whitney Portal, one begins the approach to Mount Whitney via the Mount Whitney Trail (see route 1).

Mileage Log

0	Corner of Highway 395 and Whitney Portal Road in Lone Pine. Go west on Whitney Portal Road.
13	Whitney Portal.

Whitney Portal, the parking lot at the end of the road, is often full and it is sometimes necessary to park in designated overflow parking lots. The trailhead is marked by a kiosk and is near the end of the road on the north (right) side of the canyon. This trailhead is the start for both the Mount Whitney Trail (route 1) and the North Fork of Lone Pine Creek Trail (see Eastern Approach via North Fork of Lone Pine Creek, below). Here at the trailhead, the trail is called the Mount Whitney Trail.

Eastern Approach via North Fork of Lone Pine Creek, Class 2

The standard approach for east face climbing routes on Crooks Peak, Keeler Needle, and Mount Whitney is the trail that parallels the North Fork of Lone Pine Creek. It is also the standard approach for east face routes on the Whitney satellites (Keeler Needle, Crooks Peak, and Third Needle—the last of which is described in chapter 2, Mount Muir), and also for Mount Russell (see chapter 4). The North Fork of Lone Pine Creek is narrow, brush-filled, and extremely

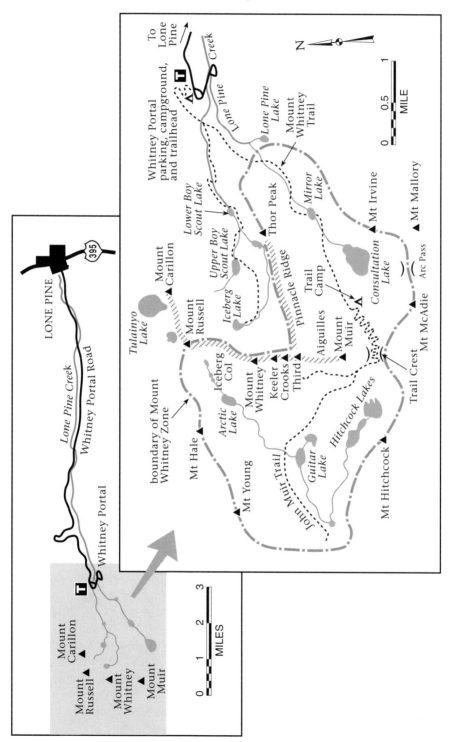

steep. The key to starting up the North Fork of Lone Pine Creek is selecting the correct creek to follow. Following the trail is difficult for the first 2 miles, and once the gorge has widened, it is easy to become disoriented among the craggy ridges and peaks. Generally, snow can be found in the gorge until midsummer, and once it has melted the dense alder provides an interesting challenge.

The North Fork of Lone Pine Creek Trail is gained by first taking the Eastern Approach to Whitney Portal (see above) and then hiking on the Mount Whitney Trail out of Whitney Portal. After following the Mount Whitney Trail for about a mile from the Whitney Portal trailhead, the North Fork is the second creek to be crossed. Head west, staying on the south side of the creek for approximately a mile or until granite slabs on the left pinch the canyon closed. Above this point the canyon is choked with alder and is very difficult to negotiate. Cross the creek to the right (north) and angle toward a large foxtail pine that can be seen on a ledge halfway up the south-facing granite wall. The ledge continues from the pine in an easterly direction. After a hundred yards the ledges cut back to the west. Follow this prominent ledge until it connects with a faint trail that resumes in the canyon, now above and beyond the alder-choked section below.

The canyon and trail eventually open up at the base of a small lake known as Lower Boy Scout Lake. Hike around the south edge of the lake and from here, a steep boulder field to the west is climbed via a trail. After gaining the top of this steep slope, it is best to cross to the north side of the drainage, over more granite slabs, before continuing west toward Upper Boy Scout Lake. To reach the east face of the Whitney group, turn south before reaching Upper Boy Scout Lake. (To go to the south face of Mount Russell, chapter 4, continue toward Upper Boy Scout Lake, hike to its west shore, and then climb talus and scree to the saddle known as the Whitney–Russell saddle.)

Turning south before reaching Upper Boy Scout Lake, enter a shallow hanging valley that gradually curves to the west. The south border of this valley is formed by Pinnacle Ridge. The farther west you go, the more serrated Pinnacle Ridge appears until it joins with Third Needle and the Whitney massif. When hiking due west, the incredible east faces of Crooks Peak, Keeler Needle, and Mount Whitney should become obvious. To gain the east face walls of Mount Whitney, Crooks Peak, and Keeler Needle, continue westward. Bivy sites are present in the talus of the moraines, but they are few and far between. This area is also very ecologically fragile and we recomend carrying out all feces.

To reach routes 2, 3, 4, 5, 6, 7, 8, and 9: as you approach and come upon the base of the east face of Mount Whitney, look for weaknesses in the small cliff to the north. At one point a faint trail ascending scree leads to the top of this moderate cliff. Obtaining the top of this rise brings one to Iceberg Lake. Iceberg Lake lies to the east of the Mountaineers Route (route 8) on Mount Whitney. Be sure to camp at least 100 feet from the lakeshore so as to keep pollution to a minimum in the lake. To gain access to routes 2, 3, and 4: hike to the west side of Iceberg Lake and scramble up to a shallow col on the ridge leading to Mount Russell. We have called this col Iceberg Col. From Iceberg Col one can drop down easy talus slopes to Arctic Lake and beyond to the John Muir Trail. Arctic Lake

The east face of Mount Whitney and the eastern escarpment; from left to right: Aiguille Extra, Third Needle, Pinnacle Ridge, Crooks Peak, Keeler Needle, Mount Whitney, and Cardiovascular Seizure; arrow shows the beginning of Pinnacle Ridge
(Photo by Steve Porcella)

and the small unnamed lakes above it in the drainage are good locations for starting routes 2 and 3. Route 4 begins at Iceberg Col.

Route 1, Mount Whitney Trail from Whitney Portal, Class 1

Use the Eastern Approach to Whitney Portal.

The Mount Whitney Trail is the easiest route up Mount Whitney. From Whitney Portal, it winds slowly up through lodgepole pines and gains nearly 7,000 feet in elevation. It crosses the Sierra Crest just south of Mount Muir at a location called Trail Crest and traverses the Whitney Massif on the west side of Muir, Third Needle, Crooks Peak, and Keeler Needle before winding through granite blocks to the summit of Whitney. The ascent requires nothing more than stamina, determination, and a good pair of hiking boots. It is almost impossible to lose this trail. There is a solar composting rest room located about halfway up the trail in the vicinity of Mirror Lake.

Descend via the same route.

Route 2, West Flank, Class 2–3

Use the Eastern Approach via North Fork of Lone Pine Creek and go to Iceberg Lake.

The numerous chutes and gullies on the western side of Mount Whitney can be seen from the John Muir Trail near the headwaters of Whitney Creek (directly west of the mountain). One of these was climbed by C. P. Begole, A. H. Johnson, and John Lucas when they made the first ascent of the mountain on August 18, 1873.

The west flank can be approached by hiking over the Iceberg Col from Iceberg Lake, and hiking west toward Arctic Lake. Passing Arctic Lake on its eastern shore places you in the vicinity of the numerous west chutes of the mountain. There are numerous variations and any of these chutes can be followed to the summit via Class 2–3 rock.

The other way to reach the west flank is to use the Eastern Approach to Whitney Portal, then hike the Mount Whitney Trail as described in route 1, Mount Whitney Trail from Whitney Portal. Where it joins the John Muir Trail take the latter to Guitar Lake. Leave the John Muir Trail from Guitar Lake and hike toward Arctic Lake and pick a chute.

Descend via the same route or the Mount Whitney Trail.

Route 3, North Face, Class 2–3

Use the Eastern Approach via North Fork of Lone Pine Creek to get to Iceberg Lake. From the lake hike over the Iceberg Col northwest towards the north face of Whitney.

The north side of Mount Whitney is similar to the west side in approach and difficulty of climbing. As with the West Flank Route (route 2), the north face can be approached via the Eastern Approach via North Fork of Lone Pine Creek and over the Iceberg Col (or via the Eastern Approach to Whitney Portal and route 1, Mount Whitney Trail, to the John Muir Trail and Guitar Lake; from Guitar Lake hike to Arctic Lake and continue up the valley to the smaller unamed lakelets). From here, there are many easy gullies and chutes between sharp, serrated ribs. Any of the chutes can be followed and the climbing, although steep, is no harder than Class 3.

Descend via the same route or the Mount Whitney Trail.

Route 4, Rowell North Arête, III, 5.7

Use the Eastern Approach via North Fork of Lone Pine Creek, or the Eastern Approach to Whitney Portal and route 1, Mount Whitney Trail.

On July 27, 1988, Galen Rowell soloed this 1,200-foot arête that lies on the north face proper of Mount Whitney. It is bounded by easy gullies on its northeast and west sides.

The start of the arête is reached from the southeast shore of Arctic Lake. From the east, hike from Iceberg Lake over the Iceberg Col to Arctic Lake. From the south and west, hike the Mount Whitney Trail to the John Muir Trail to Guitar Lake; hike upstream to Arctic Lake. The route features prominent gendarmes and it is heavily pinnacled for its length and size.

Descend via Route 1, 3, or 8.

The northeast ridge (bounded by light and shadow) and the north face of Mount Whitney from the summit of Mount Russell (Photo by Cameron Burns)

Route 5, Northeast Ridge, IV, 5.10, A1

Use the Eastern Approach via North Fork of Lone Pine Creek to Iceberg Lake.

The first ascent of this spectacular spur of Mount Whitney was made by Galen Rowell, Claude Fiddler, and Vern Clevenger on July 26, 1982.

This route is best reached from Iceberg Lake via the Iceberg Col. The route begins at the col and follows the prow of Whitney's northeast ridge. The only aid used on the climb is a short rappel. The route joins the Mountaineers Route (route 8) at the notch near the summit of the mountain.

Descend via route 8, Mountaineers Route.

Route 6, Cardiovascular Seizure, III, 5.10

Use the Eastern Approach via North Fork of Lone Pine Creek to Iceberg Lake.

The crack for which the climb is named was first climbed by Vern Clevenger and Keith Bell in September 1973.

This formation lies just to the north of the Mountaineers Route (route 8), on the northeast ridge and to the south of Iceberg Col. It is a large, prominent buttress easily seen from Iceberg Lake that contains a large, south-facing dihedral. This route ascends the prominent dihedral on the eastern prow of the formation.

Descend via Route 8, Mountaineers Route.

Route 7, The Rotten Chimney, III, 5.8

Use the Eastern Approach via North Fork of Lone Pine Creek to Iceberg Lake.

This well-named route was first climbed by Vern Clevenger, Mark Moore, and Julie X in 1973.

It starts just left (south) of Cardiovascular Seizure (route 6) and ascends the obvious chimney, which also contains a dihedral, for five pitches until it tops out on the northeast ridge.

Descend via route 8, Mountaineers Route.

Route 8, Mountaineers Route, Class 3

Use the Eastern Approach via North Fork of Lone Pine Creek to Iceberg Lake.

This route was first climbed by John Muir, solo, on October 21, 1873.

This large gully provides the easiest method of ascending the entire eastern side of Mount Whitney. It gains the obvious notch just north (to the right, when viewed from below the east face) of the summit. To reach the beginning of the gully, start from the southwest shore of Iceberg Lake and hike west. Walk toward the gully that lies just to the north of the eastern escarpment, or wall, of Mount Whitney. The gully is often snow-filled and has many loose rocks that await the unaware. Near the bottom entrance to the gully, a well-worn trail ascends shelves and ledges until it traverses out into the main portion of the gully at one-third of the height of the gully. From here, the ever-changing route winds its way up the steep talus.

Once the notch on the northeast ridge has been gained, the Mountaineers Route continues directly west for about 300 yards, traversing the north slope of the mountain until it joins the northwestern edge of the summit plateau. The summit, which lies back to the east, is obvious from this point.

The only equipment absolutely necessary for this route is a good pair of boots for kicking steps in the snow. An ice ax is thoroughly recommended, however, and if you're inexperienced in glacier travel, a small pair of instep crampons or their equivalent are also highly recommended.

Note: If you use this route as a descent route for the big-wall routes on Crooks Peak, Keeler Needle, and Mount Whitney, be prepared. The north-facing snowfield can freeze solid after sunset, making the traverse to the notch treacherous. There, boots and a pair of instep crampons will make an evening descent safer.

Descend via the same route.

Route 9, Northeast Buttress (The "Peewee" Route), IV, 5.0–5.8

Use the Eastern Approach via North Fork of Lone Pine Creek to Iceberg Lake, then follow the beginning of route 8, Mountaineers Route.

This high-quality route was first climbed on September 5, 1937, by Glen Dawson, Richard Jones, Howard Koster, Robert Brinton, and Muir Dawson, with a variation performed by Mike Carville and Joel Richnak in 1986 (route 9a).

The east face of Mount Whitney showing routes 8 through 12 and the summit shelter (Photo by Steve Porcella)

There are several variations to this route, which consists of mainly Class 4 climbing, with one pitch of Class 5.0–5.8 rock. Hike route 8, Mountaineers Route, to the base of the east face of Tower Two. At this point, it is wise to rope up. Climb the east face of Tower Two, the uphill tower (see route 10, East Face, for a description of the Towers) until 15 feet from the top of the tower. Then, traverse right on a ledge system that gains a second notch, between Tower Two and the true northeast buttress. The next lead, the first pitch on the buttress, is the crux of the climb. It is the only Class 5 pitch on the route.

Several pitches follow the very prow of the buttress until the Peewee itself is reached. The Peewee is the enormous block of granite that sits precariously upon the crest of the buttress halfway up the route. Go around the Peewee to the right (north) side. A few more pitches of Class 4 rock lead to the summit blocks. This route is recommended for novice mountaineers and offers high-quality rock with outstanding exposure.

A lightweight rope is recommended, with a small rack of eight to ten nuts and variously sized camming devices.

Descend via route 8, Mountaineers Route.

Route 10, East Face, III, 5.4

Use the Eastern Approach via North Fork of Lone Pine Creek to Iceberg Lake, then follow route 8, Mountaineers Route.

This route was first climbed by Norman Clyde, Jules Eichorn, Glen Dawson, and Robert Underhill on August 16, 1931. This famous historical route is perhaps the best documented rock climb in the Sierra Nevada. It is certainly one of the most classic.

Hiking about one-fourth of the way up route 8, Mountaineers Route, a notch appears to the left, separating two towers. These towers are known today as Tower One (the lower tower) and Tower Two (the upper tower). The four climbers ascended to the notch and found access to the face more troublesome than they'd expected. The first rope (Underhill and Dawson) began to scale the face of Tower Two. They quickly discovered that this was of no use, and retreated. Meanwhile, Eichorn had found the narrow ledge system now known as the Tower Traverse. Hidden from view from almost all sides, this very exposed catwalk leads to the northwest, across the south face of Tower Two. Once the climbers had gained the Washboard, the rock slabs below and right of Whitney's summit, they moved quickly and easily up this Class 3 section of rock. The remainder of the route is best described by the first ascensionists as in this excerpt from *Norman Clyde of the Sierra Nevada: Rambles through the Range of Light* (Scrimshaw Press, 1971):

"After an ascent of a few hundred feet, we entered an alcovelike recess where further direct advance was barred by a perpendicular wall. There we awaited rope number one, which presently arrived and after a short pause climbed over a low ridge [a traverse left (south) into another chimney], rope number two following. From this, however, progress upward could be made only by climbing a steep crack." This crack leads over the sharp arête that divides the east face of the mountain.

Apparently the youthful Eichorn and Dawson were eager to attempt the climb straight up, but Underhill and Clyde "urged that a traverse, which we had all already noticed, out to the left, be investigated," Underhill wrote in a *Sierra Club Bulletin* article in 1932. It is this traverse, around the huge buttress that splits the east face from top to bottom, that proved to be the key for the group to attain the upper part of the mountain.

Upon traversing the arête, an enormous ledge was gained. This was, and still is, an excellent place for a rest and a close examination of the upcoming Fresh Air Traverse.

As Clyde recounted in "Up the East Face of Mount Whitney" in *Touring Topics* in 1931, "We were confronted by a gap in the ledge, with a narrow platform about 8 feet below. There was the alternative of stepping across it—as far as a man of medium height could possibly reach, availing himself of rather poor handholds— or of dropping down to the platform and of climbing the other side of the gap. Some members of the party chose one method; some, the other. Once over the break in the ledge, we were obliged to pull ourselves over a rounded rock by clinging to a diagonal crack with our hands while our feet momentarily swung out over the 1,000-foot precipice. We then attacked a precipitous 'slabby' wall, availing ourselves of narrow ledges for hand- and footholds."

Soon the four climbers reached the major crack system far to the left. Several old fixed pitons are present now and indicate the direction of the course. At this point, one is below the Giant Staircase. Upon gaining the lower portion of the aptly named "Giant Staircase," the four climbers stopped for lunch. It had taken them just a few short hours to ascend 600 feet of the route, and the most difficult sections had been overcome. A traverse of the stairs of the Giant Staircase for several pitches, following the path of least resistance, was performed until the top of the staircase was gained. At the upper end of the staircase, Dawson led out a small chimney in the southwest corner. From the top of the dihedral, several Class 3–4 pitches wound up through the granite blocks to the summit. From this point, the climbers unroped and continued to the summit where Farquhar was waiting. The ascent had taken only a few hours, and the climbing had been considerably easier than expected.

An average ascent of the east face should take no more than 5 hours, if the Washboard is climbed unroped. A fully roped and belayed ascent of this route can take up to 12 hours, especially for groups of three or more.

Descend via route 8, Mountaineers Route.

Route 11, The Great Book, V, 5.9

Use the Eastern Approach via North Fork of Lone Pine Creek to reach the base of the east face of Mount Whitney.

This outstanding route was first climbed by Chris Vandiver and Gary Colliver in July 1974. This route was originally called the East Face Direct; however, it is now more commonly known as The Great Book.

The Great Book splits the right side of Whitney's dramatic east face and offers a direct start to the two Washboard pitches above. Because this route connects with the two Washboard pitches, it allows climbers the possibility of escape onto route 10, East Face, before the crux of the climb is tackled. The Great Book route should not be confused with route 13, Direct East Face, which is the most prominent "open book or dihedral-like" feature on the mountain, but which lies in the center of the east face of Whitney.

The Great Book route starts at the base of the east face of Mount Whitney, below and south of Iceberg Lake, far to the right (north) of the newer route 12, The Hairline. It follows the obvious southeast-facing crack system in the largest left-facing (south-facing) dihedral in the region of the face. Follow this crack system for many pitches (up to 5.9), until the base of the Washboard is finally reached. Follow up the Washboard to the base of a vertical left-facing dihedral (the Great Book itself). Route 10, East Face, continues off to the left (south). Several vertical pitches of 5.8–5.9 (Vandiver, 1974, Class 5.9) lead up this dihedral until the remaining 400 feet of Class 4 climbing to the summit blocks is attained. This route offers high quality rock and incredibly steep climbing, especially on the Great Book pitches.

A double set of friends and a set of stoppers is adequate on this elegant route.

Descend via route 8, Mountaineers Route.

Route 12, The Hairline, V, 5.10, A3

Use the Eastern Approach via North Fork of Lone Pine Creek to attain the massive east face of Mount Whitney.

This long route was first climbed in August 1987, by Alex Scmauss and Bernie Bindner. It is the first route to ascend the prominent wall to the right (north) of route 13, Direct East Face.

The start of this climb can be found by looking for a line of widely spaced bolts that ascend a relatively clean, white slab (5.10) at the base of the east face of Mount Whitney. Climb this face with cracks above for three pitches to a sandy ledge. Aid climb up the headwall for three pitches to a major left-facing dihedral. There is fun climbing for three to four pitches to the top of the dihedral. The dihedral tops out at the top of the Washboard. From the top of the Washboard, the route goes straight up, to the left (south) of the Great Book crack described in route 11, using aid till you reach a big, wide crack. The big, wide crack is followed for two pitches. The remainder of the route involves many small, easier pitches that lead to the top. During these last pitches to the summit, a haul bag may take on an evil persona all its own.

At the publication date of this book, there was a report that this route had been free climbed in the range of Class 5.11+. We are unable to gather or substantiate more information on this subject.

Descend via route 8, Mountaineers Route.

Route 13, Direct East Face, V, 5.9, A3

Use the Eastern Approach via North Fork of Lone Pine Creek to reach the east face of Mount Whitney.

This route ascends the most obvious structural feature on the east face of Mount Whitney: the incredible and obvious crack system up the prominent dihedral, or open book, in the center of the face. The route lies left (south) of

The east face of Mount Whitney showing routes 9 and 11 through 15
(Photo by Steve Porcella)

Galen Rowell (behind flake) and Dave Wilson leading a 5.11 crack on the first ascent of Left Wing Extremist (Photo by Steve Porcella)

the newer route 12, The Hairline, but right (north) of the prominent black water marks in an overhanging section of rock at the base of the face. The route climbs numerous pitches of Class 5 up to 5.9 following cracks, chimneys, flakes, and small ledges until the Fresh Air Traverse is reached. The most difficult pitch involves an overhanging off-width bypassed by a bolt ladder. At the Fresh Air Traverse, the route continues on route 10, East Face.

There are several different ways of avoiding the difficult start of this awesome dihedral at the base of the east face of Mount Whitney. One way is to climb up and left, gaining the small buttress that forms the base of route 15, Southeast Face (to the left—south—of the black water streaks). From the top of this large buttress, one can traverse directly right on shallow ledges, gaining the dihedral of the Direct East Face proper. Stay in the chimney for many hundreds of feet, eventually gaining the Fresh Air Traverse of route 10. Follow the remainder of route 10 to the summit.

Descend via route 8, Mountaineers Route.

Route 14, Left Wing Extremist, V, 5.11a

Use the Eastern Approach via North Fork of Lone Pine Creek to reach the east face of Mount Whitney.

In 1991, Galen Rowell and Dave Wilson returned and finished the Left Wing Extremist route originally started by Rowell and Kike Arnal the year before.

The sixteen-pitch route begins at the base of the east face of Mount Whitney, in the center of the rock buttress immediately to the left (south) of the prominent black water streaks. Two pitches of 5.8 lead up this buttress and gain a series of Class 3 ledges. The route veers right (north) up these ledges and ascends vertical and overhanging cracks that lead for four continuous pitches of 5.10–5.11. The last of these four pitches ends at the base of a prominent left-facing dihedral, or open book, that contains a man-eating off-width on the right, or south-facing, wall. This stout off-width is overhanging and, judging from the cursing and heavy breathing emanating from Rowell's lungs during his first ascent of this pitch (the authors were attempting a new line nearby), it should not be taken lightly. Numerous large camming devices are required for this full-pitch, 5- to 7-inch off-width (5.10d). The route eases after this pitch to numerous 5.8–5.9 pitches that follow a rib that stays left of the standard route 10, East Face, but that leads directly to the summit.

Descend via route 8, Mountaineers Route.

Route 15, Southeast Face, Class 4–5

Use the Eastern Approach via North Fork of Lone Pine Creek to reach the southeast face of Mount Whitney.

The first ascent of this route was made by John and Ruth Mendenhall on October 11, 1941. It ascends the most obvious line of weakness that can be found on the southeast face of the mountain. Unfortunately, this portion of the mountain has some of the poorest-quality rock in the Whitney area, and rockfall is a serious consideration when climbing here. The route is best described by John Mendenhall in the 1942 *Sierra Club Bulletin:*

"The southeast face falls in great yellow cliffs to the couloir that separates the highest summit of Whitney from Keeler Needle. A short distance north of the couloir rises an overhanging chimney. The buttress between the couloir and the chimney looked quite feasible, and it seemed possible to traverse into the chimney above the overhangs, and work up the cliffs above."

After cutting steps in the icy couloir, the climbers were able to reach the base of the buttress. They soon discovered that the climbing was actually quite easy and enjoyable, and that their ample supply of pitons would not be needed on the Class 4 rock. The remainder of the route was fairly simple: straight up on pleasant rock that required the use of two pitons. On the summit, the pair encountered an icy wind and stayed only briefly.

They made their descent by rappelling the ice-covered Mountaineers Route (route 8).

Climbing Routes on Keeler Needle

Use the Eastern Approach via North Fork of Lone Pine Creek to reach the east face of Keeler Needle. Instead of climbing north up the cliff band that leads to Iceberg Lake, continue west toward Keeler Needle. Small bivy sites can be found in the glacial moraine near the base of the spire. Routes are presented in a south-to-north fashion starting with route 16.

Route 16, Harding Route, IV, 5.10c

This route was first climbed by Warren Harding, Glen Denny, Rob McKnight, and Desert Frank in July 1960. It ascends the obvious crack system on the left-hand side of Keeler Needle's east face.

Start near the entrance to the Keeler-Crooks Couloir; caution should be exercised because the couloir periodically emits large boulders. The first pitch (5.6) ascends difficult-to-protect slabs to a small stance that is often decorated with rappel slings. The second lead ascends the base of the enormous crack system that splits the entire pinnacle.

From the stance, work a hand straight up to a fist-crack that widens below a small roof. The crack has loose red material in its recesses, and the roof is a little bit loose. There is a short section of 5.10b, followed by easier climbing above. The third lead continues straight up, using several key hand-jams to surmount a small roof (5.9). The pitch continues up a left-facing dihedral until it is possible to traverse right, around the corner, gaining a stance upon an orange boulder.

The next pitch, a steep hand-crack that becomes an off-width (5.9), lies directly above. At the top of this pitch, the broken ledge system that is so obvious from the ground is reached. Two Class 4 leads, followed by a pitch of 5.8, put one directly under the Red Dihedral, one of the most enjoyable leads on the climb. Start up the pitch by climbing a small overhanging dihedral that leads to the base of the Red Dihedral. Several fixed pins are found in the small open book, and several more are found in the Red Dihedral itself.

The next lead (5.7) puts one under the squeeze chimney, the crux of the climb. A steep, fingertip dihedral to the right appears to be a better choice; however, this is off route. Several fixed bongs are found in the back of the chimney

The east face of Crooks Peak and Keeler Needle showing routes 16 through 20
(Photo by Steve Porcella)

and, once the crux (5.10c) has been negotiated, one gains the bolt ladder used by Harding on the first ascent. Continue straight up the enormous chimney via some 5.8 stemming.

The eleventh lead climbs straight up a 5.7 squeeze chimney, then continues up progressively easier cracks and flakes until the leader decides to belay. There are many stances from which to choose. From here, a very easy lead puts one on the left shoulder of Keeler, on an enormous broken ledge system.

At this point, it is possible to traverse off the needle to the left, via easy Class 4–5 rock. In fact, this exit to the ridge separating Keeler from Crooks has been called the "Chicken Man Escape Route." The original free route, however, continues on the east face of Keeler Needle by traversing up and right, on flakes and ledges. It is very easy to know where to traverse at this point. There are two prominent dihedrals above the ledges, and right of those is a thin crack with three fixed pins. The correct traverse uses a large ledge below the fixed pins and moves directly right to the skyline. Once around the corner, a small, very comfortable ledge is gained. From here, a lead up double cracks (5.7) to a small roof, which is bypassed on its left side (5.8), is followed by a 5.4 off-width to Class 3 ground and the summit.

An average ascent takes a competent party between 10 and 12 hours, and it is not uncommon to bivouac halfway up on the Class 4 ledges. Excellent ledges for camping are located below the Red Dihedral.

A good assortment of gear includes two sets of friends supplemented with two extra large camming units (#4 Camalots), a set of wired nuts, 'biners, and runners. A lightweight haul line is recommended in case the weather turns bad and rappelling is necessary.

Descend via route 8, Mountaineers Route.

Route 17, The Crimson Wall, V, 5.12

Mike Carville, Kevin Steele, and Kevin Brown put up ten new pitches that ascend the center of the east face, slanting left, and that join with the Harding Route (route 16).

The first pitch climbs to a belay just under a 3-foot roof. The remaining pitches are comprised of corners, blank faces, cracks, and dikes. The seventh, eighth, and ninth pitches form the soul of the route and are comprised of an arching corner, a huge flake, and a sustained and steep lie-back corner, and these pitches are rated 5.11, 5.10, and 5.12, respectively.

Twenty bolts exist on the climb, and a full wall rack is required.

Descend via route 8, Mountaineers Route.

Route 18, Lowe Route, V, 5.9, A2

Jeff Lowe and John Weiland climbed this route on the right (north) side of Keeler Needle in September 1973.

Starting on the right side of Keeler, ascend six pitches into the obvious red dihedral (not to be confused with the Red Dihedral mentioned in route 16, Harding Route). Work left on a good ledge system into the center of the east face. Strenuous direct aid leads up incipient cracks, eventually joining the Harding Route for its final pitches.

A complete big-wall aid rack is essential.

Descend via route 8, Mountaineers Route.

Climbing Routes on Crooks Peak

The approach for Crooks Peak is the same as that for Keeler Needle: Use the Eastern Approach via North Fork of Lone Pine Creek. Instead of climbing north up the cliff band that leads to Iceberg Lake, continue west toward Keeler Needle. When you are hiking toward Keeler Needle, Crooks Peak is just to its south. Bivy sites can be found throughout this Crooks–Keeler Needle–Mount Whitney basin. Routes are presented from south to north starting with route 19.

Route 19, East Face, IV, 5.7, A2, or 5.9

The east face of Crooks Peak was first climbed by Fred Beckey and Rick Reese in September 1963. There are many variations to this route, depending on how close one stays to the easternmost prow of the peak. The most straight-forward line of ascent lies just next to, but south of, this prow. Any attempt to stay on the true crest of this prow could result in a lot of aid climbing and difficult routefinding.

The East Face Route starts in the Class 3–4 snow gully that lies between Crooks Peak and Third Needle. As with the Keeler-Crooks gully, this gully also has numerous rocks coming down it. An often wet chimney with a small roof is surmounted on the right while in the gully. A large roof looms above and the route moves right, onto a steep face (facing south) that has protectable cracks (5.8). Turning the corner right (north), the route enters the large southeast portion of Crooks' east face. The route continues up, angling right (north), but staying just left of the eastern prow of the peak. Cracks, dihedrals, blank faces, and small roofs (all 5.8–5.9) are followed for numerous pitches. Eventually, a fixed bong (piton) in a flaring dihedral (5.9) leads to easier ledges. From here, the route can traverse left of the final headwall to the ridge leading to Whitney (Class 4–5), or it can continue up any number of varying-difficulty crack systems. As with the lower sections of the route, the farther right (north) you go, the more sustained and steep the climbing.

For free climbing this route, a full rack of stoppers and friends are needed.

Descend via route 8, Mountaineers Route.

Route 20, The Illywacker, IV, 5.10b

First done by Steve Porcella and Cameron Burns in 1991, this variation of route 19, East Face, follows the line as described in route 19.

At the base of the final headwall, the last three pitches of this route go up a crack that lies 5 to 10 feet to the left (south) of a very large, prominent, overhanging off-width that can be seen from the base of the peak. Runout, vertical, spectacular knobby face climbing (5.10b) on the second to last pitch comprises the crux of this variation.

Descend via route 8, Mountaineers Route.

References

Bade, William Frederic. "On the Trail With the Sierra Club." *Sierra Club Bulletin* 5 (January 1904).

Baker, Charles L. "Physiography and Structure of the Western El Paso Range and the Southern Sierra Nevada." *Bulletin of the Department of Geology of the University of California* 7 (December 1912).

Beckey, Fred. *Mountains of North America.* San Francisco: Sierra Club Books, 1982.

Bohn, Dave and Mary Millman, eds. *Norman Clyde of the Sierra Nevada: Rambles through the Range of Light.* San Francisco: Scrimshaw Press. 1971.

Bowie, William. "Leveling Up Mount Whitney." *Sierra Club Bulletin* 14 (February 1929).

Campbell, W. W. "The Spectrum of Mars as Observed by the Crocker Expedition to Mount Whitney." *Lick Observatory Bulletin* 5 (1908–10).

Church, J. E. J. "Notes and Correspondence." *Sierra Club Bulletin* 5 (June 1905).

———. "Up From the Land of Little Rain to the Land of Snows." *Sierra Club Bulletin* 7 (June 1909).

Clyde, Norman. "High-Low." *Touring Topic* 22 (November 1930).

———. "Up the East Face of Mount Whitney." *Touring Topics* 22 (December 1931).

Colby, William E., J. N. Le Conte, and E. T. Parsons. "Report on the Kings River Canyon and Vicinity." *Sierra Club Bulletin* 6 (January 1907).

Daughenbaugh, Leonard. "On Top of Her World: Anna Mill's Ascent of Mount Whitney." In *Mountains to Desert, Selected Inyo Readings.* Independence, Calif.: Friends of the Eastern California Museum, 1988.

Dawson, Glen. "Mountain Climbing on the 1931 Outing." *Sierra Club Bulletin* 17, no. 1 (February 1932).

Eichorn, Jules. Interview by authors. Redwood City, Calif., August 1989.

Everman, Barton Warren. "Experiences in an Electrical Storm on Mount Whitney in 1904," in "Notes and Correspondence." *Sierra Club Bulletin* 17 (February 1932).

Farquhar, Francis. "The Sierra Nevada of California." *The Alpine Journal* 46 (May 1931).

———. "The Story of Mount Whitney." Parts 1–4. *Sierra Club Bulletin* 14 (February 1929); 20 (February 1935); 21 (February 1936); 32 (May 1947).

Gunthe, A. E. "The Sierra Nevada of the Upper Kern River, California." *The Alpine Journal* 41 (November 1929).

Hague, James D. "Mount Whitney." *The Overland Monthly* 11 (November 1873).

Harding, Warren. Interviewed by authors. Moab, Utah, January 1990.

Hittel, Theodore H. "On the Tip-Top of the United States." *Sunset* 10 (February 1903).

Jepson, Willis Linn. "Mount Whitney, Whitney Creek and the Poison Meadow Trail." *Sierra Club Bulletin* 4 (February 1915).

Johnston, Anna Mills. "A Trip to Mount Whitney in 1878." *Mount Whitney Club Journal* 1, no. 1 (May 1902).

Jones, Chris. *Climbing in North America.* 1976. Reprint, Seattle: The Mountaineers Books, 1997.

King, Clarence. *Mountaineering in the Sierra Nevada.* Boston: James R. Osgood and Co., 1872.

Lawson, Andrew C. "The Geomorphogeny of the Upper Kern Basin." *University of California Bulletin of the Department of Geology* 3 (February 1904).

Le Conte, Joseph N. "The High Mountain Route Between Yosemite and the Kings River Canyon." *Sierra Club Bulletin* 7 (January 1909).

Matthes, Frances E. "The Geologic History of Mount Whitney." *Sierra Club Bulletin* 11 (February 1937).

McAdie, Alexander G. "Mount Whitney as a Site for a Meteorological Observatory." *Monthly Weather Review* 31 (November 1903). Reprinted in Sierra Club Bulletin 5 (June 1904).

————. "Mount Rainier, Mount Shasta, and Mount Whitney as Site for Meteorological Observatories." *Sierra Club Bulletin* 6 (January 1906).

————. "The Observatory on Mount Whitney." *Sierra Club Bulletin* 7 (January 1910).

Mendenhall, John. "Mountaineering Notes." *Sierra Club Bulletin* 27 (August 1942).

Off Belay Magazine. "News and Notes." (December 1974).

Popular Mechanics. "Aerial Tramway to Scale Mount Whitney." *Popular Mechanics* 45 (June 22–26, 1926).

Roper, Steve. *A Climber's Guide to the High Sierra.* San Francisco: Sierra Club Books, 1976.

Rose, Eugene. *High Odyssey.* Berkeley, Calif.: Howell North Books, 1974.

Rowell, Galen. *High and Wild.* San Francisco: Sierra Club Books, 1979.

Sierra Club Bulletin. "Mountaineering Notes." *Sierra Club Bulletin* 27 (August 1942) and 34 (June 1949).

Stetson, Frank Owen. "A Pack Trail Up Mount Whitney." *Monthly Weather Review* 32 (September 1904).

Underhill, Robert L. M. "Mount Whitney by the East Face." *Sierra Club Bulletin* 17 (1932).

United States Military Reservations, National Cemeteries, and Military Parks. Washington, D.C.: Government Printing Office, 1916.

Wallace, W. B. "A Night on Mount Whitney." *Mount Whitney Club Journal* 1 (1902).

Wood, Crispin Melton. "A History of Mount Whitney." Master's thesis, Dept. of History, College of the Pacific, 1955.

Chapter 4
Mount Russell

*I was so stoked . . . a first ascent of a great, hard route, with good pro(tection)
on mostly great rock. . . . I didn't know rock in the Sierras could be this good!*

Alan Bartlett, after the first ascent of the Mithral Dihedral,
from an unpublished manuscript, 1990

The 14,000-foot mountains of the
southern Sierra Nevada are some of the highest in the range. These peaks are not
only tall, their relief is dramatic. Rising an incredible 10,000 feet above the floor
of the Owens Valley, the mountains take off skyward in great ridges, buttresses,
and ramparts. Their canyons and gullies are the deepest in the whole range, and
their summits offer some of the finest vistas in all California.

Because it is the highest peak in the contiguous United States, Mount Whitney
receives more attention than any other mountain in the area. Hikers, climbers,
and peak-baggers, interested in achieving only the highest summit in the state,
often leave the area unaware of the smaller, lesser-known mountains that surround
Whitney. One such peak is 14,086-foot Mount Russell.

Named for Israel C. Russell (1852–1906), an assistant geologist with the
Whitney Survey, Mount Russell contains sweeping chasms and smooth, twisting
ridges that abut the southern side of the mountain like the flying buttresses of a
medieval church. The summit itself is like a knife-edged gable, with steep walls
falling away on all sides.

Because of the diversity of climbing opportunities available, Russell now has
over two dozen routes, ranging from Class 3 to Grade IV, 5.10+. As of this writing, many potential lines are still unclimbed.

Steve Porcella on the fifth pitch of the West Chimney Route, Mount Russell (Photo by
Cameron Burns)

Historically, Mount Russell was not climbed until relatively late. Norman Clyde made the first ascent, solo. He climbed from his camp near Tulainyo Lake on June 24, 1926. Before he even began climbing, Clyde headed east, completing a half circuit of the peak and gaining the east arête. Although the route ahead looked formidable—at times impossible—Clyde soon found that the route opened up before him as he progressed. Clyde described the ascent for the 1927 *Sierra Club Bulletin*:

"There was always a safe passage and there were always enough protuberances and crevices to afford secure handholds and footholds. Now and then I came to a gash in the ridge through which I looked with a thrill down vertical cliffs, hundreds of feet in height, to the basin below, and beyond to the flanks of Mount Whitney.

"After reaching the end of a ledge, a short scramble brought me to the eastern summit of the mountain. There, a knife-edge extends a few hundred yards to the western peak, which is apparently the higher. The whole summit, in fact, is nothing more than a knife-edge with a high point at either end. Picking my way along the crest, or along shelves a short distance below it, I advanced toward the western eminence, which I reached by hoisting myself over some large granite blocks. There was no cairn or other evidence of a previous ascent. It was just such an eyrie that delights the heart of a mountaineer."

Indeed, Clyde had stumbled onto one of the last 14,000-foot peaks to be climbed. It is quite remarkable that this 14,000-foot peak, just a mile north of Mount Whitney, remained untouched fifty years after Whitney's first recorded ascent in 1873.

Unlike many other Sierra peaks that were repeatedly climbed by a standard route for many years, Mount Russell saw a proliferation of different routes from the outset. Within six years of the first ascent, five new routes, and many variations, had been climbed. Primarily, it was the easy gullies and couloirs that were picked off first.

Norman Clyde (Photo by Glen Dawson)

Then, for almost forty years, no significant new routes were established on Russell. The east face of Whitney was climbed in 1931, and routes were established on several other peaks in the 1940s and '50s, but the most dramatic cliffs remained unscaled. When the seventies arrived, Mount Russell, like many other peaks, experienced a new route explosion.

The climbers of this period were beginning to experiment with pure rock climbing, and tops of mountains were not the ultimate goal. Belaying was introduced to California in the early thirties, and direct aid was quickly being developed. Thus, Yosemite Valley, where high-angle rock climbing could be practiced, became the place to climb. The high country was considered, in many ways, a climbing backwater.

Galen Rowell comments on this situation in his 1979 book *High and Wild:*

"When I first climbed in Yosemite in 1957, none of the big walls had been ascended. Since that time, all of Yosemite's major cliffs had been climbed by at least one route; El Capitan now had eleven; the front face of Half Dome, four. The simple joys of exploration were on the wane; in their place was a trend to count and compare experiences with those of others who had climbed the same routes. I had no doubt that many Yosemite climbs demanded greater skill than the hardest routes of the highest ranges, but a big red flag went up when I saw climbers far more talented than myself unwilling to test in the nearby wilderness the skills acquired in this fair-weather womb. There was little I could do person-ally to reverse what I considered an unfortunate trend, except to bow out of it."

In the early 1970s, after Yosemite's biggest walls had been conquered, a few climbers, like Rowell, began to rediscover the high Sierra. Armed with substantial big-wall experience, they again looked at the unclimbed faces and ridges.

Fred Beckey and Galen Rowell were both extremely active during the period. Rowell, with Chris Jones, established the first route on Russell's west face, while Beckey, with various partners, climbed three new routes on three different sides of the mountain.

The well-known British mountaineer John Cleare, who made the first ascent of the Fishhook Arête with Gary Colliver in 1974, never realized at the time just how popular and sought-after this route would become. John Cleare wrote about Mount Russell in *Mountains:*

"Snow slopes led to a narrow rocky col, and suddenly there ahead was the great south flank of Mount Russell, across a wide snow-streaked desert of scree.

"We gazed at the spiky summit ridge—a mile long—and at the half dozen ribs and spurs which buttressed it on this southern side. 'West Face—the profile left of the highest top—is the route Galen Rowell and Chris Jones did in '71,' said Gary. 'Fred Beckey did a line on the northeast face, but they're the only modern routes. Which line shall we try?' As far as we knew, they were all virgin."

And on September 1, 1974, just three months after the first ascent of the Fishhook Arête, Gary Colliver joined T. M. Herbert and Don Lauria for a new route on the southwest buttress.

During the rest of the seventies, many more new routes were added, many of them clustered around the Yosemite-like rock of the southwest buttress. Particularly noteworthy was the Mithral Dihedral, considered by many to be the finest route on the mountain. Lying just a few feet to the right of the Direct South-west Buttress Route, this beautiful dihedral was first climbed by Alan Bartlett and Alan Roberts in 1976. After this ascent, Bartlett remained active on Russell, even-tually becoming the mountain's most prolific climber, ascending more new routes than Clyde and Beckey put together.

During the early eighties, the last major arêtes on the southern side of the mountain were climbed, and many more routes were added to the west face.

Although the peak seems inundated with a plethora of routes, many impressive walls and crack systems remain unclimbed.

Climbing Routes on Mount Russell

The routes are described from north to south, counterclockwise on the mountain. The southwest buttress, on the very southwesternmost corner of Mount Russell, contains a number of excellent routes, and the potential for several more. The north face of Mount Russell is actually divided into two faces by the north arête. To avoid confusion, the face to the east of the north arête is called the northeast face and the face to the west of the north arête is called the northwest face.

Eastern Approach via Whitney-Russell Saddle

Of the following routes, 1 through 20 lie on the south side of the mountain. The most direct approach to the south side of Russell is via the North Fork of Lone Pine Creek, the same approach used for east-face routes on the Whitney massif (see chapter 3, Mount Whitney, Eastern Approach via North Fork of Lone Pine Creek). Routes on the east, northeast, and west side of the mountain (21–26) can also be approached this way. Climbing route 22, however, is required for gaining the north side of the mountain and accessing routes 24–26. The approach diverges from the Whitney approach at Upper Boy Scout Lake. Here, a chasm that feeds the lake turns slightly to the north, toward Russell's southern flanks. This approach continues northwest, up the chasm to a saddle known as the Whitney-Russell saddle.

The first obstacle to negotiate is Upper Boy Scout Lake. A good trail exists on the right-hand (east) side. Then, following the creek above the lake (the head-waters of the North Fork of Lone Pine Creek), climb a steep boulder field. A thick layer of lush grass makes this climb easy and enjoyable. Another very small lake (often dry) is soon reached, and above this another steep gravelly talus slope is climbed to a short cliff band. The easiest route, and there are many, lies near the middle of the cliff (directly east), but care should be taken not to climb too far left, where the precipice steepens and the climbing becomes more difficult. Some Class 4 may be encountered if the route is not carefully picked. Directly above the cliff band are the soaring ridges of the southeast face, routes 20 and 21.

Eastern Approach via Sierra Crest

For the west face, southwest buttress, and south face, routes 1 through 18, it is necessary to cross the Sierra Crest, the sharp ridge that joins Mount Whitney to Mount Russell. That is easily accomplished from the top of the cliff band described in the Eastern Approach via Whitney-Russell Saddle (see above) by traversing the gravelly slopes above the cliff band in a westerly direction. The closer one approaches the saddle, the steeper and more exposed this traverse becomes. By carefully picking one's way across the large ledge systems, the rock climbing should get no harder than Class 3.

Chris Jones on the first ascent of the west face of Mount Russell (Photo © Galen Rowell/ Mountain Light)

Eastern Approach via Iceberg Col

Another, perhaps much easier way of approaching the west face of Russell is to hike from Iceberg Lake over the Iceberg Col (see chapter 3, Mount Whitney, Eastern Approach via North Fork of Lone Pine Creek). This approach is a little longer in distance than the approach described above, but it is easier once you are over the col. Camp at one of the little lakelets above Arctic Lake.

Western Approach via John Muir Trail

Another approach involves circumnavigating the Whitney massif completely. Follow the Mount Whitney Trail to the Sierra Crest (see chapter 3, Mount Whitney, Eastern Approach to Whitney Portal, and route 1, Mount Whitney Trail), where it joins the John Muir Trail (just south of Mount Muir). From here, follow the John Muir Trail toward Guitar Lake (obvious from its shape when it comes into view), then cut north, across the western slopes of Mount Whitney. The enormous U-shaped valley containing Arctic Lake and separating Russell from Whitney curves toward the east, and soon the west face of Russell comes into view. There are a few small lakelets above Arctic Lake, which provide water for camping, but there is no vegetation whatsoever.

Although Russell's west face routes require a great deal of effort to approach this way, they are easily worth it. These climbs are some of the finest high-mountain routes in all of California.

Route 1, West Couloir, Class 4

Use any of the approaches.

This route, lying on the extreme northern end of Mount Russell's west face, was descended by Jules Eichorn, Glen Dawson, Walter Brem, and Hans Leschke on July 28, 1932. The four climbers had just ascended the south face, left side, of Mount Russell.

Although this route is fairly straightforward, caution should be taken in surmounting the huge boulder that is wedged halfway up the couloir. Surmount this obstacle on its left side, using the wall of the gully for hand- and footholds. Loose gravel exists throughout the length of the couloir and caution should be exercised in most areas. This route is cold most of the day and often contains patches of snow.

This is an excellent descent route for parties climbing west-face routes.

Route 2, West Chimney, IV, 5.10

Use any of the approaches.

This route, which follows the deep chimney system on the northern side of Mount Russell's west face, was first climbed by Steve Porcella and Cameron Burns over two consecutive days, September 4 and 5, 1989.

The West Chimney Route starts by ascending slabs and shelves for several hundred feet until a pitch of 5.4 climbing leads to an obvious roof with a deep cave beneath it. Surmount this roof by climbing first the left wall of the cave, then the crack above. Sustained 5.8 and 5.9 climbing leads to a point where the steepness lessens, and the slab to the right can be traversed to gain a gravelly

The west face of Mount Russell showing routes 1 through 4 (Photo by Cameron Burns)

gully. Ascend the gully past several large chockstones, and belay on some big ledges to the left. The fourth lead ascends a 5.8 squeeze chimney to a belay among a pile of large blocks. To avoid the next big roof, the fifth lead ascends loose blocks and ledges on the wall to the left. This crux pitch is sustained (5.9) and difficult to protect. Caution is advised. The exposed sixth lead surmounts more chockstones. Above that, a boulder blocking upward progress forces one to climb left, up a diminutive dihedral on small face holds. This 5.10 face lead is poorly protected.

Several easy pitches lead up to the top of the chimney. Easy scrambling up granite blocks soon puts one on the summit.

A variation, designated as Route 2a, starts just right (south) of route 1, West Couloir. This variation ascends four or five pitches of Class 5.0–5.7 rock to connect with the West Chimney Route (main route 2) about halfway up.

Descend via route 1, West Couloir.

Route 3, Beowulf's Revenge, IV, 5.8

Use any of the approaches.

Climbed in October 1978 by Fred Beckey, Mark Fielding, and Marie Grayson, this route lies on the north side of the west face.

The climbing starts among ledges in a semi-rotten chimney approximately 100 feet left (north) of an obvious right-leaning arch. The first three leads go up and left, with the climbing getting better the higher one goes. The fourth lead enjoys high-quality rock, great exposure, and roomy belay ledges. The final pitch is a traverse left that ends in a 5.7 lie-back.

Descend via route 1, West Couloir.

Route 4, New Era, IV, 5.10a

Use any of the approaches.

Alan Bartlett and Kim Walker climbed this route in October 1978.

The route starts about 100 feet left of the Rowell-Jones Route (route 5) in an obvious right-facing dihedral with numerous cracks on the left wall of the dihedral. After one pitch (5.7), a tiny stance is reached. The second pitch climbs up and right in the arching dihedral (5.10a). The third lead, 5.7, climbs straight up, then moves right, then ascends to the bottom of a long right-facing dihedral. The fourth pitch (5.8) climbs cracks on the left wall of the dihedral. Then, halfway up the fifth pitch, the route moves from the cracks in the left wall of the dihedral, traverses right, and climbs the main dihedral (5.9) as a lie-back. The last two pitches of 5.8 climb straight up jam-cracks, eventually gaining the summit ridge.

Descend via route 1, West Couloir.

Route 5, Rowell-Jones, IV, 5.10

Use any of the approaches.

This route, originally rated IV, 5.9, A2, was the first route ever climbed on Mount Russell's dramatic west face. It was ascended by Galen Rowell and Chris Jones in June 1972. The pair climbed most of the route free, but used ten pitons on the two overhangs. The first free ascent of the route was by Mark Moore and Julie X, in 1974.

Descend via route 1, West Couloir.

Route 6, Montezuma's Revenge, IV, 5.10+

Use any of the approaches.

First climbed on July 3, 1986, by Fred Yackulic and Rich Romano, this route ascends the crack system immediately to the right of route 5, the Rowell-Jones Route.

This route begins in a large, left-slanting, right-facing dihedral. The second pitch fights through overhangs to a large ledge shared with the Rowell-Jones

The southwest face of Mount Russell showing routes 4 through 13 and 15
(Photo by Cameron Burns)

Route. From the left end of this ledge, one fearfully proceeds up through a loose chimney (5.8) to another ledge. On the left end of this ledge, an arête is face climbed (5.10+) until one can enter a hand-crack that leads up into a large right-facing dihedral that is followed to the summit ridge.

Descend via route 1, West Couloir.

Route 7, Two P.C., IV, 5.10+

Use any of the approaches.

Fred Yackulic climbed this route first with Alan Kouzmanoff on June 18, 1985. According to Yackulic, the first ascent of this route was a "self-destructive process"; a large flake was trundled by the second from under the first overhang.

This route starts 40 feet to the right of route 5, the Rowell-Jones Route, in a somewhat rotten, right-slanting crack that leads up a series of overhangs in 15 feet. After the first overhang, there is an exciting fingertip traverse right to a hand-crack that goes through a second overhang. The first pitch continues up to the base of a large right-facing dihedral, which is then followed in several straight-forward pitches to the summit ridge. The first lead is hard 5.10; the rest are no harder than 5.8.

Descend via route 1, West Couloir.

Route 8, Double Dihedral, II, 5.8

Use any of the approaches.

Alan Bartlett and Robb Delinger climbed this route the day before they made the first ascent of route 11, Startrekkin'. Although they found a fixed nut high on the route, past the crux, it is not known who made the first true ascent, but it was prior to 1977.

This route is essentially the upper two pitches of route 7, Two P.C. (in other words, the first pitch of Two P.C. is a direct start to this route). It is approached from Class 4 and easy Class 5 ledges to the right (near the start of route 9, Bloody Corner). Climb two pitches up a right-facing corner, then jog left and climb a similar but smaller corner to the top. A high-quality route, this is perhaps the easiest climb in this area of the mountain.

Descend via route 1, West Couloir.

Route 9, Bloody Corner, III, 5.10

Use any of the approaches.

This route was first climbed by Alan Bartlett and Alan Pietrasanta in September 1979.

The leftmost dihedral on the southwest buttress, this route climbs several hundred feet of increasingly difficult rock until the intimidating corner itself. This two-pitch dihedral is the crux of the route. Above, the southwest ridge is gained and easier rock leads to the summit.

Descend via route 1, West Couloir.

Route 10, Direct Southwest Buttress, III, 5.8

Use any of the approaches.

The first route on the southwest buttress was put up by Don Lauria, T. M. Herbert, and Gary Colliver on September 1, 1974. Due to subsequent route de-velopment on the southwest buttress, this first route has become known as the Direct Southwest Buttress.

On the south face of the southwest buttress are two excellent cracks; the left-hand crack is the Direct Southwest Buttress Route. The first pitch ascends the very base of the Mithral Dihedral (route 12). However, Lauria noted in a 1975 issue of *American Alpine Journal,* "The first pitch is loose and requires caution if one is desirous of company on the summit." Then, traversing left, climb four pitches of 5.7 and 5.8 climbing to the southwest ridge. This was also described by Lauria in the *American Alpine Journal:* "I climbed to the base of the right crack, from whence Gary led a deceptively easy traverse to the bottom of the left crack. Colliver strung out the lead well up into the 5.8 crack. T. M. led 'the most enjoyable crack I've ever led' with only a minimal Herbertian 5.7 whimpering." Progressively easier climbing leads to the summit.

Descend via route 1, West Couloir, or route 18, South Face, Right Side.

Route 11, Startrekkin', III, 5.10

Use any of the approaches.

This route, climbed by Alan Bartlett and Robb Dellinger in July 1978, follows the high-quality crack between the Direct Southwest Buttress Route (route 10) and the Mithral Dihedral Route (route 12).

This route shares the same first pitch (and approach) as the Direct Southwest Buttress and the Mithral Dihedral. Halfway up the second pitch of the Mithral Dihedral, traverse left, to a belay below a roof. Turning the roof (5.10) is the crux of the climb. Belay in slings. The last two pitches are both 5.9.

Descend via route 1, West Couloir, or route 18, South Face, Right Side.

Route 12, Mithral Dihedral, III, 5.9

Use any of the approaches.

Alan Bartlett and Alan Roberts made the first ascent of this route in July 1976. It ascends the huge left-facing dihedral just right of the Direct Southwest Buttress Route (route 10). It shares the same approach and first pitch as routes 10 and 11 (Startrekkin'). The route is best described in this personal account provided to us by Alan Bartlett:

"We rope up and do the first pitch, which obviously is the same as the first pitch of the [Direct] Southwest Buttress. A little loose, not too bad. I continue up the corner, past where that route traverses left into its straight-in crack. The climbing is slightly harder, but the rock seems better, and I get to a small, semi-hanging stance at the base of the upper, main dihedral. From the stance, I get a good view of the awesome crack splitting the face between the two lines; the following year Robb Dellinger and I would climb this crack, calling it 'Startrekkin'.' Suddenly there's a scream and the rope goes taut. A second later there's the huge crash of rockfall hitting the talus below.

"'Alan!' I yell. No answer. 'Alan!' I scream again, louder. Still no answer.

"Oh, no. The guy's gotten hurt. I'm beginning to get really worried, when the tension slowly eases off the rope, and I faintly hear:

"'It's okay, man. I'm all right,' yells Alan Roberts from below.

"A big block had come off when he was climbing over it, so of course he had come off too. Luckily he isn't hurt at all, just stunned and unable to respond for a few seconds. He climbs up to the belay and is a little shaken, but I'm hyper to get going. After all, I didn't just almost get the chop.

"It's getting more serious, but it still looks freeable. I lead up the corner a short way to where the crack suddenly opens to a squeeze chimney. It looks hard above, so I set up a belay.

"Alan comes up, and I set off again into the chimney, which suddenly narrows back into a hand-crack. With good pro[tection], I worm my way out of the alcove at its top and into the steep crack above.

"I belay in a low-angle slabby area, where it looks like the climb should be about over, except there's a short, steep headwall above.

"After a couple of false starts on the next lead, it seems that it's going to present more of a problem than I'd thought; in fact, the only possible way seems to be an intimidating lie-back flake going up and over the right wall of the dihedral. Setting some pro at its base, I crank up the steep, ever-widening (but thankfully very short) flake, and pull onto ledges and an obvious unroping spot. It feels a little harder than the spot below, but still only 5.9.

"We continue up the steep Class 3–4 rocks to the summit, gasping for air; this was only the second time I'd been above 14,000 feet. The register is great, the best I've ever seen. Norman Clyde's in there, Beckey, Rowell, all those guys. I gleefully write our entry, but, uh-oh, a thunderstorm's moving in fast, so we head off down the ridge looking for a descent.

"A short way down, it's quickly getting worse, and all of a sudden I hear this buzzing, and my hair's doing funny things. I've never heard this before, but I know what it is and Alan sure does too. Luckily we drop off the ridge into the correct descent gulley, and a short while later I'm feeling safe again. It doesn't rain until we're well into the flats, halfway back to camp. We crawl into our tents soaked but exhilarated. Man . . . what a route . . . what a day . . . what a life."

Descend via route 1, West Couloir, or route 18, South Face, Right Side.

Route 13, Pilgrimage, III, 5.9

Use any of the approaches.

This route was first ascended by Alan Bartlett and Alan Pietrasanta in September 1979.

It lies just right of route 12, Mithral Dihedral. According to Alan Bartlett, it is the worst he's done on the mountain. The climb ascends a crack on the left side of a left-facing, broken dihedral. After surmounting a small roof, several easier pitches lead to the summit.

Descend via route 1, West Couloir, or route 18, South Face, Right Side.

Route 14, Southwest Buttress, South Face, III, 5.10+

Use any of the approaches.

Fred Yackulic and Rich Romano were in an "exploratory mood" when they made the first ascent of this route on June 30, 1986.

This route ascends Class 2–3 talus to the amphitheater between the Fishhook Arête and the southwest buttress. A stance is soon reached below a hand-crack that leads up to an obvious right-facing dihedral on the left side of the south face of the buttress. The first-ascent party third-classed it to the stance, but less experienced parties may want to rope up. The crux pitch involves difficult stemming and off-width moves in a slightly overhanging bombay section of the large left-facing dihedral two-thirds of the way up the face. It is hard 5.10.

Descend via route 1, West Couloir, or route 18, South Face, Right Side.

The south face of Mount Russell showing routes 14 through 21 (Photo by Steve Porcella)

Route 15, Fishhook Arête, II, 5.8

Use any of the approaches.

Of all the climbing routes on Mount Russell, this route is one of the most sublimely beautiful. Next to the regular East Arête Route (route 22), this outstanding arête is the most popular route on the mountain. It was first ascended by John Cleare and Gary Colliver in June 1974.

The route description for this wonderful climb is simple: stay on the arête for its entire length. The climbing is sustained, interesting, and extremely exhilarating.

Descend via route 18, South Face, Right Side.

Route 16, South Face, Left Side, Class 4

Use any of the approaches.

One of the easiest and most direct routes to the summit, this route was first climbed by Jules Eichorn, Glen Dawson, Hans Leschke, and Walter Brem on July 28, 1932. Although it appears intimidating from a distance, the greatest challenge of this climb is the tedious slog up steep sand and talus to the base of the granite.

There are two cruxes on this route. The first is entering the gully at the base of the amphitheater between the Diamond Arête (route 17) and the Fishhook Arête (route 15). This gully, which disappears behind the Diamond Arête, is very steep at its entrance. Several variations exist, most of them using either the left or right side of the gully, and some parties may wish to rope up for this short section. Above, the steepness of the slabs lessens, and ledges or shelves are ascended for several hundred feet until the face steepens again. Above a large ledge, a short but vertical chimney is ascended. Again, many parties may choose to rope up for this short section that requires a very bold lead for Class 4 rock. Above the chimney, blocks are surmounted and the summit ridge is gained. The summit lies just a few hundred feet to the west.

Descend via route 18, South Face, Right Side.

Route 17, Diamond Arête, III, 5.9

Use any of the approaches.

This short arête, which has a small diamond-shaped south face, has seen numerous ascents; however, who made the first ascent is uncertain.

The crux of this beautiful arête is getting on it. Climbing from the very base of the arête at the lower left-hand (west) side of the Diamond Face, the route ascends steep rock for 30 feet before turning the corner to the right, and ascending a strenuous 5.9 lie-back to easier rock above. Belaying from behind a huge boulder, the second lead moves right, into a shallow open book (5.6) on the very top of the arête itself. This pitch is easily the most beautiful on the climb, being wildly exposed and containing many interesting sequences. Belay on a big ledge at the top of the dihedral. The third lead mantles several ledges above the big ledge, then climbs a pinched crack before moving right, onto the knife-edge arête again. The pitch ends on a large sloping ledge. From here, ascend the block behind the ledge, gaining the crest of the arête, directly above the Diamond Face.

The route then goes north, into the mountain itself. After 100 feet of weaving through the huge granite blocks, a deep recess is reached. This is the key to the route. Drop down 30 feet into the notch and climb right, on small edges, around the corner to the right (south). This unlikely traverse, over 500 feet of air, is extremely scary, and caution should be employed not to overprotect; rope drag can be a serious problem. Around the corner, a chimney leads up between the arête and a detached block. Above the chimney a ramp leads up for 40 feet until the top of the arête is again reached. Across another notch is a broken dihedral, which is climbed to its top. Another lead along the ridge puts one between an enormous boulder and a steep headwall. This headwall, climbed via parallel cracks and numerous ledges, is another beautiful, but easy (5.5), lead. Ascend another short pitch to the summit ridge.

Descend via route 18, South Face, Right Side.

Route 18, South Face, Right Side, Class 3

Use any of the approaches.

This historic route, the second route ever climbed on Mount Russell, was climbed by A. E. Gunther in 1928.

It is similar in nature to route 16, South Face, Left Side, requiring only Class 3 rock skills and patience with steep sand. The only difficulties lie near the summit ridge. This is an excellent descent route for climbers ascending the southeast ridge.

Descend via the same route.

Route 19, Southeast Ridge, IV, 5.9, A1

Use the Eastern Approach via Whitney-Russell Saddle.

First climbed on September 15, 1974, by Fred Beckey, Greg Thomsen, and Ed Ehrenfeldt, this route is listed in Steve Roper's *Guide to the High Sierra* as being II, 5.7. However, that grade, and our own grade, are both subject to the many variations that are possible on this long arête. The closer one stays to the very crest of the arête, the harder the climbing. And it is possible to escape the arête in many places, simply by making one rappel (or, in certain places, walking) to the west.

Starting at the lowest point on the arête, stay as close to the top of the rock as possible. There are several sections of 5.9 climbing, and up to three rappels are needed to circumnavigate unclimbable headwalls. The route tops out near the east summit. This route, for lying on such a spectacular arête, is complicated and requires a keen eye for routefinding.

Descend via route 18, South Face, Right Side.

Route 20, Southeast Face, West Arête, IV, 5.9

Use the Eastern Approach via Whitney-Russell Saddle.

This was climbed in the early eighties, though the first ascent party is unknown. The route is, however, of good quality.

Descend via route 22, East Arête.

Route 21, Southeast Face, East Arête, III, 5.10-, A1

Use the Eastern Approach via Whitney-Russell Saddle.

This long arête was first climbed by Bob Harrington, Vern Clevenger, and Claude Fiddler in 1984. The route begins just west of route 22 but east of route 20. The only aid used on the route is a rappel into a notch.

Descend via route 22, East Arête.

The north face of Mount Russell (Photo © Galen Rowell/Mountain Light)

Route 22, East Arête, Class 3

Use the Eastern Approach via Whitney-Russell Saddle. Follow the description in route 23 to reach the Russell-Carillon Saddle.

This is the original route used by Norman Clyde on the first ascent of the mountain, June 24, 1926. It is also one of the easiest routes, not to mention the most popular, on Mount Russell. The main objective in climbing the east arête is to reach the saddle between Mount Russell and Mount Carillon, the arête itself.

From the Tulainyo Lake area, simply climb the 500-foot wall above the lake to gain the east arête, east of the east peak. Staying exactly on the ridge for its length is almost impossible, and there are numerous places where it is necessary to drop down on the northern side of the ridge.

Route 22a, East Arête Variation, Class 3

Use the Eastern Approach via Whitney-Russell Saddle.

The approach from the south, which joins the East Arête Route partway up, was first ascended by Homer D. Erwin and Fred Leuders on June 19, 1927. This was the third route established on the peak, and remains one of the most climbed today.

From the south, the approach to this saddle, like the approach to most south-face routes, requires a strenuous battle up loose sand and gravel. The easiest way to get to the Russell-Carillon Saddle is to follow the South Face Approach (see earlier in this chapter). Then, once the cliff band above Upper Boy Scout Lake has been surmounted, turn northeast, up a steep, gravelly chute. This steep chute gains the saddle, and from here the summit is a long ridge hike. The last hundred feet to the summit (the west summit, the highest on the mountain) requires some careful weaving among the large blocks.

Descend via the same route.

Route 23, Northeast Face, Class 5

Use the Eastern Approach via Whitney-Russell Saddle and cross over the Russell-Carillon Saddle (route 22).

The ubiquitous Fred Beckey climbed this face with Reed Cundiff on June 10, 1970.

The major portion of the northeast face of Mount Russell is monolithic and shieldlike in its appearance. This route ascends broken rock and steep snow to the right (west) of the main northeast face. Apparently, rotten snow conditions prevented the first ascensionists from gaining the central slabs, so they settled for this route, described by Beckey as "very alpine."

Descend via route 24, North Arête.

Route 24, North Arête, Class 3

Use the Eastern Approach via Whitney-Russell Saddle and cross over the Russell-Carillon Saddle (route 22).

This route was first descended by Norman Clyde on July 24, 1926.

From the moraine shelf to the west of Tulainyo Lake, follow up the rib that leads into the north arête. The difficulties of the arête can be avoided at any time by moving to the west, onto the ledges of the north face.

Descend via the same route.

The northeast and north faces of Mount Russell showing routes 22 through 26
(Photo by Steve Porcella)

Route 25, Northwest Face, Class 3–4

Use the Eastern Approach via Whitney-Russell Saddle and cross over the Russell-Carillon Saddle (route 22) or the western approach via John Muir Trail.

This route was first climbed by J. H. Czock, M. Czock, and Mary Luck in 1935.

The route goes up the east side of this face (close to the north arête) until a conspicuous ledge is reached that can be climbed right (west), to the center of the face. From here, the route continues straight up the middle of the face to the summit ridge.

Descend via route 24, North Arête.

Route 26, West Arête, Class 3

Use the Eastern Approach via Whitney-Russell Saddle and cross over the Russell-Carillon Saddle (route 22) or the western approach via John Muir Trail.

This arête, which is really the ridge that joins Mount Russell to Mount Hale, was first descended by Norman Clyde in July 1927. It was Clyde's third route on Russell.

Although an easy and exposed ridge, this arête lies so far from normal approaches that it is rarely sought out as a route in itself. Stay close to the arête on its north side, and be especially careful of the various notches that fall away to the west and south.

Descend via the same route.

References

American Alpine Journal 13 (1971); 14 (1972); 15 (1973); 17 (1975); 19 (1977).

Bartlett, Alan. "The First Ascent of the Mithral Dihedral." Unpublished manuscript. Yucca, Calif., 1990.

Cleare, John. *Mountains*. New York: Crown Publishers, 1975.

Clyde, Norman. "First Ascent of Mount Russell." *Sierra Club Bulletin* 12 (1927).

Lauria, Don. "New Route Activity." *American Alpine Journal* 17 (1975).

Rowell, Galen. *High and Wild*. San Francisco: Sierra Club Books, 1979.

Chapter

Mount Williamson

Mountain climbing would be great if it weren't for all that damn climbing.

John Ohrenschall, from an interview with Warren Harding, 1990

Mount Williamson, elevation 14,375 feet, can often be seen from Highway 395 from more than 50 miles away. Simply stated, Mount Williamson is an enormous peak. In California, it is second in elevation only to Whitney. In complexity it is rivaled only by the conglomeration of North Palisade, Polemonium, and Starlight Peak. But in overall dimensions, Mount Williamson has no rival.

On the north face of Mount Williamson, fluted arêtes and spires border steep, complex gullies. The complexity of this face is evident when trying to follow a written route description—the possibilities are endless! When enveloped in snow, Mount Williamson's north face can take on the appearance of a Himalayan giant. When storms blow over it, Mount Williamson looks like a wild peak in Patagonia. And, shrouded in mists, with the Owens Valley below, Williamson can give one the impression of an exotic African mountain.

Although not as steep as the north face, the south and west faces of the mountain are also composed of an assortment of sheer walls, steep buttresses, and twisting gullies. At the base of the west face is a massive basin known as the Williamson Bowl. This basin, carved millions of years ago by glaciers, contains five large lakes, one of which is the recently named Lake Helen of Troy.

Mount Williamson has three summits that are over 14,000 feet. The south summit is the highest and lies on the southwestern corner of the mountain plateau. Two sub-summits, Peak 14,160 and Peak 14,125, lie on Mount Williamson's northeastern side. From Highway 395, these sub-summits appear to be the highest parts

Steve Porcella bouldering above the Williamson Bowl; northwest face of Mount Williamson in the background (Photo by Cameron Burns)

of the mountain. When most mountaineers boast about "having done" Williamson, they are talking about the south summit.

Mount Williamson was named after Major Robert Stockton Williamson of the Army's Pacific Railroad Survey of 1853. Williamson was renowned for mapping and surveying skills that allowed a route for the Pacific Railroad to be built through California.

In 1875, James M. Hutchings and two others decided to try for the summit of Mount Williamson. According to the October 9, 1875, edition of the *Inyo Independent,* Hutchings and his companions "proposed to take a short cut across the country (if such gigantic, awe-inspiring mountains of rock can be called country), with a view of intersecting the Kearsarge trail, and a possible ascent of Mount Williamson. Taking a small supply of 'grub,' but no blankets, the three started afoot, the main party taking the back track. It was expected the three across country gentlemen would reach here [Independence] on the second day."

When the three intrepid adventurers didn't arrive on schedule, a search party was sent out to find them. It didn't take long. On October 11, 1875, the following item appeared in the *Independent:*

"By the time [the search party] had reached the mountains, the missing ones came trampling in, weary, footsore, and, oh, how hungry. Instead of a practical route for even expert footmen, they found sheer precipices thousands of feet high cutting square across the proposed line of travel, so that it was simply impossible to proceed in the desired direction. The mountains around appeared to tower as high above them as from this valley. By this time the party were looking for a way to reach the foot, not the top of the mountains."

JOHN MENDENHALL, in writing his 1940 *Guide to Peaks in the Sierra Nevada,* mentions that the first ascent of Mount Williamson occurred in 1881 but that the route and climbing party are unknown.

The first successful recorded ascent of Mount Williamson was performed by W. L. Hunter and C. Mulholland in 1884. They hiked up the rugged, trailless canyon known as George Creek Canyon and camped upon a high plateau deep in the canyon. From this plateau they climbed the talus of the southeast ridge to reach the south (main) summit. Although steep and loose, this route was nothing more than a long Class 2 trudge up to the summit.

Between 1892 and 1896, A. W. De La Cour Carroll and a group of four led by C. Mulholland, of the 1884 ascent party, hiked up George Creek to a base camp high in the canyon. The next day they climbed the southeast ridge, enabling the first woman, Miss Skinner, to reach the summit. They were the fourth party to accomplish this feat, and were quite proud to be in the company of the first woman to the top.

One of the most intriguing ascents was accomplished by Bolton Coit Brown and his wife, Lucy, in June 1896. Brown recounted in an 1897–99 *Sierra Club Bulletin* series of articles that, after an incredibly difficult approach from the west, battered by wind and rain the whole way, they stood at the base of the mountain.

"Mount Williamson, which is not on the main crest, but to the east of it, towered in the morning light, dark, massive, and bristling—a stupendous pile and a most impressive sight. Its shape may be likened to that of a house, with gables east and west. Having crossed the bowl, we attacked the mountain by climbing up 200 or 300 feet over a small, reddish slide at its extreme northwestern angle. Thence we followed a previously selected diagonal upward across the western end of the house, and gained a small notch near the eaves on the southwestern corner.

"The climb to this perch, though not especially dangerous, was exceedingly rough and very impressive because of the vast heights above, which seemed almost to overhang us, and the vast depths below, which we seemed almost to overhang. Looking through the notch, we saw the southern face of the peak—a wilderness of vertical crags and gullies, seemingly impassable. Yet the hope of finding there a line of ascent carried us out among them, where, after some really ticklish cliff work, we got upon the lowest seat of a bottomless amphitheater with very high and steep sides. Wallowing up to the top of a big snowbank, we managed to squirm from it onto the next ledge; thence we edged up a crack to the one above, whose smooth slope was ascended by sitting down and shoving ourselves up backward with the palms of our hands. The next step we reached by cross-bracing ourselves against the sides of a vertical crack; everything the gymnasium ever taught us, and several things it neglected, now came into play. Eventually, up the bottom of a narrow, steep chute, over patches of snow and ice, with plenty of all-over climbing, we got up the highest and steepest part of the southern wall of the peak— through the eaves, as it were—and upon the more moderate slope of the roof."

In many of the guidebooks previously published, Bolton Coit and Lucy Brown have been credited with the first ascent of the standard West Face Route (route 1). However, the West Face Route reaches a notch that allows one to look out upon the north face, not the south face as Brown described. It is not likely that Brown, a seasoned veteran of the backcountry, would get his directions backward. In addition, Brown's description of the rock and the climbing more closely resemble that found near the southwest arête on the south face of the mountain rather than the north face.

John Mendenhall in his 1940 climbing guide to the Sierra Nevada credits Joseph N. Le Conte and six other members of his party with the first ascent of the now standard and very popular West Face Route. We agree with the historical record that Le Conte and his party were the first to climb this route in July 1903.

A speed ascent was first reported by Leroy Jeffers, who claimed, on July 21, 1916, to have climbed Mount Williamson from the basin in 2½ hours.

Leigh Ortenburger and Bill Buckingham, on December 22, 1954, made the first winter ascent of the Southeast Slope Route (route 11) and seven days later, on December 29, 1954, Warren J. Harding and John Ohrenschall began an incredible four-day epic involving the first complete ascent, in winter, of the northeast ridge of Mount Williamson.

Other guidebook authors have attributed the first ascent of the northeast ridge to Norman Clyde. However, while researching for information on a one-day

The northeast ridge of Mount Williamson with Mount Tyndall beyond
(Photo by Steve Porcella)

ascent of the route from the valley, Dick Beach recounted to us that he discussed this matter with the legend himself.

"Sitting on the rear patio of the old Baker Creek Ranch in Big Pine, I focused on the bright blue eyes of Norman Clyde. I had often asked him about his routes and climbs in the hope of repeating some of them.

"I had read about Clyde's solo first ascent in H. Voge's first edition of the *Climbers Guide to the Sierra Nevada*. Yet, when I asked Clyde about his climb, his fondness for reliving past memories failed to appear. Instead, his eyes turned in with a troubled stare and his brow creased in dismay. 'I have never been up that darn ridge. I told those guys when they printed that book!'

"I was shocked. I pleaded with Norman to check his memory, even though I knew it was for naught, for Norman Clyde's memory is just as impressive as his climbs.

"'It's a grand ridge. I always wanted to do it someday,' said Norman as he lowered his stare. In the air there was the feeling of a lost, glorious day of mountaineering."

On June 13, 1969, Dick Beach and Steve Rogero climbed the ridge that Norman wished he had done. However, Beach made the ascent in the impressive time of 14 hours, a truly remarkable achievement by any standard.

Climbing Routes on Mount Williamson

As of this writing, there are areas around Mounts Williamson and Tyndall that are restricted to access during certain times of the year. It is wise to call the Forest Service ranger station in Lone Pine before you begin a trip into the Williamson area. Make sure that the time you have planned your trip does not conflict with the access restrictions currently in place. Below are the current access times, but these may be subject to change in the future.

The Bighorn Sheep Zoological Preserve encompasses an area bordering the east face of Mount Tyndall and stretching east approximately 4 miles. The preserve extends north and south for many miles. This area is open from December 15 to July 15. This means that Shepherd's Pass can be used to access Tyndall-Williamson routes anytime between December 15 and July 15. You are not allowed onto the Shepherd's Pass Trail from July 15 to December 15. It is closed and you may be fined. There are several Forest Service maps that detail different portions of the bighorn preserve, but none are comprehensive. It is best to consult the Forest Service in Lone Pine before starting out toward either peak.

The entire south face of Mount Williamson has its own restrictions. The George Creek Canyon, including the south face of Williamson, is only open two months per year, from December 15 to January 1, and from April 15 to May 15. This makes climbing routes on Williamson's south face all the more difficult. Obviously, it makes a great deal of sense to plan your climb of Williamson well in advance.

The easiest way to climb Mount Williamson is the West Face Route (route 1) and this route is the most popular route to the summit. Route 1 is reached by hiking the Shepherd Pass Trail from Owens Valley. Routes are presented in a clockwise fashion starting with route 1.

Eastern Approach via Shepherd Pass

The following mileage log explains how to get to the Shepherd Pass Trailhead. The description begins in downtown Independence, at the corner of Highway 395 and Market Street.

Mileage Log _____

0	Corner of Highway 395 and Market Street in Independence. Go west (toward the Sierra Nevada) on Market Street. Outside of town, Market Street becomes Onion Valley Road.
4.4	Turn left (south) on Foothill Road (dirt).
5.6	Road forks. Follow the right (west) fork. Also, you'll pass a sign reading "SHEPHERDS PASS TRAILHEAD."
7.2	Cross a small creekbed, near a corral.
7.6	Fork in road. Go right.
7.7	Fork in road. Go right. (There is a small "HIKER" sign here.)

8.2   Fork in road. Go right.
9.2   Symmes Creek (Shepherd Pass) Trailhead. Parking. No facilities.

A large parking lot lies at the end of the road, and from here it is a long (around 10 miles) and very strenuous hike to Shepherd Pass. It is not uncommon to take two days from the car to make the hike to Shepherd Pass.

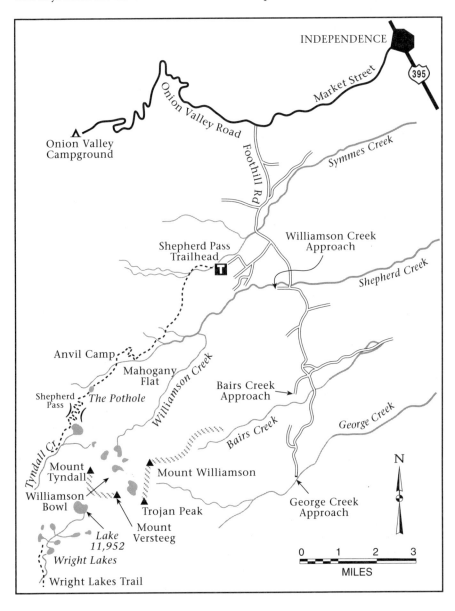

From the trailhead, the Shepherd Creek Trail parallels Symmes Creek for about 2 miles before it turns south and switchbacks up to the top of a ridge. From this ridge the north face of Williamson can be seen to the south. The top of this ridge is also the boundary for the Bighorn Sheep Zoological Preserve. From the preserve boundary, the trail drops southwest and continues into Shepherd Creek Canyon.

There are several good campsites in this canyon along the way. Mahogany Flat is the first camping area encountered on the Shepherd Creek Trail once you've entered Shepherd Creek Canyon. It is the first big, flat area up the canyon. The most popular camping area is Anvil Camp, at the 10,000-foot level, 2 miles before the pass itself. Many climbers have camped at Anvil Camp. The hike from here to start the climb on Williamson is a long one and definitely requires an early start.

To reach the Williamson Bowl, a large basin between Mounts Williamson and Tyndall, continue on the Shepherd Creek Trail to Shepherd Pass. In late summer, the pass is nothing more than a steep talus hike. In early summer, an ice ax can be very useful when snow covers much of the pass. Once on top of Shepherd Pass, hike southeast to a large basin. A 300-foot drop over talus and boulders is the final obstacle to the first large lake in the Williamson Bowl. There are four large lakes in this basin, and gravel bivy sites can usually be found near them. The Williamson Bowl provides access to routes 1, 2, 3, 4, 5, 6, 7, 8, 12, 13, and 14.

Eastern Approach via Williamson Creek

The Williamson Creek approach is arduous, involving cross-country bush-whacking and scrambling up a steep canyon. For this approach, follow the mileage log for the Shepherd Pass Approach. At the 7.6-mile mark, instead of making a right turn to go to the Shepherd Pass Trailhead, take the left branch of the fork in the road. It heads south. This leads to a small parking area at the end of the road.

There appears to be no trail from this parking area. However, the creek just to the south of this parking area is Shepherd Creek. Follow Shepherd Creek into the canyon. After about 2 miles, the creek branches with one branch coming from the west (right) and the other from the south (left). The west branch is Shepherd Creek, and following it eventually leads to Mahogany Flat; instead, follow the south branch of the creek, which is Williamson Creek. Cross back and forth over the creek as the terrain requires. Eventually you leave the steep walls of the canyon and enter into a more U-shaped canyon. Bushwhacking prevails until timberline is reached. At timberline, talus and gravel fields compose most of the terrain.

Many of the north face and northeast routes can be reached via Williamson Creek, which provides a great wilderness experience. However, the Eastern Approach via Shepherd Pass to the Williamson Bowl and then dropping down into Williamson Creek is easier. The Eastern Approach via Williamson Creek is also the best place to park when doing the northeast ridge of Williamson. This approach provides access to routes 4, 5, 6, 7, and 8.

Eastern Approach via Bairs Creek

Follow the Eastern Approach via Shepherd Pass to the 7.2-mile mark and then follow the mileage log below.

Mileage Log

7.2 Cross a small creekbed next to a corral.

7.6 Fork in the road. Turn left.

9.4 Road forks. Take right fork. Road goes straight for a while and then turns sharply to the left.

10.7 Bairs Creek parking area.

This approach is similar to that of the Eastern Approach via Williamson Creek in that there is no real trail, and bushwhacking and cross-country scrambling prevail. Follow Bairs Creek southwest to the east face of Mount Williamson. This approach provides access to route 10.

Eastern Approach via George Creek

Follow the Eastern Approach via Bairs Creek to the 10.7-mile mark, and then follow the mileage log below.

Mileage Log

10.7 Bairs Creek parking area.

12.2 Cross the south fork of Bairs Creek.

12.6 Road turns right. Go straight and cross a cattle guard. (Turning right leads 0.3 mile to a parking area for hiking up into the South Fork of Bairs Creek.)

13.5 Roads forks. Take right fork.

14.1 Parking area off to the right side of the road.

14.5 This last 0.4 mile is very rough and it may be better to park at the parking area at the 14.1-mile mark.

Park your car and hike west following George Creek up the prominent canyon leading west. The Eastern Approach via George Creek, as with the Eastern Approach via Williamson Creek and Eastern Approach via Bairs Creek, has no real trail. Hiking George Creek enables one access to the easiest route on the peak, the Southeast Slope Route (route 11), but the canyon is rough, with the trail often disappearing. As of this writing, George Creek is only open from April 15 to May 15 and December 15 to January 1, because it's within the Bighorn Sheep Zoological Preserve.

Hike up the rugged, trail-less George Creek Canyon. The trail is often faint and indiscriminate, because it is not maintained. At the end of the canyon stands a prominent buttress. There are two small creeks; one trickles down from the basin to the north of the buttress and one from the basin to the south of the buttress. Hike up the creek north of the buttress, toward Mount Williamson. A small grassy plateau is attained just north of the buttress. From here one may camp or begin climbing. This approach provides access to route 11.

Note: It is possible to reach George Creek by turning off Highway 395 at Manzanar and driving west. However, we have not included that approach because of the numerous branchings and side roads encountered. The approach via Symmes Creek is the easiest and least complicated.

Route 1, West Face, Class 3

Use the Eastern Approach via Shepherd Pass or Eastern Approach via Williamson Creek.

Joseph N. Le Conte, R. H. Butler, E. B. Gould, T. Parker, G. Cosgrove, A. Elston, and A. G. Eells made the first ascent of the now standard and very popular West Face Route on July 10, 1903. This is the most popular route on the mountain; it's fairly straightforward and not very difficult, and it is suggested for anyone with solid Class 3 climbing skills. However, for those less confident, a rope and a few stoppers are recommended.

After entering the Williamson Bowl from the north, hike south toward the second lake in the bowl. Pass the first lake, which lies at the base of the impressive east face of Mount Tyndall, on your right (west). Directly east of the second lake lies the West Face Route on Mount Williamson.

On the southern portion of the west face is a prominent rock band along the base of the mountain, containing a number of black water marks. Climb toward the most prominent black water mark and ascend the talus just to the right of it. Above the black water mark, enter a large chute and climb this chute for about 1,000 feet. At the top of the chute, a broken, rocky cliff blocks further progress. A few feet to the left (northeast) is a small notch that looks out upon the north face of Mount Williamson and Owens Valley. To continue to the summit, traverse right (southeast) below the rocky cliff for about 20 feet, to a narrow cleft. Climb up this cleft, which is moderate Class 3 and one pitch long. At the top of this pitch, the summit plateau is gained. From here it is a short walk to the south (main) summit.

Descend via the same route.

Route 2, Peak 14,160, from the main summit, Class 4

You must first gain the high south summit in order to follow this route.

This route was first climbed by Leroy Jeffers on July 21, 1916. There are several ways to reach the top of Peak 14,160, the higher of two sub-summits of Mount Williamson. All entail Class 4 climbing. But first you must choose one of the routes to the south summit of Mount Williamson.

From the south (main or highest) summit, hike northeast toward the peaklet. At the end of the plateau, drop down into a notch for 200 feet, moving east along the easier terrain as you descend. At the base of the notch, climb into a chute that connects to the top of the crest of the arête of the peaklet. From here drop about 80 feet down the opposite side of the arête, traversing northwest where one pitch of broken Class 4 rock leads to the summit.

The west face of Mount Williamson showing route 1 (Photo by Steve Porcella)

An easier approach involves staying low on the east side of the plateau as you hike toward the notch. This avoids the initial Class 4 descent into the notch.

Descend via the same route.

Route 3, Northwest Buttress, Class 5

Use the Eastern Approach via Shepherd Pass to hike to the Williamson Bowl. This route was first climbed by Galen Rowell in October 1970.

In the Williamson Bowl, starting between the first (northernmost) and second lakes, climb northeast to a notch behind a prominent tower. From the tower, continue up the northwest buttress. Some Class 5 climbing is encountered in order to gain the western edge of the summit plateau.

Descend via route 1, West Face.

Route 4, North Face, Class 5

Use either the Eastern Approach via Shepherd Pass to the Williamson Bowl, or the Eastern Approach via Williamson Creek.

John and Ruth Mendenhall made the first ascent of this route on July 6, 1957.

From the Williamson Bowl, drop down into the Williamson Creek Canyon and hike to the two smaller lakes that reside in the bowl directly northeast of Mount Williamson. Ascend into a gully that allows passage through a steep, black, water-stained rock band. Broken rocks above the rock band can be climbed. This eventually turns into a shoulder that separates two gullies. This shoulder steepens to the point where it is easier to traverse left into a gully. Work up this gully and to the left while inspecting other gullies for access to the summit plateau. Pick the easiest one and follow it to the plateau. From here it is an easy jaunt to the south summit.

Descend via route 1, West Face.

Route 5, North Rib, IV, 5.7

Use either the Eastern Approach via Shepherd Pass to the Williamson Bowl, or the Eastern Approach via Williamson Creek.

The north rib was first climbed from the north by Lito Tejada-Flores and Edgar Boyles in July 1972.

Leaving the Williamson Bowl and entering the Williamson Creek Canyon, one can see a long, curving rib ascending up to Peak 14,160. The North Rib Route lies on the rib to the right of the Peak 14,160 rib. The first half of the North Rib Route is fairly easy and is composed of moderate Class 3 and 4 climbing. The upper half of the route consists of nine to ten pitches of 5.5 to 5.7 rock. The route tops out on the summit plateau to the west of Peak 14,160.

Descend via route 7 or route 1.

The north face of Mount Williamson showing routes 5 and 6 (Photo by Steve Porcella)

Route 6, North Arête, III, 5.4

Use either the Eastern Approach via Shepherd Pass to the Williamson Bowl, or the Eastern Approach via Williamson Creek.

The north arête was first climbed by Claude Fiddler and Jim Keating in July 1984.

This route climbs the long, twisting ridge to the left (east) of the North Rib Route (route 5). The North Arête is a perfect arête that drops straight down from Peak 14,160. The climb is started by approaching from the Williamson Bowl and entering the Williamson Creek Canyon. The initial climbing is moderate, and a prominent tower, which the route aims for, can be seen high on the route. The route passes the tower on the left side and continues up the steepening ridge. The route tops out on the summit of the west horn.

Descend via route 7 or route 1.

Route 7, Peak 14,125 from Williamson Creek, Class 2–3

Use either the Eastern Approach via Shepherd Pass to reach the Williamson Bowl, then hike into Williamson Creek, or use the Eastern Approach via Williamson Creek.

This tower or horn was first climbed from the north by George Wallerstein, Andy Smatko, Barbara Lilley, Bill Schuler, and Ed Treacy on October 11, 1970. It lies to the east of Peak 14,160.

Hike up the Williamson Creek Canyon to about the 10,000-foot level. High on the north face of the mountain is a red buttress to the left of two dry waterfalls. Climb up to this buttress. After passing a cliff on the left, traverse left using a prominent chute. When near the top of this chute, traverse left again to a saddle. The saddle is the beginning of a broad chute. Continue up this broad chute to the top of the peaklet.

Descend via the same route.

Route 8, Northeast Ridge from Williamson Creek, Class 4

Use the Eastern Approach via Williamson Creek.

Homer D. Erwin, on July 26, 1925, made the first ascent of the upper portion of this ridge.

From timberline in the Williamson Creek Canyon, ascend a prominent chute up the northeast face of the peak well to the east of the two sub-summits. Once the northeast ridge is attained, follow it over Peak 14,125 and Peak 14,160 to the summit plateau.

Route 9, The Northeast Ridge from Owens Valley, Class 4

Use the Eastern Approach via Williamson Creek.

On December 29, 1954, Warren Harding and John Ohrenschall made the first complete ascent from Owens Valley during the winter. The physical and technical demands of a winter climb of this route are best described in an unpublished account of the experience by Warren Harding:

"It was winter—December 30, to be exact. The weather, deteriorating all day, had turned dark and ugly. We questioned whether we should continue on. If we went ahead with the climb, there would be no chance of getting back to our high camp at about 12,000 feet elevation. We would spend the night out somewhere on the northeast ridge. Our 'high-altitude gear' was a far cry from the high-tech, down or Gore-Tex or pile equipment commonly in use today. Rather, we made do with 'state-of-the-art' war surplus bomber jackets, navy watch caps, Swiss canteens, etc.—we did, however have Pivetta boots imported from Italy.

"We slogged on. Slippery slabs and scree slopes gave way to even more slippery Class 4–5 climbing. The storm was getting serious; we—and the rock—were getting heavily plastered with snow.

"Pitch after pitch of what, in dry conditions, would've been easy Class 4. We were having a hell of a time—frequently resorting to aid, we were not concerned with climbing ethics, doing it all free—we were, simply, rather desperate to get somewhere—anywhere—before dark. This was no place to spend the night!

"Just at dark, we reached a summit of sorts—all we could see was the rock ridge falling away ahead of us. We anchored ourselves to a small ledge, coiled the ropes for a seat—and that was it—our bivy!

"Eventually, morning came. We were still alive! Fortunately for us, hypothermia had not been invented yet. . . . But we were definitely not happy campers! Among other things, we didn't have much food. We thought that it would just be a 'summit dash'—and etc.

"The storm was breaking and with the clearing weather we could see our immediate problem: we were perched above a deep notch in the ridge; probably on the summit of the eastern, northeast peak of Mount Williamson, elevation 14,125 feet. It also meant that we still had one hell of a long way to go to reach the summit.

"We felt like 'frozen frogs' and got moving slowly and with some difficulty. Rappel into the notch—nail out. Reaching the summit of the western, northeast peak, elevation 14,160 feet, we were confronted by an even deeper notch separating us from the summit plateau. Rap down—nail out—simple as that! Then, the long dreadful slog to the main summit.

"During this phase of our jaunt, I saw—or thought I saw—a large white rabbit with short black ears sitting on a rock just off to our right. He was watching us as though he was the seer of the mountain. I thought about asking him for directions, but John didn't look like he was seeing anything unusual or seemingly out of place—so I kept my mouth shut—best not to let your partner know when you're hallucinating.

"Didn't hang around the summit very long. Scenery was spectacular and all, but it was already midafternoon and if we moved right on, we could, conceivably, get off the mountain today. However (and I think that bunny had something to do with this), it didn't quite work out that way.

"While on the summit, we discussed our descent. Actually—there was no discussion! Descending via the northeast ridge was out of the question—our only option was an easier route. We were out of food, and the stress and strain of the past three days was catching up with us. A quick look at our topo map showed that the George Creek Canyon was our best bet. So, off we headed in that direction.

"New Year's Eve: Timberline—George Creek.

"'Well, John, here we are! If we can just get a fire going, this won't be a bad New Year's Eve—lots of George Creek water to drink—we'll just pretend there are bubbles and alcohol in it. Don't be shy, John.'

"Darkness had overtaken us at timberline. Forging ahead seemed rather futile. The prospect of a fire seemed most inviting. John piled wood on a small bit of tinder and I produced our salvation: one pack of matches. Stricken with horror we watched our salvation disappear as match after match failed to light. We cussed at each other, at the matches, at the creek, at the lack of champagne. With quivering hands, John struck the last match. It sputtered and sparked—ready to die in a puff of smoke like all of its previous kin—but it lit! Soon, with the proper 'White Man's Fire' and the heady George Creek water, it turned into a grand New Year's Eve.

"It started snowing again at daybreak. At first light, we headed out—slipping and sliding down the snow-covered slopes. The snow was wet and we were soon completely soaked.

"Early afternoon found us at the base of Mount Williamson. A check of the topo showed that our car should be about 5 or 6 miles to the north. So, off across the alluvial fan. It was still snowing, visibility very limited—the car would be difficult to spot when and if we ever got near it.

"Slog-slog through the brush-choked washes that constantly crossed our path. The day wore on. We were gradually 'running out of gas.' I would stop to rest, look back to see how John was doing—often not too well, collapsed, lying face down in the snow. This didn't seem to matter very much—I just watched apathetically as he would struggle to his feet. A couple of times I thought I was walking among snow-covered buildings in some distant, foreign city. Turned out to be large rocks covered with snow—more hallucinations. Well, at least the rabbit wasn't sitting on top of one of them.

"As darkness approached—and still no car—we realized that if we failed to find it, our best chance of survival lay in heading east toward Highway 395; another 5 to 6 miles away. The idea was gut-wrenching—could we keep going that long?

"It had stopped snowing and visibility had improved somewhat. It was also getting much colder—something had to happen soon! Fortunately, it did. At the last possible moment, we spotted a grove of trees that we recognized. John's station wagon should be parked there—it was!

"My next thought was—'I hope it doesn't start!' It didn't!

"Had we got the beast going, we would have felt obligated to get back to Sacramento that night. When the trusty Chevy made only a feeble sound, we felt relieved of all responsibility except for our own well-being. First, dry clothes, then a night of endless cooking and eating, with frequent referrals to the big wine jug.

"The morning dawned bright and clear; we were completely restored in mind and body. Well, maybe not in mind: we had come to think of ourselves as 'Austrian alpinists.' We even goose-stepped the first few yards to Independence—turning back to look at 'our mountain,' we noted that it looked a lot like K-2.

"During the hike out, John, rather hesitantly, and with a perplexed look on his face, asked if I had seen anything strange up on the summit plateau.

"I looked at John, hesitant to reveal my mental state during that now-distant desperate moment—'Um, maybe a large white rabbit with short black ears?'

"'Yeah—yeah, that's it! I knew it was real!'

"We laughed so loud I was sure that rabbit could hear us."

ON JUNE 13, 1969, Dick Beach and Steve Rogero climbed the northeast ridge of Williamson in 14 hours from Owens Valley. During their ascent, Beach and Rogero stumbled onto the remains of Harding and Ohrenschall's last bivouac site. It was at the 8,000-foot level and Beach noted in his unpublished account:

"The camp was very old, since everything in it looked like post-WWI army surplus. There were unused K-rations and several Swiss-made canteens stashed about. There was even a bighorn sheep skull methodically placed as though it was a souvenir."

For Beach and Rogero, the next 3,000 feet proved to be the hardest. Snow and rain were intermittent and the climbing was slow. Just before they reached the first sub-summit, Peak 14,125, they wrapped themselves in a space blanket and napped for an hour.

By 5:00 P.M., the two climbers had reached the top of Peak 14,125. Due to deteriorating conditions, time was becoming precious. Rogero found himself a niche among the rocks, while Beach weighed the pros and cons of continuing alone. Finally, he decided to make a solo bid for the true south summit.

He descended into the notch between Peak 14,125 and Peak 14,160. After ascending Peak 14,160, Beach was unable to find the summit register. With snow piling up on the south side of the peak, Beach made a traverse to the true summit plateau. He finally reached the main summit at 6:10 P.M. After touching the highest rock with his hand, he turned and sprinted back toward the two sub-summits where his partner waited. Beach recalled:

"My panic-laced summit climb and return to the easternmost summit took an hour and a half. With the light all but gone, we entered a narrow chute close to the notch between the two summit horns and quickly descended it. Three frozen waterfalls were by-passed in the chute and by 9:00 P.M. we were safely on the northern escarpment of Williamson Creek."

Descend via route 10, Bairs Creek, 11, Southeast Slope, or 7, Peak 14,125.

Route 10, Bairs Creek, Southeast Ridge Variation, Class 3

Use the Eastern Approach via Bairs Creek.

This route was first climbed by Dick Jali, John Harding, and Dick Cowley in 1958.

Hike cross-country up the South Fork of Bairs Creek until a large cirque is confronted. Look for the easiest chute (the southernmost chute) that faces east and that leads out of the cirque. Exiting the cirque puts one onto the southeast ridge, which can be followed to the south summit.

Descend via the same route.

Bairs Creek Canyon and the upper portion of the northeast ridge leading to the summit of Mount Williamson (Photo by Steve Porcella)

Route 11, Southeast Slope, Class 1–2

Use the Eastern Approach via George Creek.

This route was first ascended by W. L. Hunter and C. Mulholland in 1884. This is the easiest route to reach the main (southwest) summit on the mountain.

To start the climb, hike directly north from the small grassy plateau just north of the buttress, and ascend the moderate talus of the south slope of Mount Williamson. The trudge up the talus gradually turns northwest and then west to reach the summit plateau. From here the climb is a short scramble over gently sloping talus to the south summit. This route is long, dry, and a seemingly endless talus hike, but it is the safest route on the mountain.

Descend via the same route.

Route 12, South Face Arête, IV, 5.8

Use the Eastern Approach via Shepherd Pass to the Williamson Bowl.

Cameron Burns and Steve Porcella made the first ascent of this route in May 1989.

This route lies on the south face of Mount Williamson. Hike south through the Williamson Bowl. Drop eastward into the headwaters of George Creek Canyon. At the base of the south face of Mount Williamson, there is a large, steep, triangular buttress that has an open book or dihedral on its east side. This open

The south face of Mount Williamson from Mount Whitney. The south face arête is the continuous arête just left of center (Photo by Steve Porcella)

book starts at the lower right corner (east) and angles left (northwest) to the top of the buttress. Start at the base of the open book and climb six exciting pitches up the triangular buttress. The seventh pitch is a delicate traverse left (west) and then right (east) around a spectacular, huge box-basin on the mountain. The crux is on the sixth pitch and involves a steep, slightly overhanging lie-back. From here, the rest of the climb is all Class 4 and 5, depending on how close one stays to the crest of the arête. At one point you must traverse east across an orange and dark green rock ridge in order to stay on the arête as it curves right (east) and then left (west). The climb tops out on the summit register box.

Descend via route 1, West Face.

Route 13, Southwest Face, Class 3–4

Use the Eastern Approach via Shepherd Pass to the Williamson Bowl.

This route has come to be known as the Southwest Route. Bolton Coit Brown and Lucy Brown first climbed this route in June 1896.

From the Williamson Bowl traverse upward, southeast, across the western face toward a small notch where the southwest ridge joins the southwest corner of the mountain. The south face of the peak can be seen from the notch. Climb east out onto the south face. Routefinding through gullies, broken buttresses, and chutes eventually leads one to the summit plateau. Go west to reach the south (main) summit.

Descend via route 1, West Face.

The southwest ridge of Mount Williamson (Photo by Steve Porcella)

Route 14, Southwest Ridge, Class 3

Use either the Eastern Approach via Shepherd Pass to Williamson Bowl, or the Eastern Approach via George Creek.

This route was first climbed by R. S. Fink on August 18, 1933.

From the southernmost lake in the Williamson Bowl, known as Lake Helen of Troy, climb onto the southwest arête. Follow the arête all the way, crisscrossing back and forth along the crest to avoid loose blocks and difficulties.

Descend via route 1, West Face.

References

Beach, Dick. "The Northwest Ridge of Mount Williamson." Unpublished manuscript. Bishop, Calif., 1989.

Bohn, Dave and Mary Millman, eds. *Norman Clyde of the Sierra Nevada: Rambles through the Range of Light.* San Francisco: Scrimshaw Press, 1971.

Brown, Bolton Coit. "Wanderings in the High Sierra Between Mount King and Mount Williamson." Part 1. *Sierra Club Bulletin* 2 (1897–1899).

De La Carroll, A. W. "The Route Up Mount Williamson." *Sierra Club Bulletin* 1 (1893–1896).

Farquhar, Francis. *History of the Sierra Nevada.* Berkeley, Calif.: University of California Press, 1965.

Harding, Warren J. Interviewed by the authors. Moab, Utah, September 1990.

———. "Northeast Ridge of Mount Williamson, First Winter Ascent." Unpublished manuscript. Moab, Utah, 1990.

Inyo Independent. Local Affairs, September 27, 1873; October 9, 1875; October 11, 1875.

Mendenhall, John. Letter, courtesy of Valerie Cohen. June 9, 1957.

———. "A Climber's Guide to Peaks in the Sierra Nevada." *Sierra Club Bulletin* 26 (February 1941).

Off Belay. 18:63 (December 1974).

Parsons, E. T. "The Notable Mountaineering of the Sierra Club in 1903." *Sierra Club Bulletin* 5 (1904-1905).

Robinson, John. "Mount Williamson: Giant of the High Sierra." *Summit Magazine,* October 1970.

Roper, Steve. *The Climbers Guide to the High Sierra.* San Francisco: Sierra Club Books, 1976.

Sierra Club Bulletin. "Mountaineering Notes" *Sierra Club Bulletin* 43 (1958).

Sierra Register Committee Archives. *Mount Williamson Summit Register, 1903–1931.* Berkeley, Calif.: University of California Berkeley, courtesy of the Bancroft Library; unpublished.

Tejada-Flores, Lito. Personal correspondence with the authors, June 1990.

Voge, Hervey H., and Andrew J. Smatko. *Mountaineers Guide to the High Sierra.* San Francisco: Sierra Club Books, 1972.

Chapter 6
Mount Tyndall

The climb was made as upon a tree . . .
cutting mere toeholds and embracing the whole column of ice in my arms.

Clarence King, ice climbing near the summit of Mount Tyndall,
in *Mountaineering in the Sierra Nevada,* 1872

An incredibly picturesque peak, 14,015-foot Mount Tyndall's eastern escarpment falls away dramatically, giving it a shape that imitates many other peaks in the immediate area, Mount Whitney for one.

Despite the relatively small number of routes that have been done on this peak, it offers climbs of every grade, length, and steepness.

Mount Tyndall was named for the famed English geologist/glaciologist and mountaineer John Tyndall (1820–1893), and is the site of Clarence King's first great climbing faux pas.

For three years the Geological Survey explored California. But it was not until 1863 that the adventurous group really began exploring the Sierra Nevada. Unfortunately, in 1864, the legislature rewrote the Survey's original charter, prompting the scientists to concentrate on more profitable exploration: the search for gold and silver. Pure science was deemed a less noble cause. Although Professor Whitney himself headed to the ore-rich areas of the north, the majority of the Geological Survey headed south, into the mountains.

In the summer of 1864, William Brewer, James Gardiner, Dick Cotter, and the newly hired Clarence King trekked up the western slope of the great range, and made camp below a towering peak. On July 2, Brewer, the leader of the group,

Dave Wilson leading during the first ascent of the Direct East Face Route on Mount Tyndall (Photo © Galen Rowell/Mountain Light)

125

accompanied by his topographer, Charles Hoffman, climbed the mountain later named Mount Brewer, and were perhaps the first white men to realize the extent of the great Sierra.

From the summit of Mount Brewer, the pair also caught sight of the tallest peak in the range, perhaps the tallest in the nation. It was dubbed Mount Whitney. Two other tall peaks, Mounts Tyndall and Williamson, were also observed and sub-sequently named.

Upon their return to camp, Brewer and Hoffman related their find to the other members of the group. King became utterly obsessed with the high peak to the south, and as soon as Brewer had described the "impossible" journey one would have just to reach the high peaks of the southern Sierra, King was hooked.

In his highly acclaimed account *Mountaineering in the Sierra Nevada,* published in 1872, King wrote about the night of July 2, 1864:

"I lay awake thinking of [Mount Whitney]; but early the next morning I had made up my mind, and, taking Cotter aside, I asked him in an easy manner whether he would like to penetrate the Terra Incognita with me at the risk of our necks, provided Brewer should consent. In a frank, courageous tone he answered after his usual mode, 'Why not?'"

Thus Cotter consented to join King, and even though Brewer, as reported in *Mountaineering in the Sierra Nevada,* "freely confessed that he believed the plan madness," King and Cotter set off the following day, heading east across the Sierra Nevada for the high peaks of the southern Sierra. They took only six days' provisions.

Brewer, Gardiner, and Hoffman accompanied King and Cotter to the first ridge, and from there wished the two adventurers luck. Upon reaching the ridge, King saw, for the first time, the wall of peaks that he and Cotter were to penetrate. In *Mountaineering in the Sierra Nevada,* King later reflected about his departure:

"I did not wonder that Brewer and Hoffman pronounced our undertaking impossible . . . when we shook hands there was not a dry eye in the party."

In his book, King also admitted that his goals were not of a scientific nature. "Professor Brewer asked me for my plan, and I had to own that I had but one, which was to reach the highest peak in the range." Undoubtedly, Clarence King was one of the first men to visit the Sierra whose primary objective was moun-tain climbing.

After three days of circuitous travel, the pair reached a bivouac site close to the base of the mountain. The following morning they began their final assault on the peak. King's account continued:

"I closed my eyes and slept soundly until Cotter woke me at half past three. When we arose, we breakfasted by the light of our fire, which still blazed brilliantly, and, leaving our knapsacks, started for the mountain with only instru-ments, canteens, and luncheon."

Upon reaching the base of the north side, King and Cotter toiled over blocks of enormous size. The pair found themselves continually jumping from the path of a shifting boulder. Even after the larger blocks at the base of the north

The incredible east face of Mount Tyndall (Photo by Steve Porcella)

side were surmounted, danger still lurked in the form of boulders frozen into the ice above. King observed:

"It communicated no very pleasant sensation to see above you these immense missiles hanging by a mere band, and knowing that, as soon as the sun rose, you would be exposed to a constant cannonade."

Soon the irrepressible duo was standing on the summit of the mountain. Looking south, both men realized that they had made a mistake and were not on the high peak that Brewer had described. Undiminished, King, with his usual dramatic flair, "rang" his hammer upon the topmost rock. Although King had missed Mount Whitney, he had made the first ascent of a very unique and spectacular peak. King and Cotter shook hands and King reverently named the grand peak Mount Tyndall.

Although Clarence King had made one of the most widely recounted mistakes in mountaineering history, he had just achieved the summit of the tallest mountain ever climbed in the Sierra Nevada.

After taking a series of scientific observations, King and Cotter began their descent. They quickly decided that the route of ascent was far too dangerous in its icy condition. King's account in *Mountaineering in the Sierra Nevada* continued:

"Having completed our observations, we packed up the instruments, glanced once again around the whole field of view, and descended to the top of our icicle ladder. Upon looking over, I saw to my consternation that during the day the upper half had broken off. Scars traced down upon the snowfield below it indicated the manner of its fall, and far below, upon the shattered debris, were strewn its white relics. I saw that nothing but the sudden gift of wings could possibly take us down to the snow ridge. We held a council and concluded to climb quite round the peak in search of the best mode of descent."

Although King describes his descent with Cotter as extremely hazardous, it was made by the easy southwest slope.

The first winter ascent of Mount Tyndall was made in January 1930 by Orlando Bartholemew, solo, shortly after his conquest of Mounts Langley and Whitney.

A visit from Fred Beckey and Charles Raymond meant the first ascent of the couloir just south of the true east face. In 1972, Galen Rowell, Dave Wilson, and Steve Brewer made an ascent of the most direct line on the east face, from the base of the glacier to the summit. Once again Rowell had been the first to climb the sheerest wall on a big peak in the Sierra Nevada.

Climbing Routes on Mount Tyndall

The quickest and easiest way to climb Mount Tyndall is via route 1, Northwest Ridge, after following the Shepherd Pass Trail from the Owens Valley.

Routes are presented in a clockwise fashion.

Eastern Approach via Shepherd Pass or Williamson Bowl

Follow the Eastern Approach via Shepherd Pass described in chapter 5, Mount Williamson, to Shepherd Pass. After you gain Shepherd Pass, Mount Tyndall comes into view. Routes 1, 2, and 3 are gained by hiking west or south from the pass. Tyndall's sharp eastern escarpment is not visible, but can be approached by heading south, into the Williamson Bowl. There are many good campsites around the lakes here, and morning approaches to east-face routes are short. Also, this is one of the most spectacular campsites in all the Sierra Nevada; a camera is often the best piece of equipment to have here.

East-face routes begin above the snowfield below the east face. Clothing has a tendency to get soaked here (and it's cold), and it is not uncommon to find the rock wet, even late in the summer. Also, caution is advised on all east-face routes, because the face has recently seen a number of rock and snow avalanches. This approach can be used for all routes in this chapter.

Eastern Approach via Tyndall Creek

For north-side routes on Mount Tyndall, the approach is easier, and many of these routes can be done in a day from Anvil Camp. Follow the Eastern Approach via Shepherd Pass described in chapter 5, Mount Williamson, to Shepherd Pass and, rather than dropping down into Williamson Bowl, from the pass continue on the trail as it follows Tyndall Creek. The trail passes around the north side of the mountain, allowing easy access to climbing there. The most obvious ridge from Shepherd Pass is the northwest ridge (route 1), which descends to a point about 0.5 mile west (right, when viewed from Shepherd Pass) of the pass. The north side (route 2, Sierra Crest Rib) lies 0.5 mile to the left (east) of that, and the northeast arête (route 3) lies about 0.5 mile left (southeast) of that.

Western Approach via John Muir Trail

From the west, Mount Tyndall can be approached via the John Muir Trail, which begins in Yosemite National Park and ends in Sequoia/Kings Canyon National Park. To reach the Southwest Slopes (route 8), in the vicinity of Tawny Point leave the trail and hike south around the point to turn west and hike on the Wright Lakes Trail into the Wright Lakes basin. To reach the west and north sides, from the John Muir Trail where it crosses Tyndall Creek, take the Shepherd Pass Trail and head east. The Shepherd Pass Trail follows Tyndall Creek up the western slope of the Sierra Crest. The trail passes around the west and north sides of the mountain, allowing easy access to these easy-to-hike slopes.

Route 1, Northwest Ridge, Class 2

Use the Eastern Approach via Shepherd Pass or the Western Approach via John Muir Trail.

The first ascent of this ridge is unknown, but was probably made during the 1920s or '30s.

This easy route starts near the base of a prominent ridge that descends from the summit northward to a point about 0.5 mile west of Shepherd Pass. The route ascends the right side (west) of this sharp ridge, as a twisting rocky trail. Near the top of the slope, the ridge joins another ridge that rises from the right (northwest). Where these two ridges meet is an obvious notch, which splits both ridges from east to west. From here, the climb along the final summit ridge is somewhat exposed. Turn around the large, towering gendarme above the notch on the right (west) side, and then work around behind it until the summit ridge is gained. Stay on this side of the ridge all the way to the summit. The sheer east face drops away to the left, and caution should be taken not to wander too close to the edge. Its Class 2 nature makes this the easiest method of gaining Mount Tyndall's summit from the north. There are also many variations available.

Descend via the same route.

Route 2, North Rib (Sierra Crest Rib), Class 3

Use the Eastern Approach via Shepherd Pass or the Western Approach via John Muir Trail.

This route, the original route up the mountain, was first climbed by Clarence King and Richard Cotter on July 6, 1864.

The route follows a small but well-defined rib, the Sierra Crest, up the northeastern slopes of the mountain. The route is only Class 3, yet the many blocks

The northeast face of Mount Tyndall showing routes 1 through 3
(Photo by Cameron Burns)

strewn across it are loose and require caution. As mentioned in the chapter introduction, even Clarence King observed the serious potential for rockfall on this
route. The size and quantity of the boulders decreases the higher one climbs. In
poor conditions this route also can become a gigantic slip and slide, since the
majority of the climbing involves friction on smooth slab.

Descend via route 1, Northwest Ridge.

Route 3, Northeast Arête, III, 5.9

Use the Eastern Approach via Shepherd Pass/Williamson Bowl.

This route was first climbed by Cameron Burns and Steve Porcella on
June 12, 1989. While scanning the east face for a new line of ascent, the authors

witnessed multiple rock and snow avalanches pummel the entire east face. Not surprisingly, we opted for the unclimbed northeast arête. This route boasts very high-quality rock, exposure, spectacular views along the edge of the east face abyss, excellent protection, minimal rockfall, and sunny exposure for much of the day.

From Shepherd Pass, continue to the north side of the mountain. The route starts in the obvious chimney on the corner between the north side of the mountain and the steep east face. It is best recognized as a tall, Y-shaped crack that goes straight up before melding into the arête above.

Climb several hundred feet of Class 3 rock to the base of the chimney. The rope-up spot is a ledge on the left side of the chimney, just below the point where the chimney steepens to vertical. The crux is the first pitch. After climbing up 10 feet, cross the chimney onto ledges on the right-hand side. Above is a black roof, the steepest part of the route. Cross the chimney again and ascend steep rock just a few feet left of the crack itself. Continue up and slightly left on sustained 5.8 rock until a series of small ledges are attained. A small triangular rock is surmounted, and then, moving right on small face moves (5.9), the route moves up and right, regaining the crack system. From here the route is obvious: Follow the crack straight up for multiple pitches of moderate to easy 5.7–5.8 climbing until the climbing becomes Class 4. Continue following the brink of the eastern precipice to the summit ridge, then to the summit.

Descend via route 1, Northwest Ridge.

Route 4, Direct East Face, V, 5.10, A2

Use the Eastern Approach via Williamson Bowl.

First climbed by Steve Brewer, Dave Wilson, and Galen Rowell in September 1983, over a two-day period, this steep and demanding route lies in the center of the east face, between the two prominent gullies.

The route starts on the lower left-hand side of the large buttress, directly beneath the summit. Using some aid, the first two pitches traverse up and right, surmounting the obvious overhangs in the less obvious gully that splits the central buttress. Above the overhangs, the route eases off for several pitches, then 5.8 to 5.10 cracks split the final headwall. The route finishes at the summit of the mountain.

In the *American Alpine Journal,* Rowell noted: "Like earlier parties, we were surprised by the extreme difficulty of the lower face. . . . We fixed the first 300 feet one afternoon, and returned at dawn to complete the climb. Even with considerable 5.10 climbing, we couldn't avoid several points of aid on the first two pitches. The haul line sometimes hung out 35 feet from the face." Although this route has yet to see an all-free ascent, its reputation for being wet might be a factor.

Descend via route 1, Northwest Ridge.

Route 5, East Chimney, IV, 5.8

Use the Eastern Approach via Williamson Bowl.

This east-face route was first climbed by Bill Sumner and Michael Heath in August 1972.

This route also ascends the incredible east face, just left of the Direct East Face Route (route 4). Left of the summit is a faint chimney system that drops to the snow. Surmount a series of overhangs at the base of this feature on their right side. Then follow the obvious chimney system above for many leads until the summit ridge is gained.

Descend via route 1, Northwest Ridge.

Route 6, East Gully, III, 5.8

Use the Eastern Approach via Williamson Bowl.

This route was climbed by Fred Beckey and Charles Raymond on May 31, 1970. It follows the most obvious gully south of the summit point. Although the majority of the route consists of steep snow and ice, there is a short section of rotten rock, the crux, near the top of the gully.

As recounted by Raymond in an interview in 1990, the climbing wasn't that difficult and the climbers moved quickly up the gully. At one point, Raymond

The east face of Mount Tyndall showing routes 4 through 6 (Photo by Cameron Burns)

was leading and placed a piton in a horizontal crack using only his hands. "I didn't pound it in because I thought it was solid just placed there," Raymond notes. "When Fred took it out, he fell. He pulled on it, expecting it to be solid, and then went over backward." Apparently Raymond was witness to one of mountaineering's rarest events: Fred Beckey taking a fall.

Ice axes and crampons are recommended for this route, and caution is strongly advised due to the hazard of rockfall.

Descend via route 1, Northwest Ridge.

Route 7, East Face, East Pillar, II, 5.6

Use the Eastern Approach via Williamson Bowl.

This route was first climbed by Daniel Roitman, Gus Benner, and Sergio Aragon in 1994.

The route lies on the rock wall that is between the northeast arête and the easternmost gully or chute on the east face. The climb starts in the middle of the face, ascends toward right-facing lie-back cracks, crosses the Northeast Arête Route (route 3), and leads out onto the north face. We assume that the route eventually joins with the northwest ridge and continues onto the summit.

Descend via route 1, Northwest Ridge.

Route 8, Southwest Slopes, Class 2

Use the Western Approach via John Muir Trail.

This route was the descent route used by Clarence King and Richard Cotter, after they had made the first ascent of the mountain on July 6, 1864.

Hike to the Wright Lakes basin. Hike east to the largest Wright Lake, below the east face of Mount Versteeg. From here, the south slopes are evident and they rise to the northeast of Versteeg. The southwest slopes can be ascended by any number of routes, all of which are Class 2. There are several more developed trails through the boulder fields, but it requires the skill of the mountaineer to pick the easiest way through the geological debris.

Descend via the same route.

References

American Alpine Journal. 13, (1971); 15 (1973); 26 (1984); 32, (1990).

Brower, David. "Far from the Maddening Mules: A Knapsacker's Retrospect." *Sierra Club Bulletin* 20 (February 1935).

King, Clarence. *Mountaineering in the Sierra Nevada.* 1872. Reprint, Lincoln, Neb.: University of Nebraska Press, Bison Books, 1970.

Raymond, Charles. Interviewed by Cameron Burns, March 1990.

Robinson, Doug. Private correspondence with Cameron Burns, 1990.

Roper, Steve. *A Climber's Guide to the High Sierra.* San Francisco: Sierra Club Books, 1976.

Rose, Eugene. *High Odyssey: The First Solo Winter Assault of Mount Whitney and the Muir Trail Area.* Berkeley, Calif.: Howell-North Books, 1974.

Rowell, Galen. Interviewed by authors, 1990.

Chapter 7
Split Mountain

*. . . to the northeast . . . the crest rises into a huge mountain
with a double summit . . . which I called Split Mountain.*

Bolton Coit Brown, from the summit of Arrow Peak
in 1895, *Sierra Club Bulletin,* 1896

The geology of Split Mountain, elevation 14,058 feet, is unique. The black rock that composes the majority of the mountain is actually a prehistoric remnant of an extensive sedimentary layer that once covered the Sierra Nevada. Known as a "roof" that overlaid igneous granitic rock, uplift accelerated erosion of the bulk of this layer. These "roof pendants," as they are known today, are scattered throughout the range. Split Mountain is a classic example of a roof pendant. The lighter-colored rock at the base of Split Mountain is the newer, intrusive granite that predominates throughout the Sierra Nevada.

A steep, polished gully divides the center of both the east face and the west face of Split Mountain. Both of these gullies meet at the top of the mountain and are connected by a notch that separates the north summit from the south summit. On the east face of Split Mountain, bordering the central couloir, are several prominent arêtes that join up with either the south or north summit. Some of these arêtes are more than 2,000 feet long and rival those found on Temple Crag as being the longest climbs in the Sierra Nevada.

On the west face of the mountain, the west couloir is surrounded by a complex maze of spires, gullies, and cliffs that defy logical order and symmetry. The most noticeable feature associated with the west face is a massive U-shaped arête/ridge that curves its serrated crest northward for 3½ miles before joining with the south summit.

The east face arêtes of Split Mountain (Photo by Steve Porcella)

The first ascent of Split Mountain can probably be attributed to the Indians of Paiute or Shoshone ancestry. The close proximity of Indian passes and Indian-named peaks, and the relative ease of gaining the summit via the north ridge, suggest this. Although no record exists, Indians of this area, like the great naturalist John Muir, were not always inclined to leave a summit cairn on the mountains they climbed.

From 1875 to 1879, the U.S. Geological Surveys, under the leadership of Captain George M. Wheeler, occupied several desert stations in the Owens and Bishop Valleys. One of their duties was to accurately fix the positions of some of the prominent main-crest peaks. Capt. Wheeler gave the name "Southeast Palisade" to Split Mountain and measured it at 14,051 feet. In some climbing circles this name is still used today.

Wheeler's survey was the first recorded description of a peak in the Upper Basin, but according to Sierra historian Chester Versteeg in a *Sierra Club Bulletin* article in 1921, many of the first explorers of this area, primarily shepherds, left no record of their discoveries:

"When the sheepmen first threaded old Indian trails into this watershed is not definitely known . . . we are prone to forget the debt we owe him for preserving Indian routes and establishing new trails. The perils he faced alone with his flock in combating early snows; the passes he traveled, driven by the whip of dire necessity, years before they were 'discovered' by the mountaineer; the profound love he often held for the high reaches of the Sierra—all these are unwritten pages of Sierra history."

Versteeg also revealed that Joseph N. Le Conte was not the first to gain the summit of Split Mountain, as had been previously reported. Frank Saulque and four others climbed the peak by an unknown route in July 1887. These men were Basque shepherds and may have climbed the peak via the north ridge.

In July 1895, Bolton Coit Brown made the first ascent of Arrow Peak (12,927 feet) using an ice ax made from a wagon-spoke. From the top of Arrow Peak he drew sketches of and named the mountain known today as Split Mountain.

On July 23, 1902, Joseph N. Le Conte, Helen M. Le Conte, and Curtis M. Lindley made the first recorded ascent of the north ridge from the west. Shortly after his ascent, Le Conte suggested to members of the U.S. Geological Survey that Split Mountain was in an excellent location for mapping triangulation purposes. The Survey team climbed the peak and made measurements in 1902, 1905, and 1907.

It wasn't until Norman Clyde came to the mountain that three new routes were climbed. On one occasion, Clyde soloed the northwest shoulder of Split Mountain and on another, he descended the west face by keeping close to broken arêtes and ribs. Clyde also teamed up with Jules Eichorn to climb Split Mountain for the first time from the east.

In 1923, Eichorn and Glen Dawson completed the first traverse of the south ridge from Cardinal Peak to Split Mountain.

More than thirty years later, on October 3, 1965, Ed Lane and Gary Lewis became the first to climb a new route on Split Mountain. They reached the summit by following the ridge north from Peak 13,803.

In 1976 Galen Rowell left his mark on the mountain by climbing two of the most impressive arêtes on the east face. Each of these routes boasts the potential of sixteen or more pitches of climbing.

In December 1981, Bob Harrington and Bill St. Jean started up the central couloir that divides the east face. This route contains some 65- to 70-degree ice and a step of 75- to 80-degree water ice.

In September 1983, Dean Hobbs and Gary Slate climbed the arête to the south (left) of the Rowell/Beldon route. They reported this to be over twenty pitches of varied climbing with a Class 5.9 crux.

Steve Porcella and Cameron Burns made the first ascent of the Horseshoe Arête in July 1990. This arête, approximately 3½ miles long, begins at Lake 11,599, which lies directly below the west face of Split Mountain. The arête curves south, southeast, and finally east, to a point where it joins with the south ridge of Split Mountain. The couloir that leads to the notch in the Horseshoe Arête adjacent to the south ridge we named Good Couloir after Bob Good. Good was killed in June 1989 when a section of the ridge he was traversing from Cardinal Mountain to Split Mountain gave way. The southern flanks of Split Mountain tend to be loose and often dangerous. Caution is advised.

The northwest face of Split Mountain (Photo by Steve Porcella)

David Belden leading during the first ascent of the east arête, south summit of Split Mountain (Photo © Galen Rowell/Mountain Light)

Climbing Routes on Split Mountain

The easiest and quickest way to climb Split Mountain is the North Ridge Route (route 1) by way of the Eastern Approach via Red Lake. A detailed discussion and map showing how to get to the east face are included here. Other approaches are given a brief outline.

Routes are presented in a counterclockwise fashion.

Eastern Approach via Red Lake

The north, east, and south sides of Split Mountain are best reached by hiking the Red Mountain Creek Trail to Red Lake. As of this writing, the road to the Red Mountain Creek Trailhead may require four-wheel-drive. Conditions change every year and whether four-wheel-drive is needed may be more dependent upon the amount of snowfall and runoff for that particular winter than anything else. Call the White Mountain Ranger Station beforehand to check the status of this approach. To reach the trailhead for the Red Mountain Creek Trail, begin in the town of Big Pine.

Mileage Log _____

0   Corner of Highway 395 and Crocker Street in Big Pine. Go west on Crocker Street toward Glacier Lodge.

2.5   Crocker Street crosses Big Pine Creek. Take a dirt road that cuts left, heading south off Crocker Street. The road quickly forks with one branch heading west, parallel to Crocker Street, and the other heading southwest. Take the southwest branch. This dirt road is in good condition.

2.6   Continue straight across the third dirt road that turns to the left.

6.4   Cross a cattle guard.

6.6   Cross a road that cuts off to the right.

8.2   Continue straight (south) through an intersection of a road leading east-west.

8.7   Pass through a fence. A wire gate may be strung across the road. Be sure to close the gate after passing through, to ensure that cattle do not cross.

9.4   Continue to the left, passing a road that turns to the right. The road now winds around, becomes rough, and crosses two creekbeds.

9.8   Continue to the left, passing another road that turns to the right.

10.0   Pass through a gate. Once again, be sure to close the gate after yourself.

10.9   Continue straight past a road that turns sharply to the left.

11.8   At this intersection, follow the road to Tinemaha Creek, which curves right (south). As you follow this road, the range fence is on your left.

12.5   Turn right (heading west) on the road labeled 10501A.

13.1   Continue straight past a road that branches left.

13.3   Again, continue straight past a road that branches left.

13.6   At the split in the road, take the left branch, labeled 10501. The road now winds left, then right, and ends near a Forest Service kiosk. The actual trail starts northwest from the kiosk. You can drive (100 yards) to where Red Mountain Creek Trail starts.

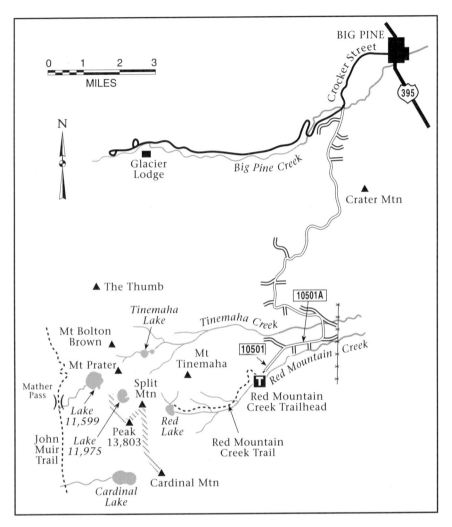

Starting from the trailhead, the climber quickly notices that the trail into Red Lake is steep, narrow, poorly marked, and often dust-choked during summer months. The trail follows along the right side of the canyon all the way to Red Lake, which lies at the base of the east face of Split Mountain. Red Mountain Creek usually has water, but it is a scramble to get to it from the trail. From Red Lake, routes 9–14 are easily accessed.

To gain routes 1–3 from Red Lake, continue toward the north face by hiking up talus and creekbeds northwest of Red Lake to a saddle in the ridge between Split Mountain and Mount Prater to the north. It is important to carry water during this approach because the hike is a long, dry one. There is one section of steep, loose talus (Class 3) that must be negotiated just before reaching the saddle between Mount Prater and Split Mountain. From the saddle, the north ridge can be climbed easily and quickly.

To gain routes 4, 6, and 7 from the northwest, continue northwest of the Prater–Split Mountain saddle and drop west over the saddle toward Lake 11,599, which is relatively easy if one descends north before heading southwest. Hike into the upper basin of the South Fork of the Kings River. Campsites are available in the upper basin. Once you are in the upper basin, the Horseshoe Arête should be visible coming down from the south summit of Split Mountain. To continue to route 7, hike south on the John Muir Trail, and then east along the drainage creek leaving Cardinal Lake. The south ridge is obvious.

To gain routes 7 and 8 from the south, from Red Lake hike southeast over a large, rounded ridge coming off of Split Mountain. To the south of this ridge is the large canyon that separates Cardinal Mountain from Split Mountain. Hike west up this canyon toward the notch in the ridge between Split and Cardinal. To the west of the notch lies Cardinal Lake, from which the south ridge may be climbed.

Western Approach via John Muir Trail

Routes 1, 2, 3, 4, and 6 may also be reached from the west via the John Muir Trail where it passes through the upper basin of the South Fork of the Kings River. From the north, cross Mather Pass, then head east through the upper basin around the south shore of Lake 11,599 toward the Split-Prater saddle. Here, routes 1–3 may be climbed. From the south, on the John Muir Trail hike east before Mather Pass, toward Lake 11,599.

To gain route 7 from the south, hike on the John Muir Trail north to the drainage creek from Cardinal Lake, and hike east up this toward Cardinal Lake.

Route 1, North Ridge, East Approach, Class 3
Use the Eastern Approach via Red Lake.

First ascent, date unknown, was by Jules Eichorn and Norman Clyde.

This route is identical to route 2, North Ridge, West Approach, except that it uses the slightly more difficult eastern approach. Both routes climb the north face of the mountain. This route is the most common way to reach the summit. From Red Lake, hike northwest to the Prater-Split saddle. The last several hundred feet to the saddle consists of Class 3 rubble and talus. Once on the saddle, follow the north ridge up to the summit.

Descend via the same route.

Route 2, North Ridge, West Approach, Class 2
Use the Western Approach via the John Muir Trail.

First recorded ascent of this route was made on July 23, 1902, by Joseph N. Le Conte, Helen G. Le Conte, and Curtis M. Lindley.

This route, approached from the west, is the easiest route to the top of Split Mountain. From the upper basin of the South Fork of the Kings River, or Lake 11,599, hike east to the saddle that joins Mount Prater and Split Mountain. From the saddle, hike south up Split Mountain's gently sloping north face.

Descend via the same route.

Route 3, Northwest Ridge, Class 2
Use either approach.

Split Mountain from the southeast showing routes 1 and 8 (Photo by Steve Porcella)

Norman Clyde made the first ascent of this route at an unknown date.

Hike to the Prater-Split saddle and drop down and to the west. The route lies somewhere between the Class 2 talus of the north ridge (routes 1 and 2) and the steeper gullies and arêtes of the west face.

Descend via route 1 or 2.

Route 4, West Face, Class 3–4

Use either approach.

Norman Clyde made the first descent of this route at an unknown date.

He came directly down the west face from the summit, but only the old gaffer himself knows exactly where this route goes. Clyde did mention that it is better to stick to the arêtes than the gullies because of the numerous dropoffs in the gullies.

Descend the north ridge via route 1 or 2.

Route 5, South Summit from North Summit, Class 3

Use either approach and any route to gain the north summit.

This climb was first performed by Norman Clyde and Jules Eichorn at an unknown date.

From the north summit, this climb is a Class 2 descent into the notch, angling to the southwest, and a Class 3 ascent up the opposing north-facing side of the south summit. The rock is good quality with a steep Class 3 section.

Descend the route back to the north summit, and then descend the north ridge via route 1 or 2.

Route 6, Horseshoe Arête, IV, 5.5

Use either approach.

First ascent was in August 1989 by Cameron Burns and Steve Porcella.

This is the prominent arête that almost encircles Lake 11,975. The arête starts near the north shore of Lake 11,975, curves south, east, and finally north to join with the south summit of the mountain. The arête is 3.5 miles long and consists mostly of Class 3–5 climbing if one stays near the crest. The crux involves traversing a notch (while staying on the crest) east of the point where the ridge between Split Mountain and Cardinal Mountain joins to Split Mountain. The crux is composed of very loose rock. The route was done in two days, but it can probably be done in one long day.

Descend via the north ridge, either route 1 or 2.

Cameron Burns during the first ascent of the Horseshoe Arête on Split Mountain (Photo by Steve Porcella)

Route 7, South Ridge, Class 3–4

Use either approach and hike to Peak 13,803.

The first south ridge ascent was October 3, 1965, by Ed Lane and Gary Lewis.

From Peak 13,803, traverse northward along the top of the ridge toward the north summit of Split Mountain. The view from this route is very spectacular.

Descend via either the north ridge, routes 1 and 2, or via the southeast chute, route 8.

Route 8, Southeast Chute, Class 3

Use the Eastern Approach via Red Lake.

From Red Lake, hike up talus toward a notch south of the white rock buttresses that make up the southeast face of Split Mountain. Continue from this notch west toward a notch between the south ridge of Split Mountain and the north ridge of Cardinal Mountain. While hiking to this notch, the climber suddenly sees a large gully on the southeastern face of Split Mountain. This large, unmistakable, U-shaped gully extends all the way up to the south summit. Enter this gully and cross back and forth between both sides to avoid steep rock. Near the south summit, some Class 2–3 climbing is encountered.

The south ridge of Split Mountain with Peak 13,803 in the distance
(Photo by Cameron Burns)

To reach the north summit from the south summit, climb down steep Class 3 rock on the north face of the south summit. At the notch, hike northwest and enter a gravel-filled gully (Class 2) that leads to the top of the north summit. A word of caution on this route: Because it is almost a perfect "U-shaped gully," this route can become a very "sporty" bowling alley in the event rocks come down it.

Descend via the same route.

Route 9, Hobbs/Slate Route, IV, 5.9

Use the Eastern Approach via Red Lake.

First ascent was in September 1984 by Dean Hobbs and Gary Slate.

From Red Lake, to the left (south) of the east arête of the south summit (route 10) is another arête that joins up with the ridge south of the south summit. Climb the Harrington Variation (route 12) and traverse left (south) to the base of the arête. Twenty pitches of varied climbing lead to the summit ridge where the south summit may be reached.

Descend the south summit via route 8, Southeast Chute, or the north summit via route 1, North Ridge, East Approach.

Route 10, East Arête of South Summit, IV, 5.9

Use the Eastern Approach via Red Lake.

First ascent was in February 1976 by Galen Rowell and David Belden.

This route starts to the left (south) of the permanent ice field below the opening of the east-central couloir above Red Lake. Several hundred feet of easy rock climbing lead to the base of a steep wall. A Class 5.9 crux leads to the top of the arête. The next 1,000 feet above consists of giant blocks of rock interspersed by a ridge crest rarely wider than 6 feet. The second crux is a Class 5.8 headwall. Easier climbing leads to the south summit. The complete climb consists of sixteen pitches or more. Although listed as a grade IV, it may be difficult for many parties to finish the climb in one day.

Descend via either the north ridge, routes 1 and 2, or via the southeast chute, route 8.

Route 11, East Arête of North Summit, IV, 5.8

Use the Eastern Approach via Red Lake.

In October 1976, Rowell returned with Fred Beckey to the east face of Split Mountain and camped at Red Lake. Their goal was to climb the arête that borders the central couloir and leads directly to the north summit. This arête was not as steep as the east arête of the south summit, which Rowell climbed in February 1976, but it was longer due to the large gaps within its crest.

After two pitches of loose rock, Beckey, disgusted with the loose rock, rappelled down. Rowell continued climbing, taking a few nuts and runners in case he would need to protect himself across a difficult section. Much of the climb consisted of Class 5.7 climbing with one strenuous Class 5.8 squeeze chimney. The climbing eased until a number of large gendarmes appeared. One gendarme in particular appeared to be featureless and sheer on all sides. Rowell considered retreating but, after a few moments of inspecting the situation, found a 5.8 lie-back traverse above a small ledge. From here he quickly gained the summit and noticed that the

The east face of Split Mountain showing routes 9 through 14 (Photo by Steve Porcella)

entire climb, from the point where Beckey had retreated, had taken no more than an hour and forty-five minutes.

Descend via the north ridge, routes 1 and 2.

Route 12, Harrington Variation, Class 5

Use the Eastern Approach via Red Lake.

Bob Harrington made the first ascent at an unknown date.

From the permanent ice field at the base of the east-central couloir, the route traverses to the left (south) and continues up the arête, following the rest of the East Arête of South Summit Route (route 10).

Descend via the north ridge, routes 1 and 2.

Route 13, East-Central Couloir of East Face, Class 4

Use the Eastern Approach via Red Lake.

This prominent east-central couloir, first climbed by Norman Clyde at an unknown date, rises above Red Lake and divides the east face of Split Mountain.

Climb up 65- to 70-degree snow or ice at the base of the central gully. After steep Class 3 and 4 rock climbing for 300 feet, a 100-foot cliff is seen. One can work to the left (south) to avoid the cliff, which may be covered in water ice. The rest of the climb is Class 3–4. Rockfall has been reported on this route.

Descend via route 1, North Ridge, East Approach.

Route 14, St. Jean Gully, Class 3–4

Use the Eastern Approach via Red Lake.

First ascent was in December 1981 by Bill St. Jean (solo). This route appears to be fairly direct and may be the quickest way, via some Class 4 climbing, to get to the top. However, it is not known if rockfall is a danger on this route.

To the right (north) of the east-central couloir above Red Lake is another couloir or chute. This gully is much easier than the central couloir and does not contain any noticeable difficulties.

Descend via route 1, North Ridge, East Approach.

References

Beach, Richard. "Goodale Mountain to Split Mountain Traverse." Unpublished manuscript. Bishop, Calif., 1990.

Brown, Bolton Coit. "A Trip About the Headwaters of the South and Middle Forks of Kings River." *Sierra Club Bulletin* 1, no. 8 (May 1896).

Le Conte, J. N. "Identification of the Great Peaks of the Southern Sierra." *Sierra Club Bulletin* 11 (1921).

Matthes, Francois. *Francois Matthes and the Marks of Time.* San Francisco: Sierra Club Books, 1962.

Norris, Robert M., and Robert W. Wood. *Geology of California.* New York: John Wiley and Sons, 1976.

Sierra Club Bulletin. "Notes and Correspondence." *Sierra Club Bulletin* 11 (1921).

Sierra Register Committee Archives. *Split Mountain Register Box, 1902–1933.* Berkeley, Calif.: University of California Berkeley, courtesy of the Bancroft Library; unpublished.

Versteeg, Chester. "The Peaks and Passes of the Upper Basin, South Fork of the Kings River." *Sierra Club Bulletin* 11 (1921).

Woods, Don M. "Fourteen Pacific Coast Fourteen-Thousanders." *American Alpine Journal* 5 (1943–1945).

Chapter 8
Middle Palisade

Struck on the back of the neck by a flying fragment of ice,
I wheeled about to see a great mass of snow . . . course down the chute . . . and
pour over the notch in the cliff from which I had [just] emerged. . . .

Norman Clyde, of his solo first ascent of the north face
of Middle Palisade, *Touring Topics,* 1931

Off in the distance, beyond Glacier Lodge, the dark, east face of Middle Palisade, elevation 14,040 feet, broods over the basin of South Fork of Big Pine Creek. At the base of this giant lies the Middle Palisade Glacier. Once thought to be the vestigial remnant of a colossal sheet of ice that shaped the east face, the Middle Palisade Glacier is now known to be a new arrival, perhaps no older than 700 years.

The Sierra Nevada was once covered by hundreds of large, individual glaciers. Over a time span that ended just 10,000 years ago, one of these glaciers cut the steep, shallow grooves that dominate the east face of Middle Palisade. Over the years, subsequent freeze-fracturing of the rock fine-tuned the face by creating intricate ledges and cracks throughout. The combined action of glacial carving and ice fracturing has created one of the most exhilarating climbs on a 14,000-foot peak in the Sierra Nevada.

Middle Palisade's west face, with a wide range of deep couloirs, arêtes, and buttresses, is very similar to the west faces of North Palisade, Thunderbolt, Starlight, and Polemonium. On the west face of Middle Palisade, after many attempts the first ascent took place.

The spectacular east face of Middle Palisade in winter conditions; Disappointment Peak on the left and Middle Palisade Glacier in the foreground (Photo by Steve Porcella)

The first recorded exploration of Middle Palisade occurred in 1875, when Gustave Eisen and a party from San Francisco made a knapsack hike up the Middle Fork of the Kings River. They followed Palisade Creek and noted that they climbed a small peak near Middle Palisade.

Surprisingly, no one recorded any further information about Middle Palisade until 1904, when Joseph N. Le Conte, in his report of the first ascent of North Palisade, listed Middle Palisade as elevation 14,070 feet and still unclimbed.

The first attempt to climb Middle Palisade was made in 1919 by J. Milton Davies, A. L. Jordan, and H. H. Bliss during a hike up the Middle Fork of the Kings River. They attempted a chute on the southwest face of the peak. After reaching a high point on the ridge, they were dismayed to see to the north, aloof and waiting across an impassable ridge, the true summit of Middle Palisade. The three climbers built a rock cairn and left a note naming the false summit upon which they stood "Peak Disappointment" (now known as Disappointment Peak). They descended their route and prepared for the next day's attempt. The following morning, Davies, Jordan, and Bliss entered the northernmost chute on the mountain. Halfway up the treacherously loose chute, they were hit by a severe storm and were forced to retreat. So ended the first attempt to gain the summit.

On August 24, 1921, Francis Farquhar and Ansel F. Hall, park naturalist of Yosemite National Park, hiked over Bishop Pass, Thunderbolt Pass, and Potluck Pass. It took them two days to reach the base of Middle Palisade. After observing the peak, the two men decided that the high point of the mountain was on the extreme right or southern portion of the ridge. They entered the farthest chute to the southwest and soon, like Davies, Jordan, and Bliss three years before, found themselves looking north across an unclimbable ridge toward the true summit.

As a testament to Farquhar and Hall's strength and determination, the two men descended the southwestern chute, crossed the talus fans, and entered the northernmost chute. Several times the two climbers were discouraged by the difficulty of the climb and thought of turning back. At one point Farquhar found himself in a particularly nasty situation, recounted in a 1921 *Sierra Club Bulletin* article:

"Presently I found myself standing on a ledge to the right of Hall, who was in the main chimney. I had reached the point with difficulty and was now absolutely blocked from further progress upward. The way across the ledge toward Hall did not seem very inviting, and I studied the rocks carefully, with the thought of descending a few feet and rejoining him by a lower route. But the more I looked at the enormous depth below, the worse I felt. Even the ledge to which I was clinging began to seem insecure, although, as a matter of fact, I had a perfectly safe hold. This feeling could not have lasted long, but I did a good deal of scared imagining during the time.

"Hall, too, seemed to be in a situation from which further progress was doubtful. He was only about 15 feet away, but that seemed a long distance to me just then.

"At length I pulled myself together, subdued my fears, and began to concentrate my attention on the firm granite at hand, paying no heed to what was below.

I promptly recognized how easy it was to work the ledge, and in a moment I was across.

"We then held a brief consultation and, after examining the rocks above, concluded that we had had about enough and definitely decided to go down. We looked around for a route for the descent, and then instead of climbing down, we both began to climb up. It was one of those spontaneous impulses that sometimes occur at critical moments."

The two men quickly gained the summit and were elated to find no sign of previous parties.

The prolific soloist Norman Clyde made the first ascent of the northeast face of Middle Palisade on June 7, 1930. Three years later, on July 30, 1933, Jules Eichorn and Glen Dawson, two of the most talented climbers in the United States, climbed Clyde Peak, lying north of and connected to Middle Palisade by a long serrated ridge. Eichorn and Dawson proceeded to traverse this difficult ridge to Middle Palisade. The route was challenging, to say the least, and it was composed of overhanging gendarmes and precipitous walls that dropped away on both sides.

On July 20, 1939, exactly twenty years after the first ascent of Disappointment Peak, David Brower, along with his two friends Bruce Meyer and Keith Taylor, performed the first traverse of that seemingly impossible ridge lying between Disappointment Peak and Middle Palisade.

On January 5, 1960, John Mendenhall and Tom Condon made the first winter ascent of Middle Palisade via the Class 3, standard East Face Route (route 1). Sixteen years later, Mendenhall returned with Tim Ryan and climbed a new route on the southern portion of the east face.

ONE OF THE SIERRA NEVADA'S best attributes is the possibility of "enchainments" of high ridges. Don Jensen was a driving force behind ridge traverses in the Palisades, as noted in a 1990 interview with longtime Palisade climber and guide John Fisher:

"Jensen was very much into the concept of enchainments.... By September 1970, Thunderbolt-to-Sill traverses were popular.... It had been guided over twenty times and done privately about ten times.... This became Jensen's dream workout. The [actual] Palisade Crest has been traversed about four or five times (at least as of '89). Jensen was the first, of course...."

In reference to the Palisade traverses, Steve Roper, in his 1976 *A Climber's Guide to the High Sierra*, stated:

"Traverses of sections of the main crest have always been popular. In 1938 Jack Riegelhuth and W. K. Davis made the Winchell–North Pal[isade] traverse in 13 hours. Thunderbolt-to-Sill traverses, and vice versa, are very common, as is the Clyde–Middle Pal traverse. The tortuous course between Bishop and South Fork Passes has probably never been done; it will be a multiday classic."

Fisher, and a client by the name of Jerry Adams, decided in June 1978 to pick up this gauntlet and try to be the first to traverse from South Fork Pass to Bishop Pass. On this first attempt, they were stopped by a sudden snowstorm on Clyde

Peak. Of their successful second attempt of the traverse, Adams wrote in an un-published article in 1990:

"In 1979, John Fisher and I made our second attempt to traverse all of the peaks on the Palisade Ridge from South Fork Pass to Bishop Pass. Five of eleven 14,000-foot peaks of the range are found in an 8-mile section of this ridge, and the largest glacier in the Sierra is on the northeast side of it."

In late July 1979, Fisher and Adams spent a week placing caches of food along the Palisade Crest. Then, on July 28 they started in to South Fork Pass. During their first night out, the pair reviewed their game plan. Adams' account continued:

"We decided that during this attempt of the traverse we would climb in light vibram-soled klettershoes and forego carrying crampons or regular ice axes. I had a Northwall hammer and John carried a short ice climbing ax. My internal-frame expedition pack had a Gore-Tex bivouac extension, so I could sleep in it with a two-pound down bag. John carried a bivouac sac, a down parka, and down pants for sleeping. John would do all the leading and routefinding, while together we would use a moving belay on a shortened rope. A set of friends would enable us to place and remove protection easily and quickly.

"From South Fork Pass we climbed up to the summit of Disappointment Peak. We quickly traversed over Middle Palisade to a small peak on the way to Clyde Peak. On our attempt the year before we had reached this point on the ridge and found a small film canister with a note in it. The note was written by Jules Eichorn and Glen Dawson on July 30, 1930, and described their naming of this peak: Bivouac Peak. We slept here, on a small ledge, tied in, in a sitting posi-tion. The next morning a lone climber yodeled loudly from Clyde Peak and looked very surprised when I yodeled back. We traversed to Clyde Peak and since it was late decided to bivouac on the summit.

"The next morning we discovered that all we had for breakfast was one pack-age of dates, which I hate with an unbridled passion, and a packet of orange-flavored Gatorade. We heated the Gatorade so I could swallow the dates with a minimum of gagging. With hunger on our minds and dates on my breath, we left the summit of Clyde Peak and dropped down a steep couloir to get the food cache I had placed. We spent 3 frustrating hours searching for that cache. Suddenly, John found it and an overwhelming sense of relief filled our hearts. I should have put a flag on that cache because everything looked different coming off of the ridge. Not to worry, though, we had the food."

The Palisade Crest now stood before the climbers. Eleven major pinnacles of the long knife-blade ridge called the Palisade Crest (13,440 feet) had to be sur-mounted or delicately traversed around. They decided to go to sleep early, and try to complete the crest traverse in one long day. It was the crux of the route. Adams continued:

"Our moment of self-doubt was upon us. We started climbing at 5 A.M. and our route wound in and out and over the pinnacles for 12 hours that day. We had to bivouac on separate narrow shelves only halfway through the crest. John was climbing phenomenally well and maintained high spirits throughout. The next day it took 8 more hours of Class 5 climbing to reach the end of the crest."

Jules Eichorn (Photo by Glen Dawson)   *Glen Dawson* (Photo courtesy of Glen Dawson)

Out of food, hungry, and dehydrated, the weary climbers staggered over Jepson Peak to reach the summit of Mount Sill at 8:00 P.M. They recovered their cache, took their choice of bivouac sites, and passed out. The next day they climbed over Polemonium Peak, passing through the top of the V-Notch couloir, dropped into the U-Notch, and climbed the chimney to the summit of North Palisade. On the summit of North Pal, they encountered the first person they had seen in five days.

Fisher and Adams saw two more climbers rappelling from the northwest point of the summit, and eagerly picked up their abandoned slings. The slings were new and Fisher and Adams desperately needed anchors for rappels.

"After so many days at 14,000 feet, we felt incredibly well acclimated," Adams recalled. "As we climbed over Starlight Peak to Thunderbolt Peak, we knew that even though John was out of cigarettes, we could finish the route without stopping for the third cache. My hands were a mass of tape, my clothes were in shreds, my pants were falling down, we looked and smelled like goats, we were stiff, sore, and itchy all over, yet we were so energized by the fact that the wind had settled down."

On their sixth night, the two climbers bivouacked on Thunderbolt Peak. The next morning they gazed upon the jagged and very technical ridge leading to Mount Winchell. Fisher and Adams decided to descend the north-northeast gully of Thunderbolt to the glacier, climb the regular route on Winchell, descend its north couloir, and scramble to the top of Mount Agassiz from the south. As Fisher recounted in his 1990 interview:

"Jerry and I asked each other and ourselves as we descended from Thunderbolt (thereby avoiding the much more technical ridge of Winchell), 'Why? Why

Left to right: the east faces of Middle Palisade and Clyde Peak (Photo by Steve Porcella)

are we not completing the traverse?' In answer to our questions, I said to Jerry, matter-of-factly, 'We've traversed from South Fork Pass to Thunderbolt and now we're climbing Winchell and Agassiz for good measure, so there and that's it.' In retrospect, we did not make the traditional, first pure traverse of the Palisade Ridge, but we did complete the most extensive traverse of the ridge to date, perhaps in the western United States. I don't think a complete and ethically pure traverse will ever be done."

CAMERON BURNS AND STEVE PORCELLA climbed the west buttress on the west face of Middle Palisade in July 1989. The route has been named the Smoke Buttress after the late Smoke Blanchard, a longtime east-side resident and prolific Sierra Nevada climber.

A new traverse of the crest was made by Bela Vadasz, Tom Birch, Jeff Jarvi, and Dave Riggs over a two-year period. The quartet traversed from Baxter Pass to Mount Sill in 1993 and Mount Sill to Mount Agassiz the next year. One hundred sixty roped pitches up to 5.9 and six bivouacs over 13,000 feet were required.

Climbing Routes on Middle Palisade

The easiest route to the top of Middle Palisade is via route 1 on the east face. A detailed discussion and map showing how to get to the east face is included here. Other approaches and routes are briefly described.

Routes are presented in a counterclockwise fashion.

Eastern Approach via Glacier Lodge

The following mileage log to Glacier Lodge starts in Big Pine.

Mileage Log

0	Corner of Highway 395 and Crocker Street in Big Pine. Go west on Crocker Street toward Glacier Lodge.
13.5	Turnoff to the right leads to overnight parking for backpackers.
14.0	End of Crocker Street, and Glacier Lodge. Backpackers and climbers can be dropped off here to save some walking.

From the end of Crocker Street, the South Fork and North Fork of Big Pine Creek Trails are one and the same. The trail starts at the end of Crocker Street, which is about 100 yards to the north from Glacier Lodge; the trail begins as a rough dirt road. After about 0.25 mile, a sign designates the start of the South Fork trail; take this trail. It follows the South Fork of Big Pine Creek, leading south. Soon the trail switchbacks up a prominent rock buttress to eventually top out near Willow Lake. During wet times of the year, Willow Lake is breeding ground for billions of mosquitoes. If they are in season, you might want to sprint through this area to avoid being eaten alive. The trail, which sometimes may be narrow or faint due to its infrequent use, climbs to Brainard Lake, a beautiful little lake with several nice campsites.

There are two possible ways to reach the east face of Middle Palisade from Brainard Lake. One involves hiking west around Brainard Lake and gradually moving up ledges to Finger Lake. The other leads around the east side of Brainard Lake, and follows the inlet creek to eventually bypass two small lakes on the right (west). Beyond the second small lake, turn right (west), hiking beneath a large rock prow several hundred feet high. Several basins containing small glacial tarns are encountered. The east-facing glaciers at the base of Middle Palisade and Disappointment Peak are soon reached. Hiking left (east) of the prow leads to South Fork Pass. This approach is useful for routes 1, 2, 3, 7, and 8.

Eastern Approach via South Fork Pass

To reach the west face from the east, follow the Eastern Approach via Glacier Lodge, to South Fork Pass. Once across the pass, turn right (west) and traverse over steep rock and grass-covered slabs. The sheer cliffs that make up the southwest ridge of Disappointment Peak are to the right (west). Once around the southwest ridge, a short hike northwest over granite slabs leads to the base of the west face of Middle Palisade. This approach is useful for routes 3–7.

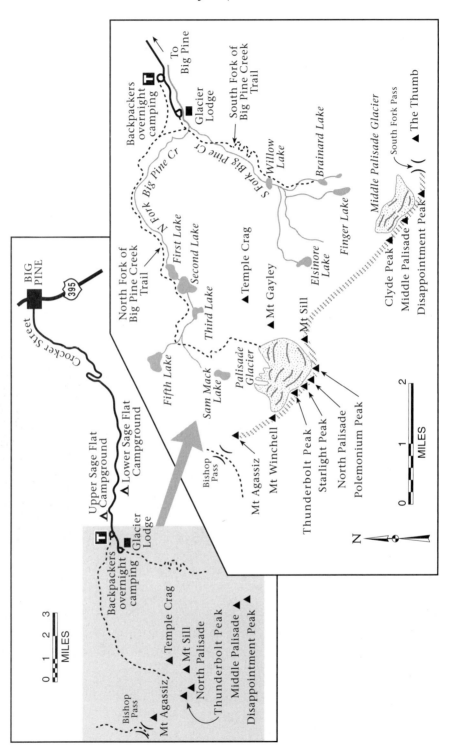

Eastern Approach via Bishop Pass Trail

From the north, the mountain may also be reached by crossing Bishop Pass, and traversing southward along the west side of the crest. To reach Bishop Pass, follow the Eastern Approach via Bishop Pass Trail in chapter 9, Mount Sill. After crossing Potluck Pass it may be best to hike southwest to the John Muir Trail and follow it south to Palisade Lakes. This approach is long, arduous, and, in general, not recommended.

Western Approach via John Muir Trail

Middle Palisade's west face can be approached from the west via the John Muir Trail as it heads north from Mather Pass and alongside the east shore of Palisade Lakes. Leave the John Muir Trail from the northernmost lake and hike northeast toward the west face of Middle Palisade. The east ridge of Disappointment Peak is on your right (south). This approach is useful for routes 3–7.

The east face of Middle Palisade showing routes 1, 2, and 8 (Photo by Cameron Burns)

Route 1, East Face, Class 3

Use the Eastern Approach via Glacier Lodge.

The first ascent party is unknown. This is the easiest and most straightforward way to get to the summit of Middle Palisade. There are many variations to this route. They mainly involve crossing into alternate couloirs or following the arêtes that border the gullies. The following description chronicles the most popular route for gaining the summit of Middle Palisade.

The starting point begins on the right (north) portion of the Middle Palisade Glacier. Climb up the snow of the glacier between a rock moraine on the left (south) and the small rock ridge that separates the Middle Palisade Glacier from Clyde Glacier to the north. About halfway up the snow, climb onto a ledge/chimney system that leads up the buttress to the right. Follow the ledge into a large, broad couloir and climb up this couloir. When the couloir begins to end, cross over to the next couloir to the north (right). After a short distance this couloir divides. The right or left branch may be followed, depending on which looks easier. Both reach a notch to the north or south of the summit.

Much of this route is continuous Class 3 with some portions of Class 4 encountered if climbers get off route. A rope is recommended if you're not totally comfortable on Class 3 rock. The first ledge/chimney system becomes somewhat exposed and is the most difficult part of the climb.

Descend via the same route.

Route 2, Northeast Face, Class 4

Use the Eastern Approach via Glacier Lodge.

On June 7, 1930, Norman Clyde, climbing solo, made the first ascent of this route.

The route begins to the right (northwest) of the prominent buttress that divides the Middle Palisade Glacier. Ascend the snow and move into a chute, keeping to its sides as much as possible. Near the top of the chute, cut right (north) and climb over rocks to the mouth of a broad couloir. From here, one can alternate between the arête and the shelves that flank the south side of the arête. Move right, over broken rocks, to eventually gain the summit.

There is a chimney near the beginning of the climb that joins the glacier and the rock, and bypasses some of the initial steep sections of the climb.

Descend via route 1, East Face.

Route 3, Northwest Ridge Traverse, Class 5

Use any of the approaches.

Jules Eichorn and Glen Dawson traversed this route on July 30, 1933.

This route starts at Clyde Peak and follows the ridge to Middle Palisade. We recommend using R. J. Secor's book *The High Sierra*, pages 178–81, to pick a route to the summit of Clyde Peak. The traverse has been listed as Class 4–5, with a possible rappel somewhere along the way. Dawson's entry in the Middle Palisade summit register mentions that the climb was fairly difficult and that a bivouac may have been performed.

Depending on where your camp is, descend to the west via route 4, Northwest Bowl, or route 6, Southwest Chute; descend to the east via route 1, East Face.

Route 4, Northwest Bowl, Class 4

Use the Eastern Approach via South Fork Pass or the Western Approach via John Muir Trail.

First ascent was by David Brower and Hervey Voge at an unknown date.

This route starts in the northwest-facing bowl on the west face of Middle Palisade. It starts at the top of a prominent snowbank at the base of this bowl. The route angles sharply to the south–southeast as it ascends. Three-fourths of the way up, it gains the top of the buttress and joins route 5, The Smoke Buttress. From here the primary crux of the route appears, and consists of Class 4 climbing to the summit ridge.

Descend via the same route, or route 6, Southwest Chute.

The west face of Middle Palisade showing routes 4 through 6 (Photo by Steve Porcella)

Route 5, The Smoke Buttress, IV, 5.9, A1

Use the Eastern Approach via South Fork Pass or the Western Approach via John Muir Trail.

On July 10, 1989, Cameron Burns and Steve Porcella made the first ascent of this direct route up the west face of Middle Palisade.

In the center of Middle Palisade's west face is a steep buttress bound on the right by route 1's northern chute and on the left by a narrow and shallow chimney/couloir system. The route ascends the center of the buttress for eleven pitches of 5.5–5.8 climbing. The crux of the route is a steep headwall (5.9) on the tenth pitch. After the eleventh lead, the top of the buttress is reached and a rappel becomes necessary. From here the route traverses a Class 3 ridge. Two Class 4 pitches up a chimney on the right are encountered. The second pitch in the chimney tops out on the summit ridge. A short scramble to the north puts one on the actual summit.

Descend via route 6, Southwest Chute.

Route 6, Southwest Chute, Class 4

Use the Eastern Approach via South Fork Pass or the Western Approach via John Muir Trail.

On August 26, 1921, Francis Farquhar and Ansel F. Hall made the first ascent of this route.

On the west side of Middle Palisade, between the summits of Middle Palisade and Disappointment Peak, there are three distinct chutes. Ascend the northernmost chute. Loose rock and gravel are very plentiful on this route, so be careful not to knock debris on other people. Upon reaching the upper section of the chute, cut left onto a broken face. Exposure and loose rock are in abundance here also. At the top of this face, enter a Class 4 chimney. This chimney tops out south of the main summit. The summit is a quick scramble left (north) across the ridge.

Descend via the same route.

Route 7, Southeast Ridge, Class 4

Use the Eastern Approach via South Fork Pass.

This route, once considered impossible, was climbed on July 20, 1939, by David Brower, Bruce Meyer, and Keith Taylor.

We recommend using R. J. Secor's book *The High Sierra,* pages 178–81, to pick a route to the summit of Disappointment Peak. From the summit of Disappointment Peak, the route traverses the ridge leading north to the summit of Middle Palisade. This route is Class 4 and requires a fair amount of routefinding skill. Stick close to the northeast side of the ridge and traverse to the southeast side only when necessary.

Depending on where your camp is, descend to the west via route 6, Southwest Chute, or to the east via route 1, East Face.

Route 8, Ryan/Mendenhall Route, III, 5.5

Use the Eastern Approach via Glacier Lodge.

On August 31, 1975, Tim Ryan and John Mendenhall climbed this route.

It starts after you've cramponed up to the highest point of the Middle Palisade Glacier. The first pitch goes straight up from the glacier and then descends to the left (south) in a delicate traverse. This first lead is the crux of the route. The next pitch traverses a fairly easy 60-foot ledge, then climbs a very loose chimney. From here, the route traverses left on the face, and then up to a belay beneath an overhang. Another pitch upward, and the route traverses left around a corner into a broad chute that goes to the first notch south of the Middle Palisade summit. From this col, traverse right (north) for one pitch before ascending to the summit ridge.

Descend via route 1, East Face.

References

Adams, Jerry. Unpublished article.

American Alpine Journal. 1 (1929–1932); 13 (1962–1963); 26 (1976).

Clyde, Norman. "Up the Middle Palisade." *Touring Topics* (August 1931).

Farquhar, Francis. "First Ascent of the Middle Palisade." *Sierra Club Bulletin* 11 (1921).

Fisher, John. Interviewed by authors. Bishop, Calif., 1990.

Le Conte, J. N. "The Ascent of the North Palisades." *Sierra Club Bulletin* 5, no. 1 (1904).

Norris, Robert M., and Robert W. Wood. *Geology of California.* New York: John Wiley and Sons, 1976.

Roper, Steve. *A Climber's Guide to the High Sierra.* San Francisco: Sierra Club Books, 1976.

Secor, R. J. *The High Sierra.* Seattle: The Mountaineers Books, 1992.

Sierra Club Bulletin. 12 (1926); 20 (1932–1935).

Sierra Register Committee Archives. *Middle Palisade Summit Register 1921–1936.* Berkeley, Calif.: University of California, courtesy of the Bancroft Library; unpublished.

Voge, Hervey H., and Andrew J. Smatko, eds. *Mountaineer's Guide to the High Sierra.* San Francisco: Sierra Club Books, 1972.

Chapter 9
Mount Sill

Does a man ever give up hope, I wonder,—
Face the grim fact, seeing it clear as day?
When Bennen saw the snow slip, heard its thunder
Low, louder, roaring round him, felt the speed
Grow swifter as the avalanche hurled downward,
Did he for just one heart-throb—did he indeed
Know with all certainty, as they swept onward,
There was the end, where the crag dropped away?
Or did he think, even till they plunged and fell,
Some miracle would stop them? Nay, they tell
That he turned round, face forward, calm and pale,
Stretching his arms out toward his native vale
As if in mute, unspeakable farewell,
And so went down—'Tis something, if at last,
Though only for a flash, a man may see
Clear-eyed the future as he sees the past,
From doubt, or fear, or hope's illusion free.

Truth at Last by Edward Rowland Sill, 1841–1887

Mount Sill, elevation 14,162 feet, was named by Joseph N. Le Conte in honor of Edward Rowland Sill, a poet and professor of literature at the University of California from 1874 to 1882. This beautifully sculpted peak, unlike most of its neighbors on the Palisade Crest, has a vertical east face similar in shape to Mount Whitney and Mount Tyndall. It is appropriate that a such a magnificent peak should be named after a poet known

Mount Sill from the Palisade Glacier (Photo by Steve Porcella)

for his descriptive wilderness prose. Robert Frost, an admirer of Edward Rowland Sill, was fond of and influenced by Sill's poem *Truth at Last*.

As with so many mountains all over the world, the story of the first ascent of Mount Sill is linked to a taller neighbor, in this case North Palisade. On July 24, 1903, James Hutchinson, J. K. Moffitt, Robert Pike, and Joseph N. Le Conte were sitting in the U-Notch on North Palisade, staring at the U-Notch chimney and wondering whether they would be able to climb it and therefore reach the summit of North Palisade for a first ascent. While contemplating the steepness of the rock that stood before them and the summit of North Palisade, the three mountaineers turned their attention toward Mount Sill, and as Le Conte described in a 1904 *Sierra Club Bulletin* article, "after a rough scramble of about an hour along the ridge to the east, arrived without serious difficulty on that hitherto untrodden crest."

Left to right: Mount Sill, Polemonium Peak, North Palisade, Starlight Peak, and Thunderbolt Peak; Mount Gayley in the foreground (Photo by Steve Porcella)

The lack of comment about the difficulty of climbing up the U-notch wall to Mount Sill's east ridge is the most notable thing about Le Conte's account.

Most Sierra historians give credit to Jules Eichorn, Glen Dawson, John Olmstead, and Charles Dodge for making the first ascent of the west ridge of Mount Sill.

In 1938, the unclimbed northeast buttress grabbed the attention of Dick Jones and Spencer Austin. On July 3, Jones and Austin, along with three beginners, scrambled up to the base of the ridge to make an attempt. Among the inexperienced group of climbers was then-twenty-five-year-old Ruth Dyer. She had been technical rock climbing for just a few months and had already climbed every route, all five of them, at Tahquitz Rock.

Dick Jones, leader of the first ascent of the Swiss Arête (Photo by Ruth Mendenhall)

Although Dick Jones led every pitch on the route, Dyer's two neophyte ropemates, Joe Momyer and Ray Ingwersen, felt extremely shaky on the climb. After climbing the newly dubbed Swiss Arête, Momyer and Ingwersen quit climbing forever. Dyer, however, loved it. She later went on to marry John Mendenhall, whom she met at the base of Tahquitz Rock, and with him assembled one of the Sierra's most impressive lists of ascents. Of all the routes Dyer was first to climb, the Swiss Arête is unparalleled in its elegance.

Climbing Routes on Mount Sill

Because Mount Sill has three separate and distinct sides, there are three separate and distinct approaches to the peak. Two are nearly the same approaches as for the North Palisade massif: the Palisade Glacier and Bishop Pass. The third is via the South Fork Pass Trail and is nearly the same as that for Middle Palisade. The easiest and safest way to climb Mount Sill is via the southwest slopes (route 8). The best way to reach the start of this route is to use either Bishop Pass and traverse south, or use the Eastern Approach via Glacier Lodge (see chapter 8, Middle Palisade), cross South Fork Pass, and traverse north.

Routes are presented in a counterclockwise fashion.

Eastern Approach via Elsinore Lake

The east face is best reached by driving to Glacier Lodge and hiking the South Fork of Big Pine Creek Trail (see the Eastern Approach via Glacier Lodge in chapter 8, Middle Palisade). From Glacier Lodge, follow the South Fork trail to where it switchbacks up a prominent rock buttress to eventually top out near Willow Lake;

this is where the South Fork Pass trail continues south. Here, turn directly east and follow the Elsinore Lake drainage east until Elsinore Lake is reached (approximately a mile and a half after Willow Lake). From Elsinore Lake, the east face of Mount Sill should be obvious. This is the best approach for routes 1–5.

Eastern Approach via South Fork Pass

Follow the Eastern Approach via Elsinore Lake, but at Willow Lake, rather than taking the Elsinore Lake turnoff, continue on the South Fork Pass trail as if your intention was to climb the west face of Middle Palisade (see chapter 8, Middle Palisade, Eastern Approach via South Fork Pass). Once you cross South Fork Pass, continue northward, walking at the base of Middle Palisade and angling around Clyde Peak until Potluck Pass can be seen to the north. Do not cross this pass; instead, just before crossing the pass, climb northeast into the drainage that contains the Polemonium Glacier. The west face of Mount Sill is east-northeast of the Polemonium Glacier. This approach is used for routes 8 and 9.

Eastern Approach via North Fork of Big Pine Creek

The northeast face is best reached by driving to Glacier Lodge and then hiking the North Fork of Big Pine Creek Trail (see chapter 8, Middle Palisade, East Face Approach via Glacier Lodge). This approach is also used for gaining the east faces of North Palisade and Polemonium, Starlight, and Thunderbolt Peaks. At Glacier Lodge and the end of Crocker Street, the South Fork and North Fork trails are one and the same. The trail starts off as a rough dirt road. After about 0.25 mile, a sign designates the start of the South Fork trail. Take the North Fork trail at this point.

The North Fork of Big Pine Creek Trail is extremely well marked and ascends the main watershed for about 7 miles to the Palisade Glacier. Initially, the North Fork trail heads northwest, encountering the First Falls of the North Fork of Big Pine Creek. The First Falls are about 0.25 mile from the end of Crocker Street. Second Falls is 1.5 miles from Glacier Lodge. The trail winds up and to the right (north) of Second Falls. The North Fork trail continues up to the Big Pine Lakes. Like the waterfalls on the trail, these lakes are named First, Second, and Third Lakes. After passing Third Lake, the trail switchbacks up to the opening of a canyon. In this canyon is Sam Mack Meadow. It is a flat, grassy-bottomed meadow in a sheer-walled box canyon. The headwaters of Big Pine Creek tumble through the canyon, and, despite its lack of a view, this is one of the prettiest camping areas in the Sierra Nevada. Fires are not allowed here.

A sign in the middle of Sam Mack Meadow points toward Glacier Trail. The Glacier Trail turns left and switchbacks up the moraine to the foot of the Palisade Glacier. The Glacier Trail ends between the northeast side of the Palisade Glacier and the north end of Mount Gayley. Mount Sill can be seen directly west of Gayley, connected to Gayley by a steep, west-to-east-running ridge.

East and northeast routes are readily approached from anywhere on the Palisade Glacier after hiking the Glacier Trail. Bivy or small campsites, for close proximity to Sill's eastern and northeastern climbs, are generally scarce. Sites can be found in the moraine or in close proximity to Mount Gayley. This is a delicate alpine ecosystem and these bivy sites are used quite frequently by many people. It is especially important to bury human waste at least 8 inches deep and at least 200 feet away from any water sources. We have found tons of trash in this area and have spent time packing it out, only to come back and find the area littered again. Please pack out all trash even if it isn't yours. Much warmer and more comfortable campsites abound at Third and Second Lakes or in the slightly cooler and exposed Sam Mack Meadow. Camping in either of these areas requires an earlier start and longer approach for doing Mount Sill.

Several routes on Mount Sill require that the climber first surmount Glacier Notch, the ridge between Mounts Sill and Gayley. This presents a problem from the Palisade Glacier. Depending on how this problem is tackled, this approach can easily be as challenging as the routes themselves. The easiest way to gain the notch is to climb west at the base of the north side of the ridge connecting Mount Gayley to Mount Sill. Just beyond several north-facing walls on this ridge, a Class 3–4 chute appears, which leads up the ridge in a southeastern direction. This chute may have snow in it early in the season. This is also the easiest descent route for route 6, Swiss Arête, and route 7, North Couloir, and several rappel anchors may still exist in this chute. This approach is useful for routes 6–8.

Eastern Approach via Bishop Pass Trail

As with most of the Palisades, the west face of Mount Sill can also be reached by traversing south after crossing Bishop Pass. Once across Bishop Pass, many camping sites can be found in Dusy and Palisade Basins. Hiking cross-country and then crossing Thunderbolt Pass brings one into Palisade Basin. Crossing Potluck Pass and traversing northeast brings one in proximity to Mount Sill's west face. The following mileage log to South Lake and the Bishop Pass Trailhead leaves from the town of Bishop.

Mileage Log

0	At the corner of South Main, North Main, and West Line Streets (the latter of which is Highway 168) in Bishop, drive west on West Line Street.
14.9	At a large sign describing South Lake Recreational Area, turn left.
16	Jeffrey Campground is on the left.
17	Habeggers RV resort park is on the left.
17.8	Mountain Glen walk-in campground is on the left.
19	Table Mountain campground is on the left.
20	Willow Campground on the left.
20.8	Parchers General Store is on the left.
21.8	The road forks. The right branch goes down to South Lake and ends at the boat-launching facility. Take the left branch to the trailhead parking area.
22	Trailhead parking area. Wilderness permit required.

Starting from South Lake, the Bishop Pass Trail gradually climbs into the high country while bypassing many beautiful lakes; Long Lake and Bishop Lakes are

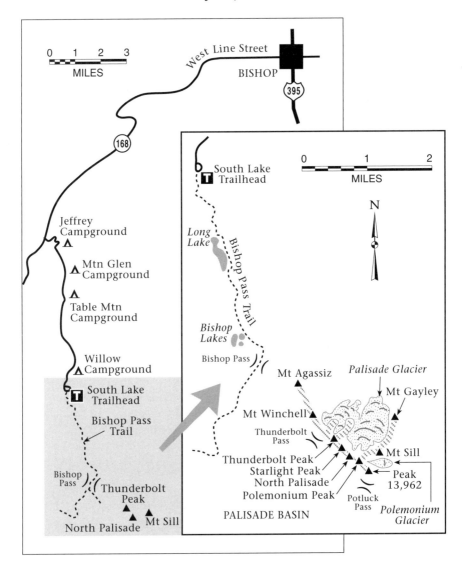

just a few of them. The hike up and over Bishop Pass follows a well-maintained trail. The trail crests Bishop Pass after about 8 miles of hiking, just west of Mount Agassiz. (From here, the trail descends to the Middle Fork of the Kings River, where it joins the John Muir Trail.)

At Bishop Pass, leave the trail and traverse southeast, across Dusy Basin, past the base of the southwestern faces of Mounts Agassiz and Winchell. After passing Mount Agassiz and Mount Winchell, cross a small northeast-southwest ridge that extends west perpendicularly from the main Palisade group. The easternmost (leftmost) notch in this ridge is Thunderbolt Pass. Thunderbolt Pass is best surmounted close to the base of the mountain itself.

Continuing across the next basin, Palisade Basin, one soon arrives at Potluck Pass. Campsites are available on the south side of Potluck Pass, but Potluck Pass is considered Class 3 and may be a little bit difficult with a pack. There is excellent camping throughout Palisade Basin; however, this basin as well as Dusy Basin are extremely fragile ecosystems. Please be sure to pack out all trash and bury feces 8 inches deep and at least 200 feet away from water sources or pack them out. This approach is useful for routes 8 and 9.

Route 1, East Couloir, Class 3

Use the Eastern Approach via Elsinore Lake.

This couloir, one of the easiest routes on Mount Sill, was first descended by Norman Clyde, David Brower, and Hervey Voge on June 16, 1934.

It lies south of the massive east face, and ascends to the prominent notch just south of the summit. Once the ridge is gained, it is a short scramble to the summit. This is a great descent route for climbs on the east face of the mountain.

Descend via the same route.

Route 2, Dead Larry's Pillar, Left Side, III, 5.9

Use the Eastern Approach via Elsinore Lake.

Mike Graber, Mike Farrell, and Kent Davenport made the first ascent of this excellent ten-pitch route in August 1986.

In the center of the 1,300-foot east face is an enormous low-profile buttress, Dead Larry's Pillar. This route, as well as route 3, Dead Larry's Pillar, starts below an overhang, then ascends a left-leaning crack before turning the overhang itself. Above the roof, this route follows the left side of the pillar.

Descend via route 1, East Couloir.

Route 3, Dead Larry's Pillar, III, 5.10

Use the Eastern Approach via Elsinore Lake.

This route was first climbed by Mike Graber and Mike Farrell in 1978.

Follow route 2, Dead Larry's Pillar, Left Side, to the overhang, and turn the overhang via the left-leaning crack. Then above the roof, move right, to the base of Dead Larry's Pillar itself. Follow the center of the pillar for many leads to the top.

Descend via route 1, East Couloir.

Route 4, East Face Mendenhall Route, III, 5.7–5.8

Use the Eastern Approach via Elsinore Lake.

This route was first climbed by John Mendenhall, Burt and Glen Turney, and Rick Gnagy on September 1, 1963.

It starts at the Palisade Glacier's highest point, just north (right) of the middle of the cliff's base, and goes almost straight up, ending 200 feet south of the summit. The first lead follows a Class 4 chimney to a huge, overhanging chockstone. The second pitch climbs behind the chockstone, then follows a thin crack in smooth rock (5.7). Two straightforward pitches of 5.6 and 5.7 rock are followed by much easier climbing that ends at the bottom of a prominent gully. The gully becomes quite steep, but it is possible to ascend the right-hand wall on 5.2 rock. Continue up the chimney system, on 5.4–5.7 rock, then an airy traverse left at the top of the gully puts one on the south ridge, just south of the summit.

Descend via route 1, East Couloir.

Michael Graber leading the first pitch on Dead Larry's Pillar (Photo by David Wilson)

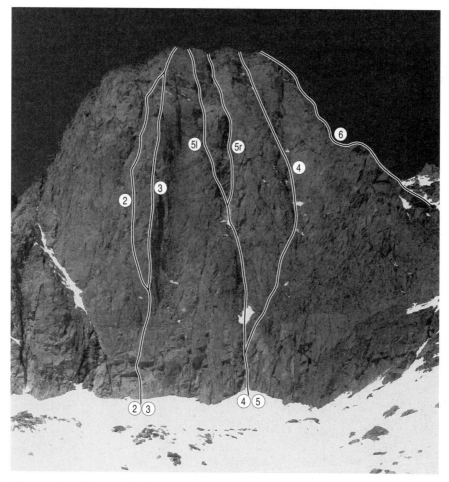

The east face of Mount Sill showing routes 2 through 6 (Photo by Steve Porcella)

Route 5, East Face, (L) or (R) Condon-Kepfelberger Route, III, 5.8

Use the Eastern Approach via Elsinore Lake.

This route, climbed by Tom Condon and Fred Kepfelberger in 1959, was the first route on the true east face of Mount Sill. It is very steep and very intimidating, but not sustained.

There is a well-defined chimney in the center of the east face, above the highest point of the Palisade Glacier. Enter the Class 4 chimney at the glacier's highest point, just north (right) of the middle of the cliff's base, and climb the chimney for two pitches. This is the same start as that for route 4, East Face Mendenhall Route. Above this, the face forms a bowl, often with a snow patch in it, and the route ascends numerous broken ledges for four leads. The climbing is wildly exposed, but easy. The seventh pitch enters the large chimney system that goes up and left. The chimney is climbed all the way to the summit ridge, just south of the peak. The summit should be obvious from here.

It is also possible to climb a fairly obvious chimney system to the right (5.7). This variation departs from the original route at about two-thirds height.

Descend via route 1, East Couloir.

Route 6, The Swiss Arête, III, 5.8

Use the Eastern Approach via North Fork of Big Pine Creek.

First climbed by Dick Jones, Spencer Austin, Ruth Dyer, Ray Ingwersen, and Joe Momyer on July 3, 1938, and originally graded 5.4, this route has been re-graded by nearly everyone who has climbed it. In his article "Climbing in the Palisades," Gordon Wiltsie states: "Very exposed in many places, it meanders steeply up pure white granite almost directly to the summit. Climbing is challenging in places, and few believe the guidebook rating of 5.4. Staying close to the top of the arête, it is closer to 5.6 or 5.7." Many entries in the summit register suggest a rating of 5.8.

Despite its ambiguous rating, this route is one of the finest in the Sierra Nevada. It provides the ambitious mountaineer with incredible views of the entire Palisade group, while keeping the climber on his or her toes with outrageous exposure—a real classic.

Quite simply stated, climb the prominent arête on the north side of the mountain. At about the midpoint on the arête, a short headwall is encountered. There are several different chimneys that surmount this steep section. They are all about 5.8. Above this, the climbing is much easier, and experienced mountaineers can turn their attention from the climbing to the views.

Descend via route 7, North Couloir.

Route 7, North Couloir, Class 3

Use the Eastern Approach via North Fork of Big Pine Creek.

Although this route is somewhat exposed, the climbing is very easy. It is the easiest way to climb Mount Sill from the Palisade Glacier. It also provides an excellent descent route for those climbing route 6, The Swiss Arête. It was first climbed by Walter Starr, Jr. on September 25, 1931.

From Glacier Notch, head south, toward the summit of Mount Sill. The Swiss Arête is on the left (east). Ascend the trough just right of the Swiss Arête for several hundred feet. Another notch, separating Mount Sill from the tower to its north, is reached. Here, an exposed traverse leads across a steep chute. Climb the opposite wall of the chute, up steep blocks, until the northwest ridge is gained. From here, the summit is just a 10-minute scramble.

Descend via the same route.

Route 8, West Ridge, Class 4–5

Use either the Eastern Approach via North Fork of Big Pine Creek or the Eastern Approach via Bishop Pass Trail.

First ascent by James Hutchinson, J. K. Moffitt, Robert Pike, and Joseph N. Le Conte on July 24, 1903.

This route involves first climbing the U-Notch of North Palisade (see chapter 11, North Palisade, routes 1–3). From the North Fork trail, climb route 14 of chapter 11; from Bishop Pass Trail, climb route 6 of chapter 11. From the U-Notch, several variations exist for climbing Mount Sill. Most of these variations have been described as Class 4; however, we found this to be somewhat of a sandbag rating, for some of the climbing can be very exposed and vertical for a Class 4 designation. If one climbs directly south out of the U-Notch toward Mount Sill, the difficulties are more akin to Class 5 and much routefinding is required to keep the Class designation down. However, there is the possibility of hiking west 100–300 feet and then climbing south over more broken terrain. This direction puts you to the west of the summit of Polemonium, and care is advised among these short cliff bands and broken arêtes. After gaining the ridge, above the U-Notch continue along its crest until Mount Sill's summit is reached. This latter portion of the route is Class 2.

Starting with the U-Notch is an excellent way for a fit climbing party to ascend the summits of Sill, Polemonium, and North Palisade in one day. For climbing south out of the U-Notch and attaining the summit of Polemonium, see chapter 10, Polemonium Peak, route 2, V-Notch. For climbing north out of the U-Notch and attaining the summit of North Palisade, see chapter 11, North Palisade, route 1, U-Notch Northeast Side.

Descend via route 7, North Couloir, if you approached from the east; or descend via route 1, U-Notch Northeast Side, chapter 11, North Palisade.

The southwest chutes of Mount Sill (Photo by Cameron Burns)

Route 9, Southwest Chutes, Class 2–3

Use either the Eastern Approach via Bishop Pass Trail or the Eastern Approach via South Fork Pass.

This is the easiest route up Mount Sill, but it is at once the most remote, least traveled, and circuitous route to the top. Not surprisingly, it has a very wildernesslike feel to it. The route is also good because it allows you the easiest opportunity of making the summit of Sill, Peak 13,962, and Polemonium while visiting the Polemonium Glacier. If this is your interest, see chapter 10, Polemonium Peak, route 1, Southeast Ridge.

If coming from the north on the Bishop Pass Trail, after hiking through the Palisade Basin, continue on to Potluck Pass; when you reach the top of the pass, hike east up the gently sloping ridge and gradually enter the large basin that contains the Polemonium Glacier. If coming from the south via South Fork Pass, when you reach the southern base of Potluck Pass, turn eastward and hike into the large basin that contains the Polemonium Glacier. The numerous chutes that lie on the southwest side of Mount Sill are directly east of the Polemonium Glacier. Climb any of these to the summit. All the chutes are similar in nature, and most Class 3 rock can be avoided by traversing into the next gully.

Descend via the same route.

References

American Alpine Club News 6 (Fall 1989).

American Alpine Journal 29 (1987).

Fisher, John. Interviewed by authors. Bishop, Calif., June 1990.

Le Conte, Joseph. "The Ascent of the North Palisade." *Sierra Club Bulletin* 5 (January 1904).

Wiltsie, Gordon. "Climbing in the Palisades." *Sierra Life* 5 (July/August 1985).

Chapter 10
Polemonium Peak

Yvon [Chouinard] was having his own problems.
The ice [in the V-Notch couloir] was so hard that his attempts to lodge an ax
or alpine hammer to pull up on yielded either ice cubes or sudden opaque cones
under the blade. Finally, he pulled up on delicate balance
and blew out a long sigh: "I haven't been gripped like that in a while."

Doug Robinson, "Truckin' My Blues Away," *Mountain*, 1970

Although Polemonium Peak, elevation 14,200 feet, was not considered to be a 14,000-foot peak for many years, the number of parties that take the few extra hours to ascend the peak from the U-Notch grows every year. The summit of this unobtrusive fourteener is as challenging as any in the Sierra Nevada. It requires not only rock climbing skill, but a good healthy set of nerves as well. The final summit block requires Class 5 climbing, no matter which side of the mountain is ascended.

Named for the small blue flower found throughout the Sierra Nevada, Polemonium Peak contains a geological feature that adds significance to its character as a mountain. On the south face of Polemonium there is a large bowl whose boundaries are formed by Peak 13,962, Polemonium's southeast face, and the southwest face of Mount Sill. Contained within this bowl is the highest glacier in the Sierra Nevada: the Polemonium Glacier. Although small by any standards, the Polemonium Glacier may be the only southeast-facing glacier in the Sierra Nevada.

Another interesting aspect of Polemonium is not the mountain itself, but the glacier that lies at the base of its north face, the enormous Palisade Glacier.

Cameron Burns soloing the last few feet to the summit of Polemonium Peak (Photo by Steve Porcella)

177

The Palisade Glacier is well known for being the largest of the more than sixty glaciers that are found in the Sierra Nevada. Polemonium's relationship to the Palisade Glacier is found in the form of the moderate, yet classic, ice chute known as the V-Notch. First climbed in 1958 by John Ohrenschall and John Mathia, the route has become a classic moderate snow-and-ice route.

It was here on Polemonium's V-Notch that the development of early ice climbing technique took place. In October 1969, Doug Robinson, Yvon Chouinard, and Tom Frost drove out of a stifling Yosemite Valley in search of cooler climbing. Robinson and Chouinard were soon standing on the Palisade Glacier, looking up at the V-Notch. The ascent, according to Robinson, was important because Chouinard was introducing modern ice climbing techniques to California. In his 1970 story "Truckin' My Blues Away," Robinson wrote:

"Chouinard had developed a technique and two tools to help us up the gully without breaking up the surface of the ice with a step. Dissatisfied with the grip of hand daggers in the right-hand Mendel couloir, he forged the back of a Yosemite hammer into a small-toothed pick with a sharp droop. Swung from the handle, this alpine hammer is driven into the ice with the force of the hammerhead behind it. I have pulled my entire weight up vertically on a single, well-placed hammer."

The relatively low-angle ice of both the U-Notch and V-Notch are excellent places for inexperienced ice climbers to hone screw- and tool-placing skills before moving onto steeper (and more dangerous) ice climbs.

One of the more interesting highlights of the V-Notch's first ascent was John Ohrenschall's report of the route in the November 1958 edition of the *Sierra Club Bulletin*. In his report, Ohrenschall noted that he and his partner, John Mathias, made a two-day traverse of the Palisade Crest, from Thunderbolt Peak to Mount Sill. Although the two climbers took only two days, Ohrenschall felt that a traverse in 24 hours or less was a distinct possibility. Then, two days later, Ohrenschall and Mathias climbed the V-Notch. Interestingly, Ohrenschall wrote:

"We called this couloir 'North Couloir'; it offers yet another route up Mount Sill requiring 600 feet of climbing with snow and ice equipment. We had some climbing to do to get past the bergschrund."

The V-Notch has been descended on skis, and in December 1989, Jim Zellers, Tom Burt, and Bonnie Leary made the first descent using snowboards.

On the opposite side of the crest, walls, gullies, and arêtes predominate Polemonium's west face. Several unclimbed buttresses are found on that side of the mountain, and it is only a matter of time before eager mountaineers explore these huge ramparts. Perhaps Polemonium Peak's significance lies less in its past and more in its future possibilities.

Climbing Routes on Polemonium Peak

The easiest but by no means quickest route to climb Polemonium Peak is route 1, Southeast Ridge, via the Polemonium Glacier. The most spectacular route has to be route 2, V-Notch. Quicker routes include the variations described in route 3, U-Notch.

Routes are presented in a counterclockwise fashion.

Eastern Approach via North Fork of Big Pine Creek

The east face of Polemonium is best reached by first driving to Glacier Lodge and then hiking the North Fork of Big Pine Creek Trail to the foot of the Palisade Glacier (see chapter 9, Mount Sill, Eastern Approach via North Fork of Big Pine Creek). This approach is used for routes 2 and 3.

Eastern Approach via Bishop Pass Trail

The west face of Polemonium Peak can be reached by crossing Bishop Pass and then traversing south. (See chapter 9, Mount Sill, Eastern Approach via Bishop Pass Trail.) Hike to South Lake and Bishop Pass; from Bishop Pass, hike south cross-country and then cross Thunderbolt Pass into Palisade Basin. Adequate campsites can be found here. This approach is useful for routes 1 and 2.

Eastern Approach via South Fork Pass

The west face of Polemonium Peak can be reached by crossing the South Fork Pass and then traversing north. (See chapter 8, Middle Palisade, Eastern Approach via Glacier Lodge and via South Fork Pass.) Hike the South Fork Trail to South Fork Pass, cross the pass, and head north, staying relatively close to the western flanks of the crest. Cross Potluck Pass (Class 3) and enter the Palisade Basin. This approach is recommended for routes 1 and 3.

Route 1, Southeast Ridge, Class 3–4

Use either the Eastern Approach via Bishop Pass Trail or the Eastern Approach via South Fork Pass.

This ridge, which joins Polemonium Peak and Mount Sill, is most commonly climbed from the summit of Mount Sill (see chapter 9, Mount Sill), from the top of the V-Notch Couloir (route 2), or from the Polemonium Glacier. From the top of either Mount Sill or the V-Notch, once you have gained the ridge, climb west, toward Polemonium. Most of this is only Class 2 hiking. The incredible chasms that slice the ridge and drop down to the Palisade Glacier can be avoided by staying south (left) on the ridge. Continue on the ridge in a westerly direction to the high point that appears to be Polemonium.

The southeast ridge can also be gained by climbing the Polemonium Glacier to the summit of Polemonium Peak. Hike from the Palisade Basin south toward Potluck Pass. Before crossing Potluck Pass, turn left (northwest) and hike up the gently sloping shoulder of Peak 13,962. Traverse east and drop into the bowl that contains the Polemonium Glacier. Hike northwest up the floor of the bowl to the southeastern foot of the glacier. Cross the glacier and continue up the southern slopes to the highest point northwest, toward the summit of Polemonium.

After reaching what appears to be the high point of Polemonium above the Polemonium Glacier, a deep gully to the southwest separates the end of the ridge from the true summit to the north. This steep gully falls away to the west, into Palisade Basin. Drop down into the gully for 100 feet while traversing east. Caution is essential because the rock here is phenomenally loose. Another branch of the gully (the next branch to the north) soon becomes visible and leads back up to the ridge. Climb this and veer to the right near the top, gaining a steep face. From the top of the face, which provides a great view into the U-Notch, the summit is obvious. The fine knife-blade ridge that must now be climbed is easy (Class 4), but stunningly exposed.

A rope is highly recommended.

Descend via the same route.

Route 2, V–Notch, III, WI 3

Use the Eastern Approach via North Fork of Big Pine Creek.

The V-Notch was first climbed in September 1957, by John Mathias and John Ohrenschall. Doug Robinson and Yvon Chouinard were the first to climb the V-Notch in full ice conditions, late in October 1970.

This couloir offers ice devotees a more challenging slope than the U-Notch in the form of 1,000 feet of 50- to 60-degree ice. Once you are at the east foot of the Palisade Glacier, the V-Notch is the obvious couloir directly left or south of the very obvious U-Notch. The first ascensionists avoided much of the ice by staying near the north or south walls of the chute. The crux, the bergschrund, changes

Left to right: Polemonium Glacier, Polemonium Peak, and North Palisade (Photo by Steve Porcella)

The west face of Polemonium Peak (Photo by Cameron Burns)

from season to season. A direct climb of the vertical ice on the bergschrund ranges WI 2–3.

Descent can be made via rappels down the U-Notch (route 3), staying close to the north side. Numerous rappel anchors exist in the form of fixed pins and tied runners.

Route 3, U-Notch, III, WI 2–3, Class 4–5

Use any of the approaches.

This is the most common way of climbing Polemonium. By climbing the U-Notch, North Palisade and Polemonium Peak can both be climbed in a day from the Palisade Glacier. (The U-Notch can also be climbed from the west at a level of Class 2–3.)

From Bishop Pass or South Fork Pass, climb route 2, U-Notch Southwest Side, as described in chapter 11, North Palisade. Or, from the North Fork of Big Pine Creek, hike to the eastern foot of the Palisade Glacier. Ascend the glacier to the base of the U-Notch gully, then either climb the vertical ice found in the bergschrund (WI 2–3), or traverse around it to the left (northwest) or right (southeast). From here, climb 900 feet of enjoyable 40- to 45-degree ice to the top of the U-Notch.

Steve Porcella on the traverse to Polemonium Peak from the south
(Photo by Cameron Burns)

Once the actual notch has been gained, start up the rock on the left (south-east) side of the gap. There are many possible routes, but none of them seem to be noticeably easier than the other. Look for the line of least resistance on this north-facing rock. By climbing straight up, one discovers that the climbing is not Class 4, as it has been described in other guidebooks, but in fact feels more like Class 5. Continue up and right on Class 5 rock, mantling blocks until the summit ridge is achieved.

Left to right: the V-Notch couloir, Polemonium Peak, and the U-Notch couloir
(Photo by Cameron Burns)

Alternatively, you may be able to hike 100–300 feet west from the top of the U-Notch and look for weaknesses in the northwest-facing rock. Summitting is possible this way, and potentially easier, but the routefinding is more difficult.

The rappel route may also be climbed. This lies just around the corner to the left (northeast), and requires that one descend the gully 20 feet to the east before turning right (southeast), toward the obvious chimney system. This can be climbed via Class 4–5 rock. However, late in the year a snow patch in this area becomes blue ice. If rappelling the route, a pendulum may be required to regain the U-Notch. This was the original route that Moffitt, Hutchinson, Pike, and Le Conte took to ascend Mount Sill; however, based on the available records, we don't believe they climbed to the summit of Polemonium.

Descend this route to the U-Notch (several rappels may be necessary), and descend the U-Notch to the west or east depending on the approach used. To the east, via the Palisade Glacier, rappel the U-Notch following the right (north) side of the chute.

References

Horwitz, Ken. "California Palisades." *Off Belay* 21 (June 1975).
Le Conte, Joseph. "The Ascent of the North Palisade." *Sierra Club Bulletin* 5 (January 1904).
Ohrenschall, John. Mt. Sill *Sierra Club Bulletin* 43 (November 1958).
Robinson, Doug. "Truckin' My Blues Away." *Mountain* 9 (1970).

Chapter 11
North Palisade

There is no more spectacular peak in the Sierra Nevada,
none more alluring to the mountaineer than the North Palisade.

Norman Clyde in 1932, *Norman Clyde of the High Sierra*, 1971

North Palisade, elevation 14,242 feet, crown of the Palisade group, is an austere diorite monolith. Guarded on its northeast side by a large ice field and on its southwest flank by huge, sheer walls, North Palisade is the spectacular culmination of the incredible ridge known as the Palisades. As a peak, North Pal (as it is commonly known) is one of the most sought-after summits in all California.

The Palisade group was first named by the members of the Brewer Party of the California State Geological Survey in 1864, the same year the party discovered and named Whitney. In his annual report on the Survey's findings, Professor Brewer wrote, according to Joseph N. Le Conte's 1904 *Sierra Club Bulletin* article:

"At the head of the Middle Fork [of the Kings River], along the main crest of the Sierra, is a range of peaks from 13,500 to 14,000 feet high which we call 'the Palisades.' These were unlike the rest of the crest in outline and color, and were doubtless volcanic; they were very grand and fantastic in shape.... All doubts as to the nature of these peaks were removed after observing on the east side of the crest, in the Owens Valley, that vast streams of lava had flowed down the slopes of the Sierra, just below the Palisades."

Although the igneous, fine-grained diorite of the Palisades bears little relationship to the lava flows of the Owens Valley, the Brewer Party were correct in their observation that the peaks were grand and fantastic in shape.

Polemonium Peak, North Palisade, and Starlight Peak from the north ridge of Mount Sill
(Photo by Steve Porcella)

In the latter part of the nineteenth century, North Palisade went through several renamings. As was common in the early history of climbing in the Sierra, lack of communication caused many mountains to receive multiple names.

In 1875, members of the Wheeler Survey recognized the terrific height of the peaks in this part of the Sierra and measured the two highest points in the range by triangulation. The two points, Northwest Palisade (North Palisade) and Southeast Palisade (Split Mountain), were determined to be 14,275 and 14,200 feet tall, respectively.

One of the earliest mountaineers to visit the region was Frank Dusy, for whom Dusy Basin is named. In 1877 Dusy explored the headwaters of the Kings River, although he made no significant ascents in the area.

Two years later, in 1879, Lil Winchell visited the Palisades and named the tallest peak Dusy Peak, after Frank Dusy. Winchell climbed and named the two peaks to the north of Dusy Peak: Mount Winchell, after the geologist Professor Alexander Winchell, and Mount Agassiz, for Louis Agassiz, the renowned French glaciologist.

Then, in 1895, Bolton Coit Brown, standing on the summit of Mount Woodworth, gained his first glimpse of the Palisades. He dubbed the tallest peak in the group (North Palisade) Mount Jordan, after the president of Stanford University.

LE CONTE EXPRESSED his desires to make a first ascent in the Palisades in his 1904 *Sierra Club Bulletin* article:

"To capture the summit of North Palisade, therefore, had long been a great desire of mine, and a number of trips through the mountains to the west and south of the peak only furnished a still further incentive to make the attempt."

In 1903, Le Conte, James Hutchinson, and James Moffitt made plans to explore the northern Palisades. Later that year, leaving the high country of the southern Sierra, where they were camped with a group of Sierra Club members, Le Conte and his wife crossed Harrison Pass and joined their fellow mountaineers Hutchinson and Moffitt in the Kings River canyon.

On July 21, having enjoyed several days of rest, the group began the long approach to the mountains. After two days' travel, Le Conte ascended Marion Peak in order to study a passable route to the northern Palisades. Le Conte was greeted with a full view of the most forbidding of Sierra peaks; in his 1904 *Sierra Club Bulletin* article, he continued:

"We turned our attention to the north Palisades, which rose in a forbidding array of jagged spires ten miles to the north. It now appeared that, although the actual summit of the highest peak was on the main crest, the whole of the great knife-edge did not constitute a portion of it. . . . One deep cleft, in particular, worried us, but of course it was impossible at so great a distance to tell whether it was passable. The western face of the mountain appeared to be totally inaccessible, though a few narrow chimneys seamed its savage face. . . . For over an hour we stayed on the summit of our peak studying the chances pro and con, and had to confess at last that the odds were against us."

That evening, the group began preparation for their final push in their trek to the Palisades. They believed they were going light, taking only the necessities, which were: an eider-down quilt for each person, a 4x5 camera with eighteen glass plates, a light plane-table, two Sierra Club registers, a small pot and frying pan, four spoons, four tin cups, and three days' worth of food.

Their plan was to attempt to climb North Palisade first; then, if the ascent proved impossible, they would try to climb Mount Sill, which they felt would be easier. The assault party consisted of Le Conte, Hutchinson, Moffitt, and Robert Pike. Robert Pike and his brother John had joined the group several days earlier. Mrs. Le Conte and John Pike were to remain in camp at the head of the Kings River.

On July 24, after two days of travel, Hutchinson, Le Conte, and Moffitt made their attempt on North Pal. They climbed up the steep southwestern chute, later known as the U-Notch, but were stymied by the sheer rock walls above. Surmounting these walls, Le Conte realized, would be the key to success. The trio spent an hour resting in the U-Notch, wondering if they would ever reach the tallest summit in the Palisades. To pass the time during their indecision, the three men began rolling rocks down the east side of the U-Notch. Apparently, as Le Conte mentioned in his 1904 *Sierra Club Bulletin* article, they found this quite entertaining:

"It was really a thrilling site [sic] to watch them go thundering down the cliff, leaping across the bergschrund, and then end over end through the snow till only distinguishable by the snow-foam when they struck."

Although boulder-rolling may have been an acceptable pastime for 1903, with the number of people frequenting the Palisade Glacier these days, it could be extremely dangerous.

Soon the three mountaineers turned their attention to Mount Sill, and scrambled out of the U-Notch and on toward Mount Sill. They summitted that peak within an hour.

The following day, the trio reascended the U-Notch chute again from the southwest. They were particularly careful to watch for access out of the huge chute to the left. Two-thirds of the way up the chute, Hutchinson and Moffitt found a crack system that they thought might yield an easy route to the upper reaches of the mountain. The climbing was difficult, however, and as the pair labored to climb the cracks, Le Conte spied a narrow ledge system lower down the chute that traversed across the steep walls that were giving the group so much trouble. Le Conte descended to the ledge, and after some nervous crawling, had discovered the key to the ascent. The three climbers quickly scrambled up the broken ledges above the "catwalk," and were soon deep in a steep ice-filled gully.

As Le Conte wrote in 1904 in the *Sierra Club Bulletin,* "Up this we climbed with the greatest care. Sometimes it was only wide enough to admit a man's body, and we had to work up with knees and elbows. In some places it was filled with clear ice, and great icicles hung directly in the way from some lodged boulder above. These had to be avoided by stepping in the narrow space between the rock and ice, or by finding footholds on the wall."

Soon the climbers were on easier ground above and the summit was within view. After entering the "bowl"-shaped area just south of the summit, the group climbed to the summit ridge just southeast of the peak. They immediately encountered the huge, precariously stacked blocks that every subsequent ascensionist of North Palisade has encountered. Le Conte's *Sierra Club Bulletin* article continued:

"Even there—even 20 feet below the top—we almost failed. The knife-edge was composed of thin blocks standing up on edge, from 6 to 8 feet apart and equally high. These had to be climbed over one by one, by letting down at arm's length between two and pulling up over the thin edge of the next. At 11:30 we crawled out upon the crown, victorious at last, after nearly 2,000 feet of difficult rock climbing."

Finally, the summit of North Palisade had been conquered.

After their triumphant return from the summit, Le Conte recounted that he and his pals engaged in a common mountaineering practice:

"That evening we celebrated by eating up practically everything we possessed that was edible, and wound up by smoking whole and complete stogies."

By 1904, when James Hutchinson, Joseph Le Conte, and J. K. Moffitt had made an ascent of the tallest Palisade, the mountain had been through so many names that Le Conte commented:

"Until further particulars of the naming of the highest point can be obtained, I shall refer to it as the North Palisade, leaving to the next *[Sierra Club] Bulletin* the result of this investigation."

Apparently Le Conte's frustration with the unknown names previously applied to the peak, and his simple reversion to the earliest name given to the mountain, were enough to promote the title North Palisade into popular usage. The name stuck, and was never debated.

IN 1921, HERMANN ULRICHS succeeded on the route originally attempted by the 1903 Le Conte party, being the first to climb the chimney route out of the U-Notch from the west.

In 1925, and during the next ten years, Norman Clyde returned many, many times to pioneer new, difficult routes in the area, often climbing solo.

The eastern face of North Palisade was one of Clyde's favorite places. In June 1928, he was the first to climb the steep ice and snow below the U-Notch to reach the summit of North Palisade. Norman Clyde climbed the U-Notch many times. During one solo descent of the U-Notch, Clyde fell and began sliding. As he picked up speed, he remembered that a gaping bergschrund lay at the base of the couloir. Rather than attempt a self-arrest that would probably not work, he launched himself over the bergschrund. The impact on the far side broke his ankle, causing him to hobble out over 10 miles for help. Although he was injured, the incident did nothing to deter Clyde from further soloing in the Sierra Nevada.

Norman Clyde's boldest ascent took place in a steep couloir on the east face of North Palisade. The Clyde Couloir, as it was subsequently dubbed, presents one of the more dangerous gully climbs in the Palisades, or in the Sierra Nevada for that matter. Subsequent ascents of the Clyde Couloir have proven that conditions in this formidable gully can change dramatically due to the east-facing aspect of the climb. Several deaths have occurred in the couloir, caused by loose rockfall from above, and it is likely that Clyde, during the first ascent, encountered very good snow and ice conditions.

Several other routes were pioneered in the Palisades during the thirties and forties, but it wasn't until the late sixties and seventies that new route activity really began in earnest. The climbers included Doug Robinson, Larry Williams, Chuck Pratt, John Fisher, Frank Sarnquist, and Bob Swift.

In July 1970, Robinson, with Allen Steck, climbed the giant open book, the Doors of Perception, on North Palisade, one of the most aesthetic lines in the Sierras. That very same month, Lee Panza and Kenneth Boche climbed a buttress just to the left of the Clyde Couloir.

Further route activity on North Palisade has been sporadic; however, one new route on the west face of the mountain did rekindle the spirit of exploration in the Palisades.

Norman Clyde with the Palisades in the distance (Photo by Glen Dawson)

In the early 1980s, Galen Rowell approached the west face with the intention of exploring the soaring ridges, buttresses, and ramparts of this massive wall. He had seen the walls of the west face from the air and realized the potential for big-wall climbing that lay hidden from view of most Palisades visitors. With David Wilson, Rowell climbed the largest wall on North Palisade. The ascent demonstrated the potential that this area of the Palisades offers.

In 1989, Cameron Burns and Steve Porcella established three new variations to the 1936 West Face Route. In 1990, the pair returned to climb the largest unclimbed formation on the west side of the North Palisade massif, the southwest buttress. This route was significant because its ascent established the first 5.11 standard on a California 14,000-foot peak.

Although North Palisade receives a great deal of attention, the rest of the western faces of the Palisades offer many mountaineering opportunities. As Doug Robinson commented in a January 1990 conversation, "The future thrust of Palisades exploration lies on these unclimbed, hardly known [west-facing] walls."

Climbing Routes on North Palisade

The easiest route to climb North Palisade is via route 2, U-Notch Southwest Side, from the west. The most popular route is route 1, U-Notch Northeast Side (Palisade Glacier), and it involves climbing the U-Notch from the east, starting on the Palisade Glacier.

Routes are presented in a clockwise fashion.

Eastern Approach via Bishop Pass Trail

The west face of North Palisade can be reached by traversing south after crossing Bishop Pass (see chapter 8, Middle Palisade, Eastern Approach via Bishop Pass Trail). From Bishop Pass, hike south cross-country and then cross Thunderbolt Pass into Palisade Basin. Adequate campsites can be found here. Treat the fragile Palisade Basin ecosystem with care to keep the area clean and pristine for future hikers and climbers. Use this approach for routes 2–9.

Eastern Approach via South Fork Pass

The west face of North Palisade can also be reached by traversing north after crossing the South Fork Pass (see chapter 8, Middle Palisade, Eastern Approach via South Fork Pass). After crossing South Fork Pass, head north, staying relatively close to the western flanks of the crest. Cross Potluck Pass (Class 3) and enter the Palisade Basin. Use this approach for routes 2–9.

Eastern Approach via North Fork of Big Pine Creek

The east face is best reached by first driving to Glacier Lodge and then hiking the North Fork of Big Pine Creek Trail (see chapter 9, Mount Sill, Eastern Approach via North Fork of Big Pine Creek). Follow the trail to the Palisade Glacier. Once at the Palisade Glacier, the U-Notch is the most obvious gash in the ridge.

East and northeast routes (routes 1 and 10–14) are readily approached from anywhere on the Palisade Glacier. Bivy or small campsites, for close proximity to North Palisade's eastern and southeastern climbs, are generally scarce. Sites can be found in the moraine or in close proximity to Mount Gayley. This is a delicate alpine ecosystem and these bivy sites are used quite frequently by many people. It is especially important to bury human waste at least 8 inches and at least 200 feet away from any water sources or pack it out. It is equally important to pack out all trash that you find. Much warmer and comfortable campsites abound at Third and Second Lakes or in the slightly cooler and exposed Sam Mack Meadow. Camping in either of these areas requires an earlier start and a longer approach hike.

Route 1, U-Notch Northeast Side (Palisade Glacier), IV, 5.2

Use the Eastern Approach via North Fork of Big Pine Creek.

This enormous notch, which splits the North Palisade–Polemonium Peak ridge, is the most obvious feature on the mountain. It was first ascended by Norman Clyde, solo, in June 1928.

Norman Clyde cutting steps on the North Palisade Glacier (Photo by David Brower)

Climbed from the east, this notch is an easy ice climb, an excellent opportunity to learn proper ice technique. Because it's an alpine route, conditions in this gully can vary from day to day, hour to hour. Conditions for the ice are usually best in August, when it is possible to climb firm, blue ice in a T-shirt and shorts.

From the head of the Palisade Glacier, any one of many routes can be followed up the steep ice. A steep bergschrund, or crevasse, exists at the mouth of the couloir and must be surmounted either by climbing the vertical-to-overhanging ice of the bergschrund itself, or by traversing completely around one of the ends of the bergschrund. Above the bergschrund, between six and ten pitches of intermediate ice climbing gain the U-Notch itself. Although the use of ice-screw belays are recommended for the center of this gully, they are by no means essential. By staying close to either side of the gully, rock-climbing equipment may be employed quite readily. The right (north) wall of the gully has numerous rappel/belay anchors, and these may be used in both the ascent and descent. (Rappelling this gully is the quickest way off the mountain and back to Glacier Lodge.)

The south-facing wall directly above the highest point of the U-Notch is characterized by a steep, almost vertical, crack system with a series of small roofs and ledges. The climbing up this route has been previously described as Class 4, but many parties find it closer to 5.2. Ascend one long pitch straight up the cracks to a small, two-piton belay below a short wall. At this point, there are several options. The easiest route moves left, into a short chimney. By climbing the chimney, and moving right onto face holds near the top, easier ground is soon reached. Keep moving right on ledges and blocks and soon a ridge is surmounted. This ridge is very obvious because it lies above the dramatic drop of the northeast face.

Traverse the rock slabs right (north) of the actual ridge to a notch in the ridge beyond. At this notch, head down into the obvious "bowl" and climb Class 3 rock north, toward the actual summit of North Palisade. In surmounting the final blocks of North Palisade, several mantles may be required.

Descend via the same route, with a rappel recommended back into the U-Notch and multiple rappels down the north side of the U-Notch.

Route 2, U-Notch Southwest Side, IV, Class 4

Use either the Eastern Approach via Bishop Pass Trail or the Eastern Approach via South Fork Pass.

This route, the original ascent route climbed by Joseph N. Le Conte, James Hutchinson, and J. K. Moffitt on July 25, 1903, has previously been called Class 3. However, the rock climbing on this route is really Class 4, and the ever-present snow in the steepest section of the key gully add up to make this route a lot more demanding than many peak baggers would like to expect. Still, it is the easiest route to the summit of North Pal.

Looking at the west face of North Palisade from the Palisade Basin, three large (about 500 feet tall) white cliffs are obvious. The gully that divides the two southernmost cliffs leads to the U-Notch, which is visible on the Palisade Crest, above. Enter the gully and climb steep, unforgiving talus to a huge flat slab about halfway up the gully. Here, the route becomes circuitous, and routefinding requires some patience. Move to the left-hand (north) side of the gully. There is a steep wall on this side of the gully, where a large, open, sloping ledge system can be seen above a vertical cliff. This cliff is often draining water, creating a very slight waterfall on its uphill end.

Gaining the ledge system is the key to the climb. From a point at the base of the vertical cliff, a very small, inconspicuous catwalk traverses down and left (west), across the cliff face itself. It is very narrow in many places and there may be cairns or "ducks" along the catwalk. Be wary of "ducks," for they may be off route.

After reaching the lower (west) end of the catwalk, move up and right (northeast), onto the large, sloping ledge system. Climb up these ledges for several hundred feet, keeping well away from the edge of the precipice to the right. After surmounting a very small ridge that cuts the ledge system north to south, a narrow, steep gully, often snow-filled, comes into view. Ascend this gully by climbing either wet gravel or the snow that lies in it. Use the walls of the gully to surmount the two small roofs formed by chockstones wedged in the gully. The rock here can be wet, making relatively easy climbing difficult.

At the head of the gully, a small ridge is surmounted, then the route drops down into a third, very broad, chute. This chute forms the lower end of the "bowl" mentioned in the chapter introduction. Follow the trough of this chute for several hundred feet, all the way to the final summit ridge. (At a point 200 feet below the summit, the U-Notch Northeast Side (route 1) drops in from the right (east), joining this chute. The West Face Route (route 7) drops in from the left (west) 100 feet higher.)

As with the Northeast Side Route, climb the gully until the summit ridge is gained and the northern precipice can be seen dropping away. Turn west and continue climbing between the huge summit boulders until the final blocks are surmounted and the summit platform is reached.

It is strongly recommended that most parties bring a lightweight climbing rope and a small selection of nuts and carabiners. This route is easy to lose and even strong 5.10 climbers have remarked on its wild exposure.

The descent of this route is the easiest descent off the mountain. The only rappels required occur in the narrow, snow-filled gully above the catwalk described above. There are obvious places to tie rappel anchors in the head of this gully.

Route 3, U-Notch Southwest Side, Chimney Variation, IV, 5.2

Use either the Eastern Approach via Bishop Pass Trail or the Eastern Approach via South Fork Pass.

This is the route that was attempted by James Hutchinson, J. K. Moffitt, Joseph N. Le Conte, and Robert Pike on July 24, 1903, shortly before they abandoned North Palisade to attempt Mount Sill. It wasn't climbed until 1921 by Hermann Ulrichs.

After surmounting the chimney, this route joins the regular U-Notch Southwest Side Route (route 2) to the summit. The crux, as with the U-Notch Northeast Side Route (route 1), is the south-facing chimney above the notch.

Also as with route 1, a lightweight rope and selection of nuts or friends are recommended. The route can be soloed, but the exposure, and potential for a fall, are considerable.

Descend via route 2, U-Notch Southwest Side.

Route 4, Southwest Buttress, IV, 5.11c

Use either the Eastern Approach via Bishop Pass Trail or the Eastern Approach via South Fork Pass.   .

This route was first climbed by Cameron Burns and Steve Porcella on June 29, 1990.

For several pitches, the route ascends the center of the middle white cliff at the base of the west face of North Palisade. The crux of the route is on the second pitch, a 5.11c overhanging off-width with marginal pro, which is just right of an even harder-looking dihedral. At the top of the white cliff, the route continues up and onto the western-facing prow of the southwest buttress. Five to six

The west face of North Palisade showing routes 2 through 9; the U-Notch and Polemonium Peak at right (Photo by Cameron Burns)

pitches continue up this face, where the climbing alternates between cracks (5.9) and runout face climbing. (5.10). At the top of the buttress, the route follows a serrated, narrow, prominent rib that continues all the way to the summit. The route is sixteen pitches of roped climbing.

Descend via route 2, U-Notch Southwest Side.

Route 5, Putterman Couloir, II, 5.5

Use either the Eastern Approach via Bishop Pass Trail or the Eastern Approach via South Fork Pass.

This variation was first climbed by Cameron Burns and Steve Porcella on July 2, 1989.

The route ascends the gully that divides the two northernmost white cliffs on the southwest side of North Palisade. After several hundred feet of very loose gravel, a smaller gully splits off to the left. Pass this gully, staying in the main chute, and climb a pinched section of very loose conglomerate rock in the main couloir. Above and left of this pinched section, an orange wall with an obvious left-angling ledge is visible. Climb the right side of this wall, angling left (west) up the ledge system. The rock quality gets progressively better. Belay at the crest of the ledge. The next roped pitch is over a straightforward traverse, left (northwest) out of the couloir itself, and onto the top of the northernmost white cliff. This route joins here with route 7, West Face, and goes to the top. This route is loose.

Descend via route 2, U-Notch Southwest Side.

The west face of North Palisade showing routes 4 through 9 (Photo by Steve Porcella)

Route 6, The White Ship, II, 5.9

Use either the Eastern Approach via Bishop Pass Trail or the Eastern Approach via South Fork Pass.

First climbed July 2, 1989, by Cameron Burns and Steve Porcella, this route ascends the center of the northernmost white cliff described in route 2, U-Notch Southwest Side. The white granite is great on this route.

The route is fairly straightforward: At the lowest point of rock, in the center of the face, there is a black water stain. Climb the dihedral just right of this stain, straight up for two pitches, traversing right at the top of the second pitch and gaining an enormous ledge. From this point, the route ascends the big dihedral above the ledge for a pitch. The fourth lead continues up the crack system, then veers right into a sloping trough. Climb this trough to its head, and surmount a small headwall via a knobby face. One more pitch, the fifth, straight up, brings the route to the top of the white cliff band. Follow the regular West Face Route (route 7) for 1,800 feet to the summit.

Descend via route 2, U-Notch Southwest Side.

Route 7, West Face, III, 5.4

Use either the Eastern Approach via Bishop Pass Trail or the Eastern Approach via South Fork Pass.

This route, first climbed in August 1936 by Richard Jones and Mary Jane Edwards, is an excellent, easy rock climb for aspiring mountaineers. However, it does have a somewhat circuitous nature and it is easy to get lost in other gullies that have boxed or dead ends. The route provides high-quality rock in a beautiful setting on the west side of the peak. It has previously been called Class 5, which does not really apply to more modern ratings. Several variations have been climbed.

As mentioned in the U-Notch Southwest Side Route (route 2), from the Palisade Basin, three white cliffs stand at the southwestern base of North Palisade. To the left (north) of the leftmost (northernmost) white cliff is a short chimney, which angles up and right (south), eventually gaining the top of the leftmost (northernmost) white cliff. The first 20 feet of this route, gaining the chimney system itself, is the crux of the climb. From the top of the white cliff, angle up and right (south), up low-angled slabs, eventually gaining a huge gully that splits the mountain all the way to the summit. Follow this gully all the way up.

Approximately two-thirds of the way up, this gully pinches very tight, and often there is snow in this steep section, which must be negotiated to achieve the easier, upper section. Once the pinch has been passed, head straight up for several hundred feet, eventually angling slightly right to the midpoint of a ridge. The summit is just 200 feet above you at this point. Turn this ridge, and drop down to the right (south) onto ledges and blocks to join the regular U-Notch routes in the "bowl" just south of the peak. Then, continuing to circumnavigate the actual summit, climb north to the summit ridge (east of the peak itself), then east, through the huge, precariously balanced boulders to the summit platform.

Descend via route 2, U-Notch Southwest Side.

Route 8, Es Lasst Sich Nicht Lesen, II, 5.10

Use either the Eastern Approach via Bishop Pass Trail or the Eastern Approach via South Fork Pass.

Steve Porcella on the White Ship (Photo by Cameron Burns)

The name of this route, taken from an H. P. Lovecraft horror story, translates to "It does not permit itself to be read." In other words, the routefinding is difficult on this route. It was first climbed by Steve Porcella and Cameron Burns on July 3, 1989, and is a variation of the upper portion of the original West Face Route (route 7).

Follow route 7, West Face, until the point where the gully pinches closed. At this point, there is an enormous white band, about 15 feet tall, that traverses right (south) across the mountain. Follow the ledges just below this band to the right (south) for approximately 200 feet. The ledges end and it is necessary to drop down Class 4 rock into a small chute. Traverse inside the top of the chute, then climb the opposite wall (south), until the original elevation is regained. Move around a corner to the right (south), and a steep, often snow-filled gully is encountered. Climb the rock face (5.10) on the right side of this gully for half a pitch, then cross the gully and ascend the left-hand (north) wall until a ledge is reached.

Above this ledge, the rock forms a series of vertical flakes and cracks that run up and left to the skyline. Follow the largest one until the crest of the ridge is reached. The next lead continues straight up the crest of the ridge until a gargantuan ledge, the "Patio," is reached. Traverse left around the very broken corner of the Patio, onto a steep (northwest-facing) wall. Traverse this wall, then belay at the base of a short chimney. After 70 feet of easy climbing, the ridge crest is regained. Drop down to the right (south) of the ridge, into the "bowl" where the regular U-Notch routes (routes 1–3) approach the summit. From here, as with the U-Notch routes, climb north to the summit ridge east of the peak, then negotiate the jumble of boulders that lead to the summit.

Descend via route 2, U-Notch Southwest Side.

Route 9, Rowell-Wilson West Face, IV, 5.10

Use either the Eastern Approach via Bishop Pass Trail or the Eastern Approach via South Fork Pass.

This sustained route was first climbed by David Wilson and Galen Rowell in July 1981.

When looking at the west face of North Palisade, a gully with water stains empties to the left (north) of the most prominent wall on the face. The route begins at the mouth of this gully and climbs easy Class 5 rock up and to the right for three pitches until a smooth, slightly overhanging headwall is encountered. Four pitches of 5.9 and 5.10 climbing lead up to the crest of the arête. Protection is adequate, but in shallow, discontinuous cracks. Continue climbing roped along the summit ridge above the face. It is necessary to drop down to either side of the ridge when faced with insurmountable gendarmes and towers. This route, for a grade IV, is very long and not to be taken lightly.

Descend via route 2, U-Notch Southwest Side.

Route 10, Starlight Buttress to North Palisade, II–III, 5.4

Use the Eastern Approach via North Fork of Big Pine Creek.

This route was first climbed by Norman Clyde on July 9, 1930, when he soloed the first ascent of Starlight Peak. A more aesthetic variation was added by Tom Naves, Ernie Spielher, Sheldon Moomaw, and R. J. Secor on June 24, 1973; this route can be used to gain the summit of North Palisade.

The route described here involves staying farther to the right (north) on the buttress immediately after crossing the bergschrund. At the top of the buttress, move right (north) into the chimney that leads south to the ridge just north of North Palisade.

Descend via route 1, U-Notch Northeast Side (Palisade Glacier).

Route 11, Clyde Couloir, III, 4

Use the Eastern Approach via North Fork of Big Pine Creek.

This steep rock and ice climb, first climbed by Norman Clyde, solo, in July 1929, has gained a bad reputation over the years, not without reason. Several

David Wilson on the Rowell-Wilson West Face Route on North Palisade (Photo © Galen Rowell/Mountain Light)

deaths have occurred on this route, due to various objective dangers such as freezing conditions, rockfall, rotten ice, etc. This route should be taken seriously. In addition to the severity and/or committing nature of the route, it has many variations.

Ascend snow slopes at the head of the Palisade Glacier to the right of the north buttress (route 13). A thin, very steep, right-angling couloir is visible above.

This is the Clyde Couloir. Clyde climbed the first 200 feet of the couloir by "kicking in" his toes. Then, for several hundred feet more, he forced his way "along the icy margin of the couloir and along the rock wall [right or north] above it." Moving off the ice, Clyde gained the rock face right of the actual chute and then veered left and right up the ledges crisscrossing the face, avoiding many of the obvious difficulties. Finally, crossing the snowfield at the head of the couloir, Clyde made his way up under the overhanging rock of the summit platform. According to Clyde's account of the ascent, he then threw a rope over an overhanging rock and hoisted himself up.

Descend via route 1, U-Notch Northeast Side (Palisade Glacier).

The east face of North Palisade showing routes 1 and 11 through 14; Starlight Peak at right
(Photo by Steve Porcella)

Route 12, Clyde Couloir Variation, III, Class 5

Use the Eastern Approach via North Fork of Big Pine Creek.

A variation of the Clyde Couloir route was performed by John Mendenhall and Dick Franklin in 1955.

It involves staying in the couloir all the way to the notch in the ridge lying between North Palisade and Starlight Peak. One can either go right (south) or left (north) near the top of the couloir to obtain the crest of the ridge. Several parties that have climbed the ice of the couloir reported its poor quality and the poor location of this variation in the event of rockfall.

Another option involves exiting the couloir to the right (north) altogether and climbing the Starlight Buttress to North Palisade Route (route 10).

Descend via route 1, U-Notch Northeast Side (Palisade Glacier).

Route 13, North Buttress, II, 5.8, A2

Use the Eastern Approach via North Fork of Big Pine Creek.

Ken Boche and Lee Panza made the first ascent of this straightforward route on July 12, 1970. Of the ascent, which was apparently Panza's first 14,000-foot peak, Boche simply wrote in the summit register: "beautiful climb, beautiful day."

Just left of the Clyde Couloir, the north buttress is the broken rib that descends onto the Palisade Glacier. Climb one pitch to a ledge. Continue climbing up and right to a small ledge below a large roof. Some aid may be required. Climb a chimney through the roof and continue up to a sloping ledge. From this ledge, the next lead climbs up and right (5.8) to the slabs below the summit snowfield.

Descend via route 1, U-Notch Northeast Side (Palisade Glacier).

Route 14, Doors of Perception, III, 5.8

Use the Eastern Approach via North Fork of Big Pine Creek.

This route was first climbed in July 1970 by Allen Steck and Doug Robinson.

The line that this route follows is the most striking feature on the northeast face of the mountain. The route is very simple: A few hundred feet to the right of the U-Notch is an enormous open book. Climb straight up three pitches of sustained 5.8 crack and chimney climbing until easier ground is reached above. The route continues to the west, where it joins up with the U-Notch routes (routes 1–3) leading to the summit.

Descend via route 1, U-Notch Northeast Side (Palisade Glacier).

References

American Alpine Journal 13 (1971); 25 (1983).

Bohn, Dave and Mary Millman, eds. Norman Clyde of the Sierra Nevada: Rambles through the Range of Light. San Francisco: Scrimshaw Press, 1971.

Le Conte, Joseph N. "The Ascent of the North Palisades." Sierra Club Bulletin 5 (1904).

McWherter, Mike. "Perspective on the Palisades." Summit Magazine, September 1981.

Robinson, Doug. Interviewed by authors. Mammoth, Calif., January 1990.

Sierra Register Committee Archives. North Palisade Summit Register, July 1940. Berkeley, Calif.: University of California Berkeley, courtesy of the Bancroft Library; unpublished.

Chapter 12
Starlight Peak

. . . a wedge several feet in length and 1 foot in width.
Being in fact the slender culmination of a great pinnacle falling away
precipitously on every side, it was an extremely airy perch.

Norman Clyde, during his solo, first ascent
of Starlight Peak, *Norman Clyde of the Sierra Nevada,* 1971

The summit of Starlight Peak, elevation 14,200 feet, offers the bold mountaineer the most exciting summit of all the peaks in the Palisades. In fact, it would be difficult to find an apex more worthy of this distinction anywhere in the Sierra Nevada. The summit is a single rock monolith standing over 30 feet high and tapering to a point only 2 feet wide. Upon reaching this diminutive point, the climber's senses are besieged by vertigo as well as euphoria. The ridge below, much like one's stomach, seems to drop out from beneath. More than 1,000 feet below to the east lies the magnificent Palisade Glacier. To the west lies the incredible expanse of Dusy and Palisade Basins. The view, like the exposure, is nothing less than exhilarating.

For many years, Starlight Peak was known as the Northwest Summit of North Palisade. It was considered nothing more than another lofty tower on a wildly serrated Pacific Crest. However, with the recent exploration of the huge buttresses, gullies, and arêtes that lead to the spectacular summit pinnacle, the peak developed a reputation of its own, justifying the acquisition of a name. Although the origin of the name is unknown, it was probably inspired by climbers gazing at the peak during a clear, star-filled night.

The first recorded ascent of Starlight was made solo by that native of the mountains, the remarkable Norman Clyde. In the early morning of July 9, 1930,

Starlight Peak; Steve Porcella at left (Photo by Cameron Burns)

Clyde crossed the Palisade Glacier and headed for the steep wall to the right of what is now known as Clyde Couloir on North Palisade. He made his way past the bergschrund by cutting steps in the ice before reaching the black speckled diorite at the foot of the buttress. He then climbed 500 feet straight up the steep rock. Clyde emerged from the walls of the couloir and soon met with some difficulty upon the face above, as he described in the 1971 *Norman Clyde of the Sierra Nevada*:

"About 30 feet up the face, after testing a rock, I began to pull myself up, but the rock began to part from the wall. With little relish for landing at the bottom of the cliff, the rock on top of me, I let go and slid down the face, the rock settling back into place as soon as it was relieved of the outward pull of my weight. Fortunately, my fall was arrested within a few feet by a shelf. After scrambling up to the rock again, I shoved it down, thereby making of the place where it had rested one of the desired holds which nature had failed to provide."

After scaling the wall for some distance, Clyde traversed through a chimney and spotted the summit monolith only a short distance away. As a thunderstorm was coming in over Dusy Basin, Clyde worked as quickly as possible to get up the pinnacle. His account continued:

"I attempted to lasso the top of the rock, but my numerous attempts proved futile. I threw one end of the rope over the summit, and after descending to the base of the spire to retrieve it, returned to my former position. After attaching one end to my waist, I looped the rope around the uppermost portion of the rock and again tied it to my waist in such a way as to prevent a fall of more than a few feet, should I happen to slip. The protruding bulge and the smooth surface rendered the short scramble a strenuous one, but eventually I pulled myself to the top of the monolith."

With the thundercloud only moments away, Clyde beat a hasty retreat. He saved himself a few valuable moments by not putting on his nailed shoes before he began to descend the route he had come up. Immediately he was struck by swirling snow and violent winds. Clyde continued down along the side of the chute to the head of a chimney. With increasingly poor visibility and snow now covering the rocks, Clyde used his rope to lower and protect himself as he descended the chimney. At the bottom of the chimney, he crept into a small alcove for shelter against the snow and driving winds. After he'd eaten a quick lunch, the snow and winds slackened and the storm passed overhead. Clyde made his way down the broad couloir and crossed the bergschrund to reach the safety of the glacier. It was nearly one year to the day after he had pioneered the Clyde Couloir route, solo, to the summit of North Palisade.

One year after Clyde's ascent, Francis P. Farquhar, Robert L. M. Underhill, Bestor Robinson, Lewis F. Clark, Neill C. Wilson, Elmer Collet, Glen Dawson, Jules Eichorn, and, of course, Norman Clyde, all members of the Palisades Climbing School, made the ridge traverse from North Palisade to Starlight Peak on August 9, 1931. Anyone who has repeated this traverse should be amazed that a group of this size could do the first ascent of this route without any complications.

Two years later, on July 13, 1933, James Wright soloed the first route on the west face of Starlight, where there had been no previous exploration.

The following summer, on June 29, Norman Clyde, David Brower, and Hervey Voge achieved the first traverse of Thunderbolt Peak, Starlight Peak, and North Palisade.

FOR OVER THIRTY YEARS, no new routes were added to Starlight Peak. It was not until the early 1960s when the natural progression of climbing saw a new level of competence arrive in the Palisades. New routes were quick to follow. A group of climbers well known for their technical and free climbs in Yosemite Valley appeared on the Palisade Glacier.

In July 1968, Doug Robinson and Carl Dreisback made the first ascent of the prominent northeast face of Starlight. This was the first new route on the east face of Starlight since Norman Clyde's first ascent. The route was a grade III, 5.7 climb and one of the first routes of such difficulty in the area.

Also in July 1968, Steve Roper guided three clients—John Clark, Jon Lonne, and Dick James—up a new route on Starlight. The X, as it was called, was the first route pioneered up the large northeast face below the summit. In June 1990, Steve Porcella and Cameron Burns climbed the spectacular arête on the west face of Starlight. The entire route was sixteen pitches.

It is unfortunate to note that at some point in time, probably after 1950, some- one drilled a hole and placed an iron bolt on the top of the summit pinnacle of Starlight. Previous climbing parties had no need of a bolt to climb and descend the pinnacle. In fact, it is very easy to protect oneself by tying a nylon runner around the top of the pinnacle or looping your rope around it as Norman Clyde did, solo. Whoever placed the bolt obviously gave no thought to the history of the pinnacle or to the aesthetics of marring a spectacular summit. The bolt's rapid and progressive deterioration on this natural lightning rod makes it currently obsolete, even dangerous to use.

Climbing Routes on Starlight Peak

There is no easy or quick route to climb Starlight Peak. The most popular route involves traversing north from the summit of North Palisade. The next most popular route involves traversing south from the summit of Thunderbolt Peak. The traverse from Thunderbolt is not bad but it requires Class 4 climbing and can be long. A just as difficult route involves climbing the west gully to the summit. This latter route is Class 4 and requires good routefinding skills and several rappels for the descent.

The summit pinnacle is arguably the most spectacular feature of Starlight Peak. To free climb it, although exposed, the route is no harder than 5.4. From the south first mantle onto the south shoulder of the pinnacle and lasso the summit with a rope or sling. The best way to lasso it is to tie something with some weight to the end of your rope or sling and throw it with enough momentum to come back around to you. You now have an anchor that is tied to the summit pinnacle.

For a real adrenaline experience, try standing on top of the summit. It feels like you are flying! . . . or, perhaps, falling.

Please do not place bolts on the summit monolith. The old-timers climbed it for decades without bolts. There is no reason why we, with our fancy high-tech gear, can't do the same.

Routes are presented in a counterclockwise fashion.

Eastern Approach via North Fork of Big Pine Creek

The east face of Starlight Peak is best reached by first driving to Glacier Lodge and then hiking the North Fork of Big Pine Creek trail to the Palisade Glacier (see chapter 9, Mount Sill, Eastern Approach via North Fork of Big Pine Creek). This approach is useful for routes 1–7.

Left: *Norman Clyde on the summit monolith, also known as the Milk Bottle, Starlight Peak* (Photo by David Brower) Right: *Francis Farquhar and Norman Clyde on the summit of Starlight Peak* (Photo by Glen Dawson)

Eastern Approach via Bishop Pass Trail

The west face of Starlight Peak can be reached using the same approach as for obtaining the west face of North Palisade and Mount Sill (see chapter 8, Middle Palisade, Eastern Approach via Bishop Pass Trail). This approach is useful for routes 8–10.

Eastern Approach via South Fork Pass

An alternative approach to the west face of Starlight Peak involves crossing South Fork Pass and hiking north across Potluck Pass into the Palisade Basin (see chapter 8, Middle Palisade, Eastern Approach via South Fork Pass). This approach is useful for routes 8–10.

Route 1, Traverse from North Palisade to Starlight, Class 4

Use the Eastern Approach via North Fork of Big Pine Creek.

In August 1931, a large group of experienced climbers composed of Norman Clyde, Francis Farquhar, Robert L. M. Underhill, Bestor Robinson, Lewis F. Clark, Neill C. Wilson, Jules Eichorn, Glen Dawson, and Elmer Collet made this first traverse. This route begins at the summit of North Palisade (see chapter 11). The most popular way to climb North Palisade to do this route is via route 1, U-Notch Northeast Side, chapter 11, North Palisade. This route is one of the predominant routes used for reaching the summit of Starlight Peak.

This route starts by descending a chimney/crack system one full pitch to the northwest of the summit of North Palisade. This first pitch is about Class 4. The route then traverses north along a broad, sloping shelf to a notch. Rappel or downclimb across this notch on the northeast side of the ridge. Face climbing into a chimney brings one back on top of the ridge. Cross over the blocks and flakes on the ridge and descend west down a small arête, eventually moving north as the climbing becomes easier. Work north up Class 3 rock toward the prominent summit pinnacle.

It generally takes between 1 and 2 hours to make the traverse if you're experienced! Also, a rope and several nuts are recommended for all parties making this traverse because the exposure is awesome.

Descend via the same route and route 1 in chapter 11, North Palisade.

Route 2, Starlight Buttress, Class 4

Use the Eastern Approach via North Fork of Big Pine Creek.

This route was first climbed by Norman Clyde on July 9, 1930.

Clyde crossed the Palisade Glacier and headed for the steep wall to the right of what is now known as Clyde Couloir. He made his way past the bergschrund by cutting steps in the ice before reaching the black speckled diorite of the buttress. He then climbed 500 feet straight up the steep rock. Clyde soon met with some difficulty on the face above. After scaling the wall for some distance, he traversed through a chimney and spotted the summit monolith only a short distance away as a thunderstorm was coming in over Dusy Basin. Clyde self-belayed himself by tying in and lassoing the narrow shaft of the summit pinnacle.

Steve Porcella on the traverse to Starlight Peak from North Palisade; the Milk Bottle in the distance (Photo by Cameron Burns)

He worked quickly to get up and down the pinnacle and was hit by a snowstorm as he descended his route. (See the chapter introduction for a more detailed account.)

Descend via route 1 above and route 1 in Chapter 11, North Palisade. Alternatively, descend via route 7 below and follow route 4 in Chapter 13, Thunderbolt Peak.

Route 3, Starlight Buttress Variation, II–III, 5.4

Use the Eastern Approach via North Fork of Big Pine Creek.

This is a variation of the route Norman Clyde first used to climb Starlight Peak. It was first climbed by Tom Naves, Ernie Spielher, Sheldon Moomaw, and R. J. Secor on June 24, 1973.

Their variation involves staying on top of the buttress. (We presume Norman Clyde climbed a shallow gully to the left [south] of the crest of the buttress.) It leads to the northernmost notch between North Palisade and Starlight Peak, to obtain the ridge just south of the summit of Starlight. Follow the ridge north to gain the summit. Although the route is called the Buttress Variation, the rock form itself is more analogous to a rib or low-profile arête.

Descend via route 1 above and route 1 in Chapter 11, North Palisade, or descend via route 7 below and route 4 in Chapter 13, Thunderbolt Peak.

Route 4, Piper at the Gates of Dawn, III, 5.7

Use the Eastern Approach via North Fork of Big Pine Creek.

In June 1968, Doug Robinson and Carl Dreisback completed the first ascent of this route.

The climb begins to the right of the Flatiron, a large triangular slab of rock, and follows the dihedral formed by its right edge for two pitches. The first pitch is often ice. During the second pitch, when possible, climb left out onto the slab. Cracks and two ceilings compose the next two pitches and lead to the top of the Flatiron. A Class 4 pitch, followed by a Class 3 pitch, take one along the right-hand margin of a right-leaning snowfield. If it is late in the season, this snowfield will have melted and will not be visible. A large chimney can be seen up ahead. Traverse left across the snowfield to a small arête (5.6). Two increasingly easier pitches lead to the summit ridge just west of the summit monolith.

Descend via route 1 above and route 1 in Chapter 11, North Palisade, or descend via route 7 below and route 4 in Chapter 13, Thunderbolt Peak.

Route 5, Piper at the Gates of Dawn Variation, III, 5.7

Use the Eastern Approach via North Fork of Big Pine Creek.

A variation of the Piper at the Gates of Dawn was done by W. Katra and D. Summers in August 1970.

Their route diverges at the right-slanting snowfield by going right of the prominent chimney ahead. The route then ascends steep flakes and cracks (5.7), traverses onto a face, and eventually goes through an overhang on the right. The route comes out to the right (north) of the summit.

Descend via route 1 above and route 1 in Chapter 11, North Palisade, or descend via route 7 below and route 4 in Chapter 13, Thunderbolt Peak.

Route 6, The X, II, 5.7

Use the Eastern Approach via North Fork of Big Pine Creek.

In July 1968, Steve Roper and his clients John Clark, Jon Lonne, and Dick James made the first ascent of this route.

At the base of the east face of Starlight Peak, there is a large, smooth slab (the Flatiron) lacking the matrix of freeze/fracture cracks that characterize many of the rock walls in the Palisades. On the northeast face of Starlight, above and to

The east face of Starlight Peak showing routes 2 through 6; North Palisade at left (Photo by Steve Porcella)

the right of the Flatiron, diagonal cracks intersect to form an X. The route begins just to the right of the Flatiron and works up over very loose rock. It continues to the right of the snow patch that lies in the junction of the cracks composing The X and continues up chimneys, cracks, and loose blocks. The route soon tops out on the northwest ridge to the left of the two pinnacles that can be seen easily from the Palisade Glacier.

Roper related that his most poignant memory of The X was being horrified at the thought that one of his clients could easily wipe out another with a car-sized block.

Descend via route 1 above and route 1 in Chapter 11, North Palisade, or descend via route 7 below and route 4 in Chapter 13, Thunderbolt Peak.

Route 7, *Traverse of Northwest Ridge from Thunderbolt Peak, Class 4*

Use the Eastern Approach via North Fork of Big Pine Creek.

Norman Clyde, David Brower, and Hervey Voge made the first ascent of this route on July 29, 1934.

To do this very popular route, you must first get to the top of Thunderbolt Peak (see chapter 13). From the summit of Thunderbolt, there are two options. One is to stay on the crest of the ridge and follow it all the way to Starlight Peak. The other option is to traverse southwest off of the ridge, eventually climbing the northwest-facing wall of Starlight. Both routes require good routefinding skills and consist of excellent and spectacular Class 4 climbing.

Descend via the same route, and from Thunderbolt Peak follows the descents described for that peak.

Route 8, *West Chute, Class 4*

Use either the Eastern Approach via Bishop Pass Trail or the Eastern Approach via South Fork Pass.

This is one of the safest routes to the summit pinnacle. It was first climbed on July 13, 1933, by James Wright.

From the Palisade Basin, this route appears to lie in the chute directly south of the second chute on Thunderbolt Peak. In other words, it is the third most prominent chute south of Thunderbolt Pass. It is also the first chute immediately north of the west buttress of Starlight Peak (route 9, West Buttress). Loose rock and steep sections of water- and ice-worn gullies predominate the route.

The chute or gully that you enter at the start of the climb is known as the Lower Chute. After entering the Lower Chute, make your way to its right (south) side and climb Class 4 rock. Follow the path of least resistance, continuing up and right as the climbing grows progressively easier. Traverse right (south) into a gully that borders the north side of the west buttress. Eventually the route leads south, to a sloping slab and notch. Go through the notch behind the buttress, and gain the Upper Chute. This is the top half of the climb and, like the Lower Chute, contains sections of Class 4 climbing. The south side of the notch drops away dramatically into the lower portion of the Upper Chute. Traverse east and downward across exposed, but secure Class 3 rock toward the center of the Upper Chute.

The Upper Chute is often filled with gravel and water from icemelt. Once in the center of this chute, move to its right side and climb steep rock for about 200 feet. Above this, the angle becomes gentler. Follow the gully, which is now composed of Class 2–3 climbing, gradually to the left (north). After nearly 500 feet of scrambling, the top of the Upper Chute is obtained. Climb left up steeper and more difficult rock (Class 4).

As the rock steepens, move up and left. There are many variations in this final section, and all are of about the same difficulty. Watch for rappel slings. Continue up this rock, which is actually a ridge that drops west from Starlight's summit. At this point, the top of the mountain may still be out of sight. The last few feet up to this ridge are exposed and strenuous. Once on top of this knife-blade ridge, the bottle-shaped summit of Starlight can finally be seen to the northeast. Scramble over a huge, precariously balanced boulder, then across to the summit monolith.

Although the route is rated Class 4, a small rack of nuts, hexes, and a rope for an ascent and rappel are useful. We have done this route many times (in addition to the other routes on Starlight) and we have found that rock climbing shoes can make this route and the summit pinnacle climb a little easier and more enjoyable.

Use the same route for descent.

Route 9, West Buttress, IV, 5.10c

Use either the Eastern Approach via Bishop Pass Trail or the Eastern Approach via South Fork Pass.

In June 1990, Cameron Burns and Steve Porcella climbed the prominent west-facing buttress on Starlight Peak.

From the Palisade Basin, looking east at the west face of Starlight, one can see immediately left (north) of the prominent west-facing wall on North Palisade a large triangular buttress. The top of the buttress joins the southwestern edge of another, very prominent, upper buttress. This arête or edge leads to the summit

The west face of Starlight Peak showing routes 8 through 10; North Palisade at right (Photo by Steve Porcella)

of Starlight Peak. The climb begins up the center of the lower buttress and involves three cruxlike pitches ranging from 5.9 to 5.10c. The most difficult crux is an overhanging crack that gains a ledge leading north to a gully. From the gully, traverse south into a notch and climb up a sustained, overhanging, white quartz dihedral (5.10), where pro is minimal. This orange dihedral is easy to see from the Palisade Basin. The quartz vein leads to the top of the buttress. Follow the right arête of the upper buttress to the summit, with much of this climbing consisting of Class 5.7–5.8. This route is comprised of fifteen to seventeen pitches of roped climbing.

Descend via route 8, West Chute.

Route 10, Starlight Chute, Class 5

Use either the Eastern Approach via Bishop Pass Trail or the Eastern Approach via South Fork Pass.

On August 28, 1985, Michael Feldmont and Jim Shirley descended this route.

From Palisade Basin, the bottom of the climb is marked by a black chute outfall to the left of the face of the west buttress of North Palisade; enter this chute. From Palisade Basin, the route rises to a notch between North Palisade and Starlight Peak. Dangerously loose rock and ice-worn chutes separated by steep and difficult chimneys pervade the route.

Descend via route 8, West Chute.

References

American Alpine Club. *Accidents in North American Mountaineering, 1988* (Annual).

Bohn, Dave and Mary Millman, eds. *Norman Clyde of the Sierra Nevada: Rambles in the Range of Light.* San Francisco: Scrimshaw Press, 1971.

Forrest, Craig. "Backpacking in the Palisades." *Summit Magazine,* December 1960.

Huber, W. L. "The North Palisade Glacier." *Sierra Club Bulletin* 9 (1915).

Horwitz, Ken. "California Palisades." *Off Belay Magazine* 21 (June 1975).

Chapter 13
Thunderbolt Peak

The wind blew so violently and the snow flew so thickly as to be almost blinding. An ice ax accidentally dislodged went hurtling down over the cliffs.

Norman Clyde, of the first ascent
of Thunderbolt Peak, *Norman Clyde of the Sierra Nevada,* 1971

Thunderbolt Peak, elevation 14,003 feet, stands as the culmination of a 1-mile-long portion of the Palisade Ridge that contains five peaks higher than 14,000 feet. For many years, due to its illusory guise of arêtes and gullies, Thunderbolt Peak remained untouched by mountaineers. Thunderbolt was the last 14,000-foot peak to be climbed in California, and yet it is one of the most spectacular.

A straightforward route to the summit of Thunderbolt Peak is not apparent from any direction. The west face of the mountain is a complex maze of gullies and arêtes. On the east face of the mountain, a massive arête known as The Prow juts eastward and practically splits the Palisade Glacier in two. The routes on the southeast face of the peak, although easily accessible, can be particularly hazardous due to seasonal rockfall. Even after you've gained the main Palisade Crest at the 13,800-foot level, the difficulties are still ahead of you. The final obstacle to the true summit is a triangular monolith lacking any noticeable features. Of all of the 14,000-foot peaks in California, Thunderbolt's summit monolith is the most difficult to surmount. The summit register is bolted to the top of this monolith, and the number of expletive comments in the register pertaining to the location of the summit box is not surprising. Thunderbolt is a unique peak with spectacular features and an exciting first ascent story.

Cameron Burns climbing the final portion of summit monolith, Thunderbolt Peak (Photo by Steve Porcella)

In 1931 Francis P. Farquhar, editor of the *Sierra Club Bulletin,* commissioned Robert L. M. Underhill to write his now-famous article "On the Use and Management of the Rope in Rock Work." Farquhar then asked Underhill to demonstrate the techniques he outlined in his article to some of the more experienced and talented climbers during the club's summer outing. After a rope-work seminar in the Ritter Range, Underhill and his students headed south with plans to utilize their new knowledge in the Palisades.

On August 13, less than a week after making the first traverse from North Palisade to Starlight Peak, Bestor Robinson, Lewis F. Clark, Glen Dawson, Jules Eichorn, Francis Farquhar, Robert L. M. Underhill, and Norman Clyde set out for an attempt on the summit of Thunderbolt Peak.

Norman Clyde leading climbers to the Underhill Couloirs during the first ascent of Thunderbolt Peak (Photo by Glen Dawson)

Storms had been sweeping over the Sierra Nevada for close to a week. On August 11, Clyde, Underhill, Eichorn, and Dawson were hit by heavy rains during an ascent of Temple Crag. By August 13, the climbers were very leery of a few white clouds that drifted over the crest of the Palisades. They entered the southernmost chute, south of The Prow, on the east face of Thunderbolt. This chute and the next one to the north are now known as the Underhill Couloirs. In order to move quickly and avoid falling rocks, the climbers roped themselves into groups of two and three before moving up the chute. They made their way north onto the arête that joins the two couloirs, and followed it upward to gain the ridge.

Meanwhile, the sky was filling with dark, threatening clouds moving in from the southwest. Despite this brewing storm, the climbers unanimously agreed to continue to the unclimbed northwest summit. The rope teams moved quickly up the face of the narrow ridge, which was broken and fissured with cracks and grooves. In the 1971 *Norman Clyde of the Sierra Nevada,* Clyde recalled:

"At the upper end of this steep pitch, we were obliged either to swing around a buttress on an exposed face with a few rounded holds, or to traverse to a couloir some 50 yards to the left and ascend that. Two of the ropes swung around the buttress; the third availed itself of the traverse and the couloir. Several hundred feet of scrambling over great rocks then brought both parties to the jagged summit arête and, an additional few hundred feet along this, to the foot of the rounded monolith that forms the top of the peak. But the storm was almost upon us.

"Arriving at the base of the monolith, one member of the party leaned across a deep crevice at its base and braced himself against the rock, forming a *courte echelle* [a human stepping stool], enabling several in turn to mount upon his shoulders and then scramble, or rather crawl, depending almost entirely upon friction, to the summit."

The storm was now upon them. The air began to hum from static electricity. Thunder boomed in the clouds above and beyond the ridge. Glen Dawson hastened off of the monolith, allowing Jules Eichorn to make his way to the top. Small blue sparks danced and flickered upon the rock. Eichorn, having gained the top of the monolith, quickly clambered off as the wind increased in intensity. Meanwhile, the party had already begun a hasty retreat eastward along the ridge. Safely off of the monolith, Eichorn moved quickly to escape the proximity of this high point and catch up with his companions. Suddenly there was a flash of light, followed by a concussive clap of thunder, as a bolt of lightning struck the summit monolith. The size and suddenness of this burst of energy was startling if not completely nerve-wracking.

When asked later how close the bolt came, in a 1989 interview Eichorn replied, "...just past my right ear!"

Somewhat dazed, if not a bit disoriented, Eichorn joined his companions as they were quickly enveloped in high winds and dense, thick snow. The climbers descended the south face, where they found a small ledge protected by an overhang. In *Norman Clyde of the Sierra Nevada,* Clyde recalled:

"As this was enough to protect us from any thunderbolt which might strike the summit and afford some shelter from the storm, we crowded together beneath it, a rather bedraggled-looking group. Within half an hour, the storm ceased for a time and we returned to the top of the mountain. The summit monolith was now too slippery to permit rubber soles to grip its rounded surface, and the other climbers were reluctantly obliged to forego its ascent."

Purely for the sake of variation, the group decided to drop down the west face of the mountain, traverse south, and cross a gap that would lead to a wide, snow-filled chute on the northern part of the mountain. Suddenly the storm surrounded their position again.

The climbers kept to their original plan, eventually reaching the head of the north-facing chute. They made their way down this chute by working the rocks on the left and right sides of the couloir, but as they approached the northern lobe of Palisade Glacier, the snow steepened and became ice. Miraculously, the ice ax that had fallen from above was recovered, as Clyde continued his account:

"As I began to cut steps with the retrieved ice ax—now broken in half—a rock came ricocheting down the ice and was presently followed by another. The storm had loosened the rocks higher up on the mountain. It being obviously very hazardous to attempt to go down the chute, more especially so because the fog which now overhung the mountains concealed the flying rocks until they were almost abreast of us, we decided to try to find a way down the end of the rock promontory which we had been following."

Unfortunately, there were several problems with this plan. The promontory was quite steep, which made climbing under the wintry conditions difficult at best. The other problem concerned the bergschrund at the base of the promontory. If the bergschrund was too wide and deep, the climbers might not be able to get across it.

They downclimbed the promontory until they came upon a protruding rock. They attached a loop of rope to the rock and tied a safety rope around the waist of Robert Underhill. Underhill rappelled down the ice to a point below a large projecting buttress that would protect the climbers from falling rock. Underhill then set up a belay while Clyde rappelled down to his position. With Underhill belaying him, Clyde chopped steps downward along the margin of the chute to a small ledge. A third member of the group rappelled down to Clyde's position and belayed him as he continued chopping steps downward. In *Norman Clyde of the Sierra Nevada,* Clyde recalled:

"Eventually, I reached a rock above the ice wall which drops into the bergschrund, over which a rope might safely be looped. Using the rope attached to my waist, together with another one which was passed down the line, I threw the doubled rope over the rock and let it down into the crevasse, whose bottom I could not see since the ice shelved for some distance before reaching the vertical or overhanging drop. I tossed rocks into the bergschrund which seemed to strike the bottom within a reasonable time. The doubled rope was somewhat over 50 feet in length.

"With the rope properly adjusted, I took off, going down the upper steeply shelving portion gradually so as to be able to cut a few steps to assist those following if I should safely get down into the crevasse, or myself, should I be obliged to come back. After going down about 30 feet, I came to the brink of the vertical ice wall. Fortunately, the bottom, apparently firm, was about 20 feet below. I therefore swung over the brink and glided down the rope to the bottom, which did prove to be firm. Luckily, too, the lower lip of the crevasse was at this point only 6 or 8 feet high. The floor was formed of material that had fallen into the crevasse. Only a few rods to one side, however, it dropped away indefinitely.

"A way having been prepared, the rest of the party came down the rope in rapid succession. All real danger past, it was rather amusing to watch one after another as they came over the top of the wall and shot down into the crevasse. After climbing out of the crevasse, we gathered up and coiled about 300 feet of rope and then sped down the glacier."

Climber being lowered onto the bergschrund during the first ascent of Thunderbolt Peak (Photo by Glen Dawson)

It is interesting to note that many of the climbers in this party remarked later, in personal communications in 1989, that if it had not been for Norman Clyde's mastery of and expertise in the mountains, they would not have made it back safely from this climb. To him, they owed their safe return to the glacier before nightfall.

IN 1933 NORMAN CLYDE returned with two men, John Poindexter and Philip Von Lubkin, to climb Thunderbolt Peak again, but this time by an entirely new route, from the west. This was the first climb of Thunderbolt from the west, and news of this would bring new climbers to this side of the mountain.

On the morning of August 11, 1938, W. Kenneth Davis and Jack Riegelhuth entered a large chute on the southwest side of Mount Winchell. They gained the summit of Winchell and then traversed across Thunderbolt and Starlight to the summit of North Palisade. The climb took a total of 13 hours. This was the first major ridge traverse to involve three peaks over 14,000 feet, and it would set the stage for longer and more encompassing traverses yet to come.

An impressive route was climbed by Charles Ray and Ulrich Brosch in 1965. They climbed the east face to the right of the Underhill Couloirs. This face is quite steep and appears to offer good-quality rock.

Over the years, many people have explored and climbed the various prominent and obscure chutes and couloirs that pervade Thunderbolt Peak. Many of the couloirs that were climbed lie on the south or north face of the east-running ridge known as The Prow. As a consequence, different sections of The Prow were climbed en route to the summit of Thunderbolt. For some time, however, a full and complete ascent of The Prow remained to be undertaken. Finally, in 1970 W. Katra and D. Sommers climbed The Prow in its entirety, from the end of its east-facing buttress to the summit of Thunderbolt. To really appreciate this route, we suggest looking down and to the east from the summit of Thunderbolt at this spectacular and narrow ridge.

Climbing Routes on Thunderbolt Peak

The easiest and quickest route to climb Thunderbolt Peak is route 1, Southwest Chute Number 1, via the west face's west chute. There are two summits on Thunderbolt Peak; both are monoliths and are separated by a short distance. The south monolith is the higher of the two and contains the summit register.

To climb the lower north summit monolith, traverse to the monolith's east side, where there is a sloping ledge, and go right (north) to a notch. Pass through the notch to gain a small ledge and climb up a 2-inch-wide crack from here to the top. This climb is considered Class 5.

There are two known methods for climbing to the top of the higher south monolith, where the summit register is located. The first, pioneered by the first ascensionists, involves having a partner brace against the east-facing side of the monolith and then climbing up and onto his or her shoulders. The move from here onto the rock requires a fair amount of balance, courage, and friction,

Steve Porcella on the summit monolith, Thunderbolt Peak (Photo by Cameron Burns)

manifested in the form of life-threatening belly crawling on the rock. The second method, perhaps more dignified, involves throwing a rope over the summit block (east to west), traversing north and then west around the block, tying in, and then climbing the west face of the monolith while being belayed from the east. The difficulty is 5.8. There are two bolts on the top (one holding the summit register down), which may be used to rappel off. If you don't trust the bolts, you can throw a runner or rope over the southwest prow of the rock and rappel northeastward off the block.

Routes are presented in a counterclockwise fashion.

The west face of Thunderbolt Peak showing routes 1, 2, and 3
(Photo by Cameron Burns)

Eastern Approach via North Fork of Big Pine Creek

The east face of Thunderbolt Peak is best reached by first driving to Glacier Lodge and then hiking the North Fork of Big Pine Creek Trail to Palisade Glacier (see chapter 9, Mount Sill, Eastern Approach via North Fork of Big Pine Creek). Routes on the northern face of The Prow can be reached by taking the Glacier Trail to the foot of Palisade Glacier, and then traversing northward on the glacier and continuing around the eastern buttress of The Prow. Northern routes on The Prow can be reached by hiking the North Fork of Big Pine Creek Trail to Sam Mack Meadow and from there to the northern edge of the Palisade Glacier.

Eastern Approach via Bishop Pass Trail

Use the Bishop Pass Trail approach (see chapter 8, Middle Palisade, Eastern Approach via Bishop Pass Trail). After crossing Bishop Pass, traverse south to Thunderbolt Pass. Cross Thunderbolt Pass and camp in Palisade Basin.

Eastern Approach via South Fork Pass

Alternatively, one can take the South Fork Pass Trail over South Fork Pass (see chapter 8, Middle Palisade, Eastern Approach via South Fork Pass Trail), and then head north over Potluck Pass into the Palisade Basin.

Route 1, Southwest Chute Number 1, Class 3

Use either the Eastern Approach via Bishop Pass Trail or the Eastern Approach via South Fork Pass.

This route was first done as a descent by the party that first ascended route 11, West Face. This is the most popular route on the mountain and probably the safest.

On the west face of Thunderbolt Peak, there is a very large and prominent chute that is the first chute directly south of Thunderbolt Pass. From Thunderbolt Pass, cross the talus and enter into this first chute. Class 2 climbing predominates. There is one point of Class 3 that involves climbing around a boulder-choked section of the chute. The route leads to a notch separating the northern summit monolith from the southern summit monolith. To reach the higher southern monolith, one can climb directly up from the notch (Class 4) or hike south along the ridge a short way and traverse west over a steep Class 3 face. This face is blessed with lots of handholds and footholds.

Descend the route either by rappelling directly down into the notch or by climbing down the Class 3 traverse.

Route 2, Southwest Chute Number 2, Class 4

Use either the Eastern Approach via Bishop Pass Trail or the Eastern Approach via South Fork Pass.

The first ascent was performed on August 3, 1933, by Norman Clyde, John Poindexter, and Philip Von Lubkin.

This is the large chute directly south of the main Thunderbolt chute described in route 1, Southwest Chute Number 1. Southwest Chute Number 2 contains some steep sections, congested with stacked rocks or cliffs. The way to surmount these obstacles is to climb the adjacent walls. This chute opens out on the ridge south of the main summit. Traverse to the northwest and then to the northeast.

A rope, for use in rappels, is very helpful when descending this chute. There are some fixed anchors in the chute for these rappels but, as always, climbers should always check the integrity of these anchors before weighting.

Descend via this route or route 1, Southwest Chute Number 1.

Route 3, Starlight West Chute, Class 4

Use either the Eastern Approach via Bishop Pass Trail or the Eastern Approach via South Fork Pass.

This is the same start as that used in chapter 12, Starlight Peak, route 8, West Chute. Enter this west chute, which is the third-largest chute south of Thunderbolt Pass. Instead of angling right (south) to go for Starlight Peak, angle left (north) following the easiest terrain in the large, wide chute. About halfway up the west chute, head northeast following smaller chutes. An upper chute is gained that allows one access to the south ridge leading to Thunderbolt Peak. Follow this ridge to the summit monolith.

Descend via the same route or route 1, Southwest Chute Number 1.

Route 4, Underhill Couloir, Class 4

Use the Eastern Approach via North Fork of Big Pine Creek to Palisade Glacier.

The first ascent of this route was climbed on August 13, 1931, by Norman Clyde, Robert L. M. Underhill, Bestor Robinson, Francis P. Farquhar, Glen Dawson, Lewis F. Clark, and Jules M. Eichorn.

On the southeast face of Thunderbolt, enter the southernmost couloir of the two couloirs that drop down from the notch separating Thunderbolt from Starlight. After climbing halfway up, work right (north) onto the rocks that form the right (northeast) side of the couloir. From here, one may continue up the wall or cross further right (northeast), gaining the crest of the arête that divides the northern couloir from the southern. Climb the arête to the notch and then head north up flat, angled slabs that are broken and fissured with cracks. The crest of the ridge is eventually attained. From here, downclimb to the northwest and traverse upward to the northeast. This leads to the notch between the two summit monoliths.

Descend via the same route.

The south face of Thunderbolt Peak showing routes 4 and 5 (Photo by Cameron Burns)

Route 5, East Face, III, 5.5

Use the Eastern Approach via North Fork of Big Pine Creek to Palisade Glacier.

This route was first climbed in August 1965, by Charles Ray and Ulrich Brosch. This route has been described as an enjoyable climb on relatively good rock. However, we have seen rockfall in this vicinity. As with all routes in this area, it is a good idea to check for rockfall before getting close to the climb.

From the base of the Underhill Couloirs (route 4), traverse right (east) over loose rock on ledges for about 200 feet. Climb up and to the left (west) toward a shallow open book. Climb this for many pitches, varying from Class 5 to 5.5, until the south summit ridge is attained.

Descend via route 4, Underhill Couloir.

Route 6, The Prow, III, 5.6

Use the Eastern Approach via North Fork of Big Pine Creek.

First climbed in August 1970 by W. Katra and D. Sommers, this route is the first full and complete ascent of The Prow.

Approach via Sam Mack Meadow to Palisade Glacier. Fifty feet left (south) of the lowest tip of the east face of The Prow, climb up a short, steep chimney. This is the crux of the route. Continue up Class 4 and 5 rock to the crest of The Prow. Follow this crest to the main ridge. The rest of the route may be completed by following routes 7–9.

Descend via route 4, Underhill Couloir.

Route 7, Northeast Couloir, III, 5.6

Use the Eastern Approach via North Fork of Big Pine Creek.

This route was first climbed in August 1968 by Bob Lindgen and Brad Fowler.

This couloir lies on the north face of The Prow. Enter the first couloir to the right (west) of the east-facing buttress of The Prow. Climb the left (east) side of the couloir, because this is the less steep of the two sides, and move up onto a broken rock ledge. Continue straight up for one Class 5.6 pitch. Easier rock pitches continue up to the top of The Prow. Follow the crest of The Prow to the main ridge, where route 8, Northeast Buttress, may be used to gain the summit.

Descend via route 8, Northeast Buttress.

Route 8, Northeast Buttress, Class 4

Use the Eastern Approach via North Fork of Big Pine Creek.

Norman Clyde soloed this route on an unknown date. This is the same route that the first-ascent party descended.

Hike to Sam Mack Meadow, and hike southwest toward the northeast face of Thunderbolt. On the north-facing side of The Prow, there is a large, snow-filled couloir that has the shape of a giant Y. Cross the bergschrund to the right (west) below a large rock bulge or cliff. Cut steps up the snow, angling left (east), all the while being protected from rocks coming down the chute by the rock buttress above. After a short distance, climb upward and east toward the crest of The Prow. Follow the crest until it joins up with the Palisade Crest, where an upward traverse brings one to a notch in the ridge. A traverse left (east) around a bulge gains a couloir that leads to the summit monolith.

Descend via the same route.

The east face of Thunderbolt Peak showing routes 4 through 8, and 10
(Photo by Steve Porcella)

Route 9, Traverse from Mount Winchell, III, 5.8, A1

Use the Eastern Approach via North Fork of Big Pine Creek or the Eastern Approach via Bishop Pass Trail.

On August 11, 1938, W. Kenneth Davis and Jack Riegelhuth made this first ascent.

We recommend R. J. Secor's *The High Sierra* for routes to reach the summit of Mount Winchell. In the morning they entered a large chute on the southwest side of Mount Winchell. They gained the summit of Winchell, then descended the south-facing skyline, performing one roped rappel, toward the notch that divides Winchell from Thunderbolt. They ascended the north-facing ridge, often encountering Class 4 and 5 rock. Many pitons were required to negotiate this portion of the climb. From the summit of Thunderbolt, the two men continued on to the summit of North Palisade. The entire climb, from Dusy Basin to the summit of North Palisade, took a total of 13 hours.

Descend via route 1, Southwest Chute Number 1.

Route 10, East Buttress, Right Side, Class 5

Use the Eastern Approach via North Fork of Big Pine Creek.

This route was first climbed in July 1959 by Richard Gnagy and Ellen Wilts.

Approach as for route 8, Northeast Buttress. Start in the farthest-west couloir (farthest one to the right) on the north face of The Prow. Climb the wall to the left (east), working upward and to the right (southwest). Eventually the top of The Prow is gained and the remaining route may be climbed via route 8, Northeast Buttress.

Descend via route 8, Northeast Buttress.

Route 11, West Face, Class 4

Use either the Eastern Approach via Bishop Pass Trail or the Eastern Approach via South Fork Pass.

This intriguing route was first climbed on September 3, 1949, by Oscar Cook, Sylvia Kershaw, Mildred Jentsch, and Hunter and Isabella Morrison.

Enter the first chute north of Thunderbolt Pass. This is the chute that gains access to the Thunderbolt-Winchell col. Follow the right (southeast) branch of

The north face of Thunderbolt Peak showing routes 7, 8, and 10
(Photo by Steve Porcella)

the chute until it is blocked by an often ice-filled chimney. Turn to the right (southwest) and work up an arête that bypasses a vein of rotting quartz and leads to another chute. A large chockstone in this chute may be bypassed by climbing on the wall to the left (north). This maneuver is Class 4. This chute leads to a spur that connects with the main ridge west of Thunderbolt. From here, follow the ridge southeast to the small notch between the two summits.

Descend via this route or route 1, Southwest Chute Number 1.

Route 12, Southwest Buttress, Class 4

The Eastern Approach via Bishop Pass Trail is the easiest and quickest approach to use.

This attractive route was first ascended on August 28, 1964, by Kim Tucker, Sten Hedberg, and Alan Jedlicka.

While standing at Thunderbolt Pass and looking east, one immediately notices a broken and fractured buttress/arête to the left (north) of the pass. Climb up this buttress and follow the crest eastward. Near the top, some gendarmes must be passed by way of a chute to the left (northeast). Regain the top of the buttress and continue until it joins up with the northwest ridge leading to Thunderbolt. Follow the ridge south to the two rock monoliths.

Descend via route 1, Southwest Chute Number 1.

The west face of Thunderbolt Peak showing routes 1 through 3 and 12
(Photo by Cameron Burns)

References

Bohn, Dave and Mary Millman, eds. *Norman Clyde of the Sierra Nevada: Rambles in the Range of Light*. San Francisco: Scrimshaw Press, 1971.

————. "Climbs in the Palisades." Letters (to David Brower), *Sierra Club Bulletin* 35 (1950).

Dawson, Glen. Personal communication with the authors, 1989.

Eichorn, Jules. Interviewed by authors. Redwood City, August 1989.

Farquhar, Francis P. "Some Climbs on the North Palisade," *Sierra Club Bulletin* 17 (February 1932).

Secor, R. J. *The High Sierra*. Seattle: The Mountaineers Books, 1992.

Sierra Register Committee Archives. *Thunderbolt Peak Summit Register, 1931–1949*. Berkeley, Calif.: University of California Berkeley, courtesy of the Bancroft Library; unpublished.

Chapter 14
White Mountain

*. . . at about A.D. 600, aboriginal groups appear to have moved into the
highest portions of the White Mountains as families and to have established
seasonal villages from which both plants and animals were procured.
This replaced an earlier pattern of alpine use—the only activity of note—
which was the short-term hunting of large mammals by small parties of males.*

Dr. Robert Bettinger, University of California Davis, 1990

Although not part of the extensive
and physically dominating Sierra Nevada, White Mountain, elevation 14,246 feet,
commands the northern portion of the White Mountain Range and is the third-
highest peak in California. The White Mountain Range forms the great eastern
wall of Owens Valley and is unique in its biology and climate.

The White Mountain Range, known as the Whites, is one of the highest desert
ranges in North America. The topography and climate of the Whites results in an
ecosystem that is fragile, unique, and incredibly diverse. More than 1,000 different plant and animal species have been cataloged and identified in these mountains. Two hundred of these species occur nowhere else in California. The gain in
elevation from the Owens Valley to the summit of White Mountain, roughly 9,000
feet over 10 to 12 miles, has partitioned the slope into different habitats based on
elevation. The fragility of the various ecosystems is related to the poor soil quality
of this desert environment. It can take more than 100 years for plants to recover
from physical disturbance. The most famous indigenous plant to thrive in this
hostile environment is the ancient bristlecone pine.

The bristlecone pine is the oldest known living organism in the world. Many
of the bristlecones in the White Mountain Range are more than 4,000 years old.

White Mountain from the south (Photo courtesy of White Mountain Research
Station)

These trees are unique for their adaptive longevity and physical beauty, which has been sculpted over the centuries by wind and extreme weather. Most of the soil in which the bristlecones grow is very alkaline and is not suitable for the growth of other types of evergreen trees. Therefore, isolated homogeneous stands of bristlecones predominate throughout the White Mountain Range. On the way to White Mountain, it is worth a stop at the Schulman and Patriarch Groves to observe these magnificent trees.

The climate of White Mountain is dry and cold, with consistently strong winds during the summer and winter months. Precipitation per year averages 20 inches along the crest, with most of it falling as snow. Because of the low atmospheric humidity and the high land elevation, the Whites have long been considered an ideal site for an observatory. However, due to access problems during severe weather, more favorable sites have been chosen in Hawaii and the coastal mountains of California. The unique high-altitude environment of the Whites, with or without bad weather, continues to attract scientists from around the world.

During World War II, many bomber and fighter pilots faced low oxygen conditions while flying at high altitudes. After the war, it was decided that an adequate site for high-altitude physiological research was needed, especially with the coming of the jet age. The Office of Naval Research began looking for possible high-altitude sites where this type of research could be carried out. Among the sites considered were the Peruvian or Bolivian Andes, El Pico de Orizaba in Mexico, Mount Wrangell in Alaska, the mountains of Hawaii, the Colorado Rockies, and the summit shelter on top of Mount Whitney. All of these sites were ruled out in favor of the White Mountain Range. Over a period of about five years, scientists decided to install and establish several permanent buildings that would comprise a permanent research and laboratory facility in the White Mountains. There are four sites: the Bishop facility, the Crooked Creek facility, the Barcroft facility, and the Summit Laboratory. The Barcroft facility lies on the south face of White Mountain at an elevation of 12,470 feet, and is named after the renowned high-altitude physiologist Sir Joseph Barcroft of Cambridge University. The Summit Laboratory is located on the summit of White Mountain.

The 136-square-foot summit laboratory, bristling with a stainless-steel roof and grounded lightning rods, is North America's highest permanent research facility at 14,246 feet. It consists of living quarters for four and a small laboratory area. The research conducted in this lab includes high-altitude physiology, meteorology, and bighorn sheep research.

The White Mountain Research Station's purpose is twofold: to provide laboratory facilities for any qualified research investigator who wishes to utilize the high mountain environment in his or her work, and to serve as teaching facilities for field courses conducted in the region. Past and present studies include research on hypoxia (oxygen depletion), physiology, cosmology, geology, archaeology, and a wide range of biological sciences.

Recently, archaeological studies in the White Mountain Range have provided clues as to who may have been the first people to climb White Mountain. Professor Robert Bettinger and co-workers at UC Davis have discovered eleven villages at elevations ranging from 10,300 feet to 12,600 feet. These are the highest known residential sites in North America.

The aboriginal diet is thought to have consisted of 50 percent marmot and 10 percent to 20 percent large game such as bighorn sheep and antelope. It is highly likely that these aboriginal people walked to the summit of White Mountain as a place for sighting game or for religious meditation.

Paiutes were known to have climbed the peak long before the arrival of the white man. Evidence has been found of a prehistoric cairn and written oral transcripts detailing the gathering of eagle feathers from the highest reaches of the mountain. In addition, there is a report that a young Paiute hunting for eagles on the summit of White Mountain was caught in a storm and died of exposure: the first reported fatality on the mountain.

Climbing Routes on White Mountain

Because the parking area for the trailhead is at 12,000 feet elevation and the trail is basically a road to the top of White Mountain, a quick hike to the peak is tempting for many people. However, proper acclimatization is very important. Many experienced climbers and hikers have staggered into the Barcroft Research Facility complaining of severe headaches, nausea, dizziness, and shortness of breath. These are the classic signs of altitude sickness, and they should not be taken lightly. The Barcroft Research Facility is available in case of emergency, but we strongly recommend that you do not plan for assistance from them. Unless you are already acclimatized to at least 12,000 feet, spend a night bivouacked at the parking area before proceeding to the summit.

No water is available once you enter the Inyo National Forest. You must carry your own water for the climb and descent of the peak. There are some snowbanks on the north side of White Mountain, but their presence or absence is related to the previous winter snowfall.

The most popular way of approaching White Mountain is from the west or east via Highway 168 to Westgard Pass. We provide approach descriptions and mileage logs for Westgard Pass approached from the west or east. Two other approaches are available for getting to White Mountain, but they are much more adventurous and involve much longer approach times and distances. They are Silver Canyon and Wyman Road. Silver Canyon Road is four-wheel-drive only with high vehicle clearance recommended. We provide limited information on these alternative approaches. Lastly, an approach for the north end start of the traverse of the White Mountain Range is included.

Routes are presented in a clockwise fashion.

Westgard Pass Approach from the West

This is the most popular and easiest way to the peak. Begin in the town of Big Pine, 15.7 miles south of Bishop on Highway 395.

Mileage Log _____

0.0	At Big Pine turn east onto Highway 168.
12.0	Continue on Highway 168 past Cedar Flat Campground on the left. Note that this campground requires advance reservations.
12.6	Turn left onto White Mountain Road.
12.7	Cedar Flat Campground entrance station.

20.3   Continue past the Sierra View vista point on the left (west). This vista point overlooks the spectacular Sierra Nevada and Owens Valley.

22.0   On the right is the turnoff for the Ancient Bristlecone Pine Forest.

22.5   The Schulman Grove Visitor Center turnoff is on the right. This is a recommended side trip on the way to White Mountain summit. The oldest living bristlecone pine trees are located in the Schulman Grove.

22.6   White Mountain Road turns into dirt.

25.5   Continue north past the Silver Canyon/Wyman Canyon intersection. Silver Canyon heads left (west) toward Owens Valley and is for four-wheel-drive vehicles only. Wyman Road turns right and heads east. Wyman Road does not require a four-wheel-drive vehicle and will eventually connect with Highway 266.

28.5   Turn right (east) toward Crooked Creek Station.

30.9   The Patriarch Grove, which contains the largest bristlecone pine tree, is on the right.

31.0   Continue past the Crooked Creek Station.

35.3   Parking area for the start of the climb to White Mountain.

As of 1994, there were two signs at the end of White Mountain Road. One sign reminds climbers (1) to please protect the delicate plants and animals that abound, (2) the hike is for foot traffic only, (3) there is no shelter at the summit, and (4) to be wary of the severe storms that are possible on the peak. The other sign mentions that the Barcroft Research Facility is 2 miles from this point and that the summit of White Mountain is 7 miles from this parking area.

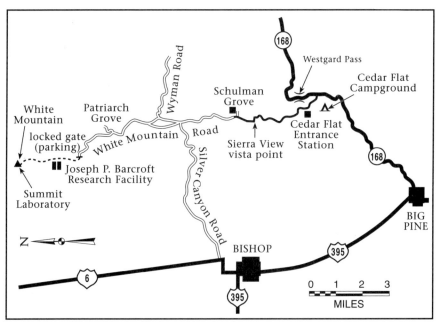

Westgard Pass Approach from the East

Whether you are driving south or west on Highway 266, take the Highway 168 turnoff. Continue west on Highway 168 toward Westgard Pass. After crossing Westgard Pass, it's 0.8 mile to the White Mountain Road. Turn right onto White Mountain Road, and follow the mileage log for Westgard Pass Approach from the West (see above), from mileage point 12.6 to the parking area.

Silver Canyon Approach

This route bypasses Highway 168, requires a four-wheel-drive vehicle with good clearance, and connects with White Mountain Road on top of the range. This is a spectacular drive to the top of the White Mountain Range and well worth it if you have a dependable four-wheel-drive vehicle. This approach begins north of Bishop.

Mileage Log

0.0   North of Bishop on Highway 395, turn right onto Highway 6.

3.6   Turn right onto Silver Canyon Road. Once the road enters the canyon it becomes rough and steep. The road switchbacks across the canyon and crosses Silver Creek many times. High vehicle clearance is needed on this road.

13.4   At the top of the White Mountain Range, at the junction with White Mountain Road, turn left and follow the Westgard Pass Approach, above.

23.5   Parking area for the start of the climb to White Mountain.

Wyman Road Approach

When heading south on Highway 266, approximately 7 miles from the Mono-Inyo county line, turn right onto a dirt road. This dirt road may or may not be marked. Immediately after turning onto the dirt road, there is a "LIMITED USE AREA" sign on the left. This is Wyman Road. The road is dirt all the way, does not require four-wheel-drive, and connects with White Mountain Road on top of the range. Follow the remainder of White Mountain Road as described in the Westgard Pass Approach from the west. Wyman Canyon is very scenic, with a creek flowing year-round. Wyman Road has many branches and side roads on it; always take the most well-worn or obvious path. All of the side roads are of much poorer quality and show less use than the main road.

Montgomery Pass Approach

The Montgomery Pass approach is used for a north approach for the traverse of the White Mountains. We do not have much information on this route or this approach at this time; suffice it to say that this is a long and very committing route in winter. Those seeking to undertake this route are cautioned that they need to explore and plan their itinerary in detail, complete with routes of escape from the ridge, and the descent toward Highway 168.

On Highway 6 out of Big Pine near Montgomery Pass, look for an area where a car can be left that is not near or on private land and that will be relatively safe for a week. Do not leave valuables in the car. Contact the highway authority prior to your trip to confirm that it is ok to leave your car in the location you have chosen. Hike or ski cross-country toward the northern escarpment of the White Mountain Range.

Route 1, South Face, Class 1

Use any of the approaches.

This is the standard and easiest route to the summit. It is a 7-mile hike from the end of White Mountain Road to the summit. The trail is the service road that goes to the Barcroft Research Facility and up to the Summit Laboratory on top of the peak. Because this road is wide and very obvious, many people have done hikes at night under a full moon. These can be cold hikes, but very enjoyable. We did it during an eclipse of the moon and it was spectacular.

Descend via the same route.

Route 2, West Ridge, Class 2

This route can be considered a classic "big" route. The climb starts in Owens Valley and climbs 9,000 feet in elevation over a distance of 10 to 12 miles. The best time to do this route is in early winter when the valley has begun to cool off from its hot summer months, and deep snow has not accumulated on the upper slopes. Another good time is in late winter or early spring, when many of the large snowdrifts have retreated and the skies are clear and cool.

The lower portion of the west ridge, which originates in Owens Valley, is split into two branches by Jeffery Mine Canyon. Either the southern or northern branch may be used as a starting point. The southern branch has a nice place to camp at the base of a steep talus slope. This talus slope is probably the toughest part of the route. The south and north branches converge at about 11,600 feet, and from this point onward the route becomes more broken and variegated. Small

The final portion of the west ridge of White Mountain; on top is the summit research laboratory (Photo by Steve Porcella)

Jay Jenson skiing off of White Mountain (Photo © Galen Rowell/Mountain Light)

gendarmes on the ridge can be easily hiked around and avoided. The final 300 feet is a little steep with some scrambling involved.

Descend via the same route.

Route 3, Winter Traverse of White Mountain Crest, rating unknown

Use the Montgomery Pass approach.

This route was first done by Galen Rowell and Jay Jenson in 1972.

This is a classic high-altitude traverse that takes two or three days to complete, offering spectacular views of the Owens Valley and the Sierra Nevada beyond and, of course, offering great skiing. The first ascensionists started at Montgomery Pass and went south to Westgard Pass. This route is very committing and we do not have much information on it at this time. Be sure not to leave anything valuable in your car and be prepared for violent winter storms that could last several days, extreme temperatures, and deep or blowing snow conditions.

Westgard Pass is usually closed for the winter, so be sure to plan ahead for the descent from the pass.

References

Bettinger, Dr. Robert. Interviewed by authors. University of California Davis, 1990.

Bowen, Thomas. "White Mountain." *Summit Magazine,* May 1975.

Jepson, Willis Linn. "The White Mountains of California." *Sierra Club Bulletin* 9 (1913).

Sierra Club Bulletin. "Mountaineering Notes" *Sierra Club Bulletin* 20 (1932–1935).

White Mountain Research Station. *Twenty-Five Years of High-Altitude Research.* University of California, 1973.

———. *Annual Report, 1989.* Clarence A. Hall, Jr., director. University of California.

Chapter 15
Mount Shasta

We enjoyed the grand uncertain form of Shasta
with its heaven-piercing crest of white, and wide placid sweep of base;
full of lines as deeply reposeful as a Greek temple.

Clarence King, *Mountaineering in the Sierra Nevada,* 1872

When one sees Shasta for the first time, whether from the northeast on Highway 93 or from the south on Interstate 5, the first impression is always one of awe. Mount Shasta, elevation 14,162 feet, is incredibly massive in bulk as well as height. It dominates northern California as the single most prominent landmark for hundreds of miles. Mount Shasta is frequently used as a readily observable landmark for commercial jets flying overhead and it has been seen from as far away as Mount Rose near Lake Tahoe. It is no wonder that a mountain as big and commanding as Mount Shasta has intrigued humans both spiritually and scientifically for hundreds of years.

Mount Shasta is a dormant volcano that belongs to the Cascade Range of volcanoes. This chain of mountains includes such notable volcanoes as Mount Rainier, Mount St. Helens, Mount Hood, Mount Adams, Mount Baker, and Mount Lassen. Geologists have calculated Shasta's most recent eruption as having occurred somewhere around 1786. However, investigations of local Indian oral history targets the most recent eruption as having occurred in the early 1850s. According to a 1926 article in the *Sierra Club Bulletin* by Ansel F. Hall,

"An authentically recorded legend told by the Indian tribes living near the base represents the mountain as a great wigwam, the home of the Great Spirit, whose lodge-fire was seen to smoke by day and to burn by night long before the coming of the white man."

Mount Shasta and the Hotlum Glacier (Photo by Steve Porcella)

Whatever the date of the last eruption, one thing is for sure: Mount Shasta is a dormant volcano and, like the other volcanoes in the Cascade chain, is sure to erupt in the future. The strength and ferocity of the next eruption is anybody's guess. Due to the recent activity of its volcanic cousin Mount St. Helens, there is now a pamphlet, distributed by the U.S. Geological Survey, that describes what to do in the event of an eruption of Mount Shasta, and where that eruption might occur on the mountain.

The Indian tribes that were present in the area surrounding Mount Shasta when the white man appeared were the Modoc, the Wintun, and the Shas-ti'ca. These tribes, whether camped in the vicinity or many miles away, used the fertile slopes of Mount Shasta to hunt and gather food. The Shas-ti'ca referred to the mountain as Wai-i'ka or Wyeka, which means "Great White" or "Great Purity." Many of the Shas-ti'ca passed on stories and legends that dealt with different aspects of the mountain. Subjects ranging from the origin of Shasta's glaciers to the origin of the small rounded hills that surround Shasta are represented in many of these Indian legends. These legends have been faithfully recorded in Rosemary Holsinger's 1982 book *Shasta Indian Tales.*

The first person from the outside world to mention Mount Shasta was Fray Narisco Duran. On May 20, 1817, during an expedition up the Sacramento River, he wrote in his diary:

"At about ten leagues to the northwest of this place, we saw the very high hill called by soldiers that went near its slope Jesus Maria. It is entirely covered with snow."

The first recorded mention of a name similar to the modern-day Shasta comes from a fur trader named Peter Ogden. On his way south from Fort Vancouver, Ogden noted in his journal on February 14, 1827,

"I have named this river Sastise River. There is a mountain equal in height to Mount Hood or Vancouver, I have named it Mount Sastise. I have given these names from the tribes of Indians."

Other explorers came through the region and also wrote down notes about the peak, describing it by the name used by the locals at that time. On October 3, 1841, Lieutenant Emmons, while on an expedition to explore the United States, mentioned a "Mount Shaste." John C. Fremont, during an exploration expedition in 1848 into northern California, in which Fremont actually made an attempt upon the summit of Shasta, designated the peak as "Shastl." Lieutenant Robert S. Williamson, for whom Mount Williamson is named, while surveying a route from the Columbia River to the Sacramento Valley, referred to the mountain as "Shasta Butte." This name of Shasta Butte was used most commonly during much of the early exploration of the mountain.

With regards to the first ascent of Mount Shasta, it must be noted that many of the Indians in the surrounding area felt that the mountain was a sacred place where God resided and therefore it was disrespectful, even foolish, to climb to the summit. In 1878, when B. A. Colonna hired Indian porters to carry his surveying instruments to the summit, he was surprised by the lack of interest displayed by the Indians in ascending the final 200 feet to the summit—"not one availing himself of the opportunity," he observed in an article in an 1880 edition of *The Californian.*

THE FIRST RECORDED ASCENT of Shasta was made by Captain E. D. Pearce, superintendent of the Yreka Water Company's sawmills, and eight other men on August 14, 1854. The party camped on the southwest side of the mountain near the present location of the Sierra Club Hut at Horse Camp. They climbed into what is now known as Avalanche Gulch and, instead of going to the right around the Red Banks, went left or north around them. They climbed Misery Hill, crossed the snowfield, climbed up to the summit, and, as Captain Pearce described in an 1854 article in the *San Francisco Daily Herald,* "[We] . . . unfurled the Stars and Stripes, and raised the standard to its long rest-place, amid the deafening cheers of the little multitude."

They discovered the hot sulfur (brimstone) springs and continued their descent in the form of an out-of-control group glissade. Pearce's article continued:

"After descending for some 2 miles, we came to a ravine of snow, and being somewhat fatigued and in a hurry to get clear of the smell of brimstone, we set sail in the following manner: The grade being on an angle of some 75 degrees, and the top of the snow soft, we set ourselves down on our unmentionables, feet foremost, to regulate our speed, and our walking sticks for rudders. At the word, off we sped . . . and the like I never saw before in the shape of coasting. Some unshipped their rudders before reaching the quarter (there was no such thing as stopping), some broached to and went stern foremost, making wry faces, while others, too eager to be the first down, got up too much steam, and went end over end; while others found themselves athwartship, and making 160 revolutions per minute. In short, it was a spirited race, as far as I can see, and that was not far, for in a thrice we found ourselves in a snug little pile at the foot of the snow, gasping for breath. After examining a little, we found that some were minus hats, some boots, some pants, and others had their shins bruised and other little et ceteras too numerous to mention."

On October 11, 1855, Israel S. Diehl made the first solo ascent of the peak. In his narrative included in a 1932–1935 *Sierra Club Bulletin* article by Charles L. Stewart, Diehl was the first person to use the word "glaciers" to describe some of the large snow masses on Shasta. The importance of this observation is interesting to note because in 1870, J. D. Whitney, of the California Geological Survey, proclaimed that there were no true glaciers on Mount Shasta. In fact, Whitney went so far as to say that nothing except scars from glaciers long gone were on the mountain. It was also at this time that John Muir (who Whitney called "that shepherd") was proposing his argument that glaciers were solely responsible for creating Yosemite Valley. In a 1926 *Sierra Club Bulletin* article by Ansel F. Hall, Whitney flatly asserted no glaciers had "ever occupied the valley or any portion of it"; and he dismissed all claims for glacial erosion as based on "ignorance of the whole subject."

On March 26, 1856, a party of three men—A. C. Isaacs, D. E. English, and Anton Roman—made the first ascent of Mount Shasta in full winter conditions. They climbed the route pioneered by Pearce and, although technically easy, this route can be quite formidable in winter conditions. After making their way up through the Red Cliffs to the base of Misery Hill, the three men were hit by fierce winds and low temperatures. A portion of their story is recounted here from the 1932–1935 *Sierra Club Bulletin* article by Charles L. Stewart, to provide an example of the ferocity of winter storms that can occur on Mount Shasta.

" . . . but, O how piercingly cold and swift comes the howling blast over this southern and eastern ridge! See the summit just above us! The drift snow is being whirled about in eddying clouds in the wildest excitement! Let us on!

"The cold becomes intense. We make way now as fast as our much exhausted limbs will let us, up the rocky side of the first summit. On the center of this side we find Roman furiously beating his sides to keep some warmth in his arms. We reach the summit (south) and come right into the teeth of an opponent whose assaults in their inconceivable might and power are irresistible! The wind, which, occasionally on the way up had, when it could get at us through the crevices of the ridge, given us sharp foretastes of what we might expect on the summit, now struck upon us as the concentrated blast of a thousand tempests! Of its incomprehensible velocity, its intense cold, its roaring and thunderous sound, as with lightning speed it tore through the clefts and crags on the edge of the cliff; of the awful, and stinging, and blinding force with which it struck our faces and eyes; of our own inability to take more than a momentary glance in the direction from which it blew, of the extreme difficulty we had to keep our feet in it (it blew us about and made us totter and reel as drunken men, and occasionally threw us down with relentless fury); of all these things 'twere vain to tell!' Aeolus reigned supreme—all the furies of his cave here let loose at once upon us. 'Look at the thermometer,' cries Roman. Twelve degrees below zero! Look at ourselves! Faces purple, and looking as if we had just been suffocated!—eyes almost closed up!—lips scarcely movable!—limbs stiffening with the cold! Shall we go on?"

They did go on and eventually struggled to the summit. However, on the descent, Roman, suffering from severe frostbite, was forced to throw away his boots and wrap his feet in pieces of blanket. In fact, as late as 1875 Roman was heard to remark that he had never completely recovered from that terrible day on Mount Shasta.

In celebration of Admission Day, on September 9, 1856, Captain E. D. Pearce led a group of five women and seven men to the trail-less summit of Mount Shasta. The first woman to scale a North American fourteener was the plucky and energetic Mrs. Olive Paddock Eddy. The media and local townspeople immediately took Mrs. Eddy to heart, spurring a host of stories and legends about her athletic achievements as a mountaineer.

In 1867, Clarence King was named U.S. Geologist in charge of the Geological Exploration of the Fortieth Parallel under Brigadier General A. A. Humphreys, the U.S. Chief of Engineers. In 1870 King and his party climbed to the top of the smaller crater, now known as Shastina, and upon reaching the notch between Shastina and the main mountain, gazed down into the gorge separating Shastina and Shasta.

King, as he recorded in *Mountaineering in the Sierra Nevada* in 1872, was awestruck, for before him lay a twisting river of ice, a ". . . glacier, riven with sharp, deep crevasses yawning 50 or 60 feet wide, the blue hollows of their shadowed depth contrasting with the brilliant surfaces of ice." King named it Whitney Glacier in honor of his former boss. King, excited about his initial discovery of apparently active glaciers on Shasta, set out to circumnavigate the mountain. He hiked and studied many of the other glaciers on Shasta's flanks, but what he marveled at most was the thought that Dana, Fremont, Brewer, and Whitney all had failed to see these rivers of ice on their visits to the peak. In fact, Whitney, Dana, and Agassiz all had claimed in their writings that no true glaciers existed in the Lower 48 states. The answer was obvious. The south face was the easiest way to climb the mountain, but it was also the only place where no glaciers existed.

IN THE FALL OF 1884, John Muir journeyed from Redding to Mount Shasta by walking, in order to experience the people and the countryside more intimately. John Muir was no ill-educated "shepherd"; after all, he had spent five semesters at the University of Wisconsin, longer than King was an under-graduate at Yale, and he had studied under Dr. Ezra Carr, a disciple of the renowned glaciologist Agassiz's teachings. Muir had written, in 1894 in *The Mountains of California,* quite emphatically, much to King's disagreement, that there were active glaciers in the Sierra Nevada and that Yosemite Valley was carved by glaciers. During his visit to Shasta, Muir described three different and active glaciers on the mountain. Of the largest he observed, it ". . . is the lowest point reached by any glacier within the bounds of California."

On April 30, 1875, Muir climbed Shasta with his companion Jerome Fay, in order to collect barometric observations for the U.S. Coast Survey. While linger-ing on the summit, both men were caught in a blizzard for 13 horrible hours. A condensed portion of Muir's story contained in *Mountaineering Essays* is included here to illustrate the ferocity of sudden storms that can occur in late April on Mount Shasta.

"Jerome peered at short intervals over the ridge, contemplating the rising clouds with anxious gestures in the rough wind. . . . I told Jerome that we two mountaineers should be able to make our way down through any storm likely to fall.

"Presently thin, fibrous films of cloud began to blow directly over the sum-mit from the north to south, drawn out in long fairy webs like carded wool, forming and dissolving as if by magic. The sky speedily darkened, and just as I had com-pleted my last observation and boxed my instruments ready for the descent, the storm began in serious earnest.

"After we had forced our way down the ridge and past the group of hissing fumaroles, the storm became inconceivably violent. The thermometer fell 22 degrees in a few minutes, and soon dropped to zero. The hail gave place to snow, and darkness came on like night. The wind, rising to the highest pitch of violence, boomed and surged amid the desolate crags; lightning-flashes in quick succession cut the gloomy darkness; and the thunders, the most tremendously loud and appalling I ever heard, made an almost continuous roar, stroke following stroke in quick, passionate succession, as though the mountain were being rent to its foundations and the fires of the old volcano were breaking forth again.

"After passing the 'Hot Springs' I halted in the lee of a lava-block to let Jerome, who had fallen a little behind, come up. Here he opened a council in which . . . he maintained, in opposition to my views, that it was impossible to proceed. He firmly refused to make the venture to find the camp, while I, aware of the dangers that would necessarily attend our efforts, and conscious of being the cause of his present peril, decided not to leave him.

"Our discussions ended, Jerome made a dash from the shelter of the lava-block and began forcing his way back against the wind to the 'Hot Springs' wavering and struggling to resist being carried away, as if he were fording a rapid stream. After waiting and watching in vain for some flaw in the storm that might be urged as a new argument in favor of attempting the descent, I was compelled to follow. 'Here,' said Jerome, as we shivered in the midst of the hissing, sputtering fumaroles, 'we shall be safe from frost.' 'Yes,' said I, 'we can lie in this mud and steam and sludge, warm at least on one side; but how can we protect our lungs from the acid gases, and how, after our clothing is saturated, shall we be able to reach camp without freezing, even after the storm is over? We shall have to wait for sunshine, and when will it come?'

"During the storm we lay on our backs so as to present as little surface as possible to the wind, and to let the drift pass over us. The mealy snow sifted into the folds of our clothing and in many places reached the skin. We were glad at first to see the snow packing about us, hoping it would deaden the force of the wind, but it soon froze into a stiff, crusty heap as the temperature fell, rather augmenting our misery.

"When the heat became unendurable, on some spot where steam was escaping through the sludge, we tried to stop it with snow and mud, or shifted a little at a time by shoving with our heels; for to stand in blank exposure to the fearful wind in our frozen-and-broiled condition seemed certain death.

"The weary hours wore away like dim half-forgotten years, so long and eventful they seemed, though we did nothing but suffer. Still the pain was not always that bitter, intense kind that precludes through and takes away all capacity for enjoyment. A sort of dreamy stupor came on at times when we fancied we saw dry, resinous logs suitable for campfires, just as after going for days without food men fancy they see bread.

"Frozen, blistered, famished, benumbed, our bodies seemed lost to us at times—all dead but the eyes. For the duller and fainter we became the clearer was our vision, though only in momentary glimpses.

"'Are you suffering much?' Jerome would inquire with pitiful faintness. 'Yes,' I would say, striving to keep my voice brave, 'frozen and burned; but never mind, Jerome, the night will wear away at last, and tomorrow we go a-Maying, and what camp fires we will make, and what sun baths we will take!'"

The next day dawned bright and clear. The two mountaineers struggled to their feet frozen, in stiff clothing, and slowly made their way down the mountain, sliding, falling, struggling through the deep, freshly fallen snow.

IN OCTOBER 1884, the same year as Muir's incredible bivouac, Captain A. F. Rodgers, along with five sailors from the U.S. Coastal Survey, hauled 3,500 pounds of metal to the summit. There, Rodgers placed a 14-foot-high cylindrical steel monument that was topped by a nickel conoid reflector. The purpose of this tower was to triangulate and eventually map the Northern California area. Although the reflector quickly became tarnished, it stood for over twenty years, until a lightning bolt toppled it over the cliffs to the east. In its heyday, the tower looked like, according to Rodgers' 1870 report, ". . . a lighthouse with brilliant lamps burning."

In 1903 and 1905 Alexander G. McAdie, by measuring the boiling point of water with a thermometer, calculated the height of Shasta as 14,200 feet. A few years later, the U.S. Coast and Geodetic Survey determined the altitude to be its currently recognized height of 14,162 feet.

In 1922 a lawyer from San Francisco, M. Hall McAllister, under the guidance of the Sierra Club, constructed the stone cabin at Horse Creek. The cabin is currently open year-round and is available to anyone who cares to use it. A natural spring produces pure clean water next to the cabin.

Because of the popularity of Horse Camp and the routes on the southwest face of the mountain, a number of climbing time records have been set from there to the summit. In 1883 Harry Babcock set a record of 3 hours and 40 minutes. Forty years later the Sierran giant Norman Clyde made the ascent in 3 hours and 17 minutes. He then rested a day and did it in 2 hours and 43 minutes.

On August 12, 1923, Barney McCoy made a phenomenally fast ascent that he reported as 2 hours and 17 minutes. However, McCoy's reputation as a climber and honest individual were blasted. Even the Sierra Club jumped into the fray, calling together a committee to "scientifically" analyze the physiological possibilities of a human being making an ascent of such speed. The committee even went so far as to consult Norman Clyde, who apparently said in the presence of McCoy, "Do not believe for a minute that he ever made the climb in the time mentioned. The snow is off and his record is next to impossible." As late as 1954, McCoy maintained that his time was 2 hours and 17 minutes. In 1925, during a Sierra Club–sponsored race to the summit, complete with a cash prize, David Lawyer, eighteen years of age, did the climb in 2 hours and 24 minutes. On July 5, 1985, Robert Webb, the current caretaker of Horse Camp, made the climb in 1 hour and 39 minutes.

Mount Shasta, because of its size, sudden violent storms, and elevation, has long been used as a training ground for future ascents of peaks in North America, the Himalayas, and the Andes. Probably the most well known warm-up on Shasta was by Allen Steck, Jim Wilson, and others who trained for their assault on the incredibly formidable Hummingbird Ridge on Canada's Mount Logan. An indication of the problems encountered on Shasta is exemplified when the climbers returned from their epic 30-day assault on Mount Logan. According to Chris Jones in *Climbing in North America,* Jim Wilson's son was overheard asking, "Dad, was it as bad as Shasta?"

Climbing Routes on Mount Shasta

Because of the general technical ease of many of the routes on Mount Shasta and the fact that climbers have been climbing all over the mountain for many years, first ascent information is often scattered and inconsistent. We have listed what we can but, in general, much of the information is lacking.

There are several ways to reach trailheads on the north side of Mount Shasta. These are broken down into three approaches: Graham/Whitney Creek, Bolam Creek, and North Gate. With all the access points on the north side, it is very important to be very conscious of your surroundings after you leave your car. When you have completed your route and are returning, you will realize just how important this is. The timberline area on the north side of the peak is composed of twisting and rolling lava flows, scattered pine tree stands, and moraines. It can be quite a hike getting to your route and quite a puzzle finding your car on the way back! Always carry a shovel when driving to north-side routes, because many of the roads may be composed of soft, deep sand. Mileage logs have been included for each of the approaches. Routes 6–10 are reached from these approaches.

Routes closest to the Sierra Club Hut at Horse Camp are presented as a group first. The remainder of the routes are presented in a clockwise fashion.

South and Southwest Approaches

This is the most popular side of the mountain for climbers attempting the summit of Mount Shasta. Most of the routes begin at the end of the Everitt Memorial Highway. The three main starting points are Sand Flat, Bunny Flat, and Ski Bowl Trailheads. The following mileage log describes how to get to these areas on the Everitt Memorial Highway from the town of Shasta.

Mileage Log

0	Corner of Lake Street and Mount Shasta Boulevard in Mount Shasta. Go northeast on Lake Street.
0.6	Turn left on Everitt Memorial Highway.
4.9	Campground on the left.
9.4	Everitt Vista Point on the right.
10.5	First Sand Flat Trailhead turnoff. Sign reads, "SAND FLAT ½ MILE, HORSE CAMP TRAIL 1½ MILES, HORSE CAMP 3 MILES."
11.1	Second Sand Flat Trailhead turnoff. Sign reads, "SAND FLAT ½ MILE, HORSE CAMP TRAIL 1 MILE."
11.9	Bunny Flat Trailhead parking area. Outhouse is present.
13.8	Panther Meadows Campground.
14.5	Mount Shasta Ski Bowl Trailhead parking area.

The Everitt Memorial Highway curves up and around the south flank of Shasta, switchbacking numerous times before reaching the trailheads. There are two access points from which to start the five routes (routes 1–5) on the south and southwest sides of the peak. One is Bunny Flat and the other is Sand Flat. If Sand Flat is your destination, we suggest taking the second Sand Flat turnoff while driving up the highway. Bunny Flat is on the left-hand side of the road and higher up the road from the second Sand Flat turnoff. At the end of the Everitt Memorial Highway is a parking lot and the Ski Bowl Trailhead. As of the writing of this guidebook, there was no overnight parking at this parking lot.

North Approach via Graham/Whitney Creek

This approach is rarely used, compared to the other north-face approaches. The condition of this road varies widely from year to year. This road requires a four-wheel-drive vehicle. Unless you are out for a little more adventure than normal, we recommend the Bolam Creek approach or the North Gate approach. Begin this approach in the town of Weed.

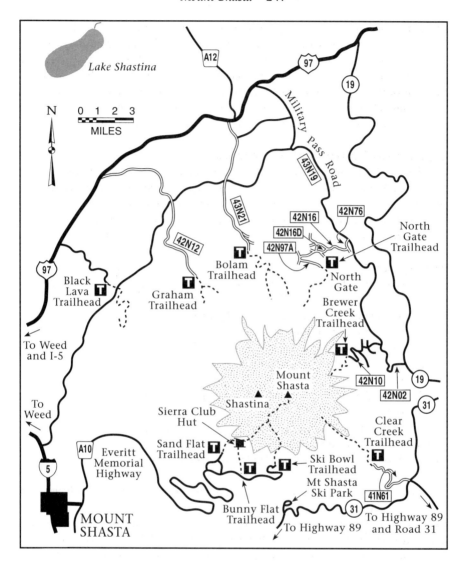

Mileage Log

0	At the stoplight in Weed, corner of Interstate 5 business loop and Highway 97, drive northeast on Highway 97.
8.5	There is a large, dark, lava-flow hill on the right side of Highway 97 at the turnoff to Graham/Whitney Creek Road, number 42N12. Turn right onto the dirt road. This road goes directly eastward for 1.3 miles, next to the lava flow, following its eastern side.
10.4	Intersection. Continue straight.
11.9	Road ends at Graham Trailhead.

A trail leads from the end of the road directly toward the Whitney Glacier. This trail is often unmarked and hard to follow. This approach is for routes 6–7.

North Approach via Bolam Creek

Bolam Creek is the access of choice for attempting climbs on many of the north and northwest routes on Shasta. A four-wheel-drive vehicle is mandatory for this road. The road varies in conditions from year to year. Begin this approach in the town of Weed.

Mileage Log

0	At the stoplight in Weed, corner of Interstate 5 business loop and Highway 97, drive northeast on Highway 97.
11.8	Turn right onto a dirt road that heads south. If you come to the county road A-12 on the left, you have gone approximately 0.3 mile too far.
12.2	Fork in the road. The left branch (with a gate) is marked 43N16 and the right branch is marked 43N21. Veer right and take 43N21.
12.7	At the fork in the road, take the right branch, 43N21, continuing southwest.
13.5	At the railroad tracks and intersection with a dirt road that runs east-west, continue straight to the trailhead.
15.5	About 4.0 miles from Highway 97, the road ends at the Bolam Trailhead.

About 4 miles from Highway 97, the road ends at the Bolam Trailhead. Directly south of the trailhead, 1½ miles away, is the Whitney Creek Falls. When leaving your car for the hike to Mount Shasta, make an extra effort to keep track of your surroundings. Due to the nature of the terrain, this area can become confusing, and a small landmark such as a tree or boulder begins to look like every other tree or boulder you have passed. In other words, it is easy to become disoriented on the return hike. Many a climber has spent hours walking in circles, searching for the hidden car. This approach is recommended for routes 6–10.

North Approach via North Gate

This access is the most popular for getting near the north and northeast face routes and it does not, at this time, require a four-wheel-drive vehicle. Begin this approach in Weed.

Mileage Log

0	At the stoplight in Weed, on the corner of Interstate 5 business loop and Highway 97, drive northeast on Highway 97.
14.6	Turn right onto Military Pass Road. Technically this road is listed as 43N19, but it does contain a number of road signs marked Road 19.
16.4	Go under a railroad trestle. From here the road is generally in good condition.
23.6	Turn right onto a dirt road that is marked with a sign that says, "NORTH GATE." This road is 42N76.

23.8   At the dirt road on the right, continue straight.

24.4   Turn right, heading west. This is road 42N16.

25.4   Continue straight through the intersection.

26   Road forks. Take the left branch, which is 42N16D.

26.3   Three-road intersection. Turn right, continuing southwest up a slope.

27.1   The road turns left.

27.1   The road turns left again. These two successive left turns complete a 180-degree turn so that the road is now heading east-southeast next to a large clear-cut.

27.7   The road gets progressively rough and eventually ends at the North Gate Trailhead.

The trailhead is located at the base of the north-northeast side of the North Gate hill, and the trail leads south. Make sure you keep track of your surroundings when leaving your car for Shasta. The nature of the terrain and area is such that it is easy to become disoriented on the return. North Gate hill is a good landmark to keep track of. This approach is recommended for routes 7–10.

Northeast Approach via Brewer Creek

Use this approach for routes 11–13. Begin this aproach from the town of McCloud.

Mileage Log _____

0   At the corner of Highway 89 and the turnoff for the town of McCloud continue south on Highway 89.

3.0   Turn left onto Pilgrim Creek Road.

8.2   Turn left onto Widow Springs Road. This road is also marked 41N15.

13.2   Intersection with McKenzie Road or Road 31. Turn right onto Road 31 and drive northeast and avoid the Old Brewer Creek Road turnoff.

19.2   Turn left onto Road 19 and follow it north-northeast.

19.3   Turn left onto Road 42N02 and drive west.

22.1   Turn left onto 42N10, heading west-southwest. This should be the third left from the 42N02/Road 19 junction.

22.2   Continue straight through the intersection.

23.0   Turn left at the T-intersection.

23.1   Turn right at the next T-intersection. The road goes northeast for a while and then turns south for 1 mile. It then goes through a hairpin turn, which is the second switchback.

25.1   The road now heads northwest for 0.5 mile, when it ends at the Brewer Creek Trailhead.

Follow the old access road until it turns to trail. This approach is recommended for routes 11–13.

East and Southeast Approach via Clear Creek

Use this approach for routes 14–16. Begin at the town of McCloud.

Mileage Log

0   At the corner of Highway 89 and the turnoff for the town of McCloud continue south on Highway 89.

3.0   Turn left onto Pilgrim Creek Road.

8.2   Turn left onto Widow Springs Road. This road is also marked 41N15.

13.2   Intersection with McKenzie Road or Road 31. Continue straight on through the intersection. There are minor branches off the main dirt road, but you should avoid these.

14.5   At a Y-intersection, take the left branch. You should now be heading west.

16.0   Reach the parking area. It's possible to continue on 0.5 mile to Clear Creek Trailhead, depending on road conditions and your vehicle's ability.

This approach is recommended for routes 14–16.

Route 1, Avalanche Gulch, Class 3

Use the South and Southwest Approaches.

This route was first climbed on August 14, 1854, by Captain E. D. Pearce and party. This was the first known route on the mountain and remains the most popular route for reaching the summit. From the Sierra Club Hut at Horse Camp, the one-day climb is roughly 4.1 miles but it involves an elevation gain of more than 6,000 feet.

Starting from Sand Flat Trailhead, one has a longer hike to get to the Sierra Club Hut. However, because of its proximity and ample cover, Sand Flat is a great place to camp the night before climbing the mountain. Bunny Flat avoids the hill out of Sand Flat and is shorter, but lacks ample campsites. Some of the purest water in California is found in a spring next to the Sierra Club Hut. A stone pathway leads northeast from the hut toward the mountain. This is the Olberman Causeway, built by and named after the first inhabitant of the Sierra Club Hut, J. M. (Mac) Olberman.

Follow the causeway as it eventually turns into trail. The trail curves to the left (northwest), ascending talus slopes to eventually gain a small plateau or shelf where Helen Lake resides. The lake is very small and may often be frozen or covered with snow. The rock bench around Helen Lake is a good area for spending the night en route to the peak. The area beyond Helen Lake involves a 2,000-foot snowfield. This is the most difficult part of the climb, and also the most dangerous.

Beyond Helen Lake, stay generally to the right (east) side of Avalanche Gulch. As its name entails, avalanches frequent this area from early to late summer. Most avalanches seem to originate from the Heart and the Red Banks, which lie to the northwest and north, respectively. It is always a good idea to keep your eyes on these two formations at all times. You can usually see or hear these avalanches long before they become a threat. Continue up the gulch and angle to the right (southeast) of the Red Banks. Reach the saddle between the Red Banks and The Thumb, a large gendarme on Sargents Ridge. The snowfield normally connects

The southwest face of Mount Shasta showing routes 1, 2, and 3; arrows indicate Misery Hill (left) and The Thumb (right) (Photo by Steve Porcella)

to the ridge that separates Avalanche Gulch from the Konwakton Glacier. Recently, during the late summer months, a bergschrund next to the ridge opens up due to the movement of the Konwakton Glacier and the large snowfield between the Red Banks and The Thumb. When almost level with the Red Banks, angle left (north) toward them and climb up the southeast portion of the Red Banks. This route basically ascends loose, red, pebbly rock to the left of the snowfield and to the right of the Red Bank couloirs. It can be somewhat steep here and some routefinding may be in order to find the easiest way. At the worst it is loose Class 3.

Continue along the top of the Red Banks to a prominent hill to the north. This hill is called Misery Hill and it is well named if you are feeling tired. The top of Misery Hill is the summit plateau. Directly north is a point of rock. This is the summit and it is usually climbed via a sandy slope that faces west. Just before the slope starts up to the summit, off to the left (northwest), are the fumeroles or sulfur hot springs. There are many variations to this standard and very popular route.

Descend via the same route.

Route 2, Sargents Ridge, Class 3

Use the South and Southwest Approaches.

From the end of Everitt Memorial Highway at Ski Bowl Trailhead, hike up and onto Sargents Ridge. The route follows the ridge while traversing left or right around obstructions. This route is long (one to two days) but offers spectacular views the whole way.

Descend via the same route.

Route 2a, Sargents Ridge Alternative Start, Class 3

This variation on route 2 takes one to two days. From the Sierra Club Hut, ascend a small, rounded, talus-covered ridge known as Green Butte Ridge, which rises to the east and joins up with Sargents Ridge two gendarmes south of The Thumb.

Route 3, Casaval Ridge, Class 4

Use the South and Southwest Approaches.

Casaval Ridge offers technical challenges, expansive vistas into Avalanche Gulch and Hidden Valley, and safety from the avalanche-prone Avalanche Gulch. The ridge has an incredible assortment of rock towers and traverses where climbers can basically pick the level of difficulty they want. Climbers can avoid some of the difficulties of the towers by traversing low to the left (north) or, less frequently, to the right (south).

From the Sierra Club Hut, begin hiking north up the talus slope that is the start of the Casaval Ridge. The ridge starts off fairly easy, but later on the difficult towers are encountered. There are a number of places to escape from the ridge. Some of these escape points lead into Avalanche Gulch, while others lead into Cascade Gulch to the north. We suggest avoiding the upper areas of Avalanche Gulch due to the potential of rock avalanches from the Heart or Red Bank areas. Casaval Ridge tops out to the left (north) of the Red Banks, directly west from Misery Hill. Continue up Misery Hill and onto the summit plateau.

Descend via route 1.

Route 4, West Face Gully, Class 2–3

Use the South and Southwest Approaches.

North of Casaval Ridge in the middle of the west face of Shasta is a long, narrow, curving gully that, near the top, goes between two prominent red-rock outcroppings.

The route starts high in the eastern end of Hidden Valley. The start of the route can be reached by traversing to the north across the lower southwest bulge of the Casaval Ridge. Hidden Valley holds snow longer than the other barren slopes to the north or south of it and therefore offers a pleasant snow alternative to dry, shifting talus.

Descend via the same route.

Route 5, Cascade Gulch, Class 2–3

Use the South and Southwest Approaches.

This route was first climbed by the well-known geologist and Sierra pioneer Clarence King around 1870. This route, which is much less traveled than the popular Avalanche Gulch Route (route 1), offers some incredible views of the Whitney

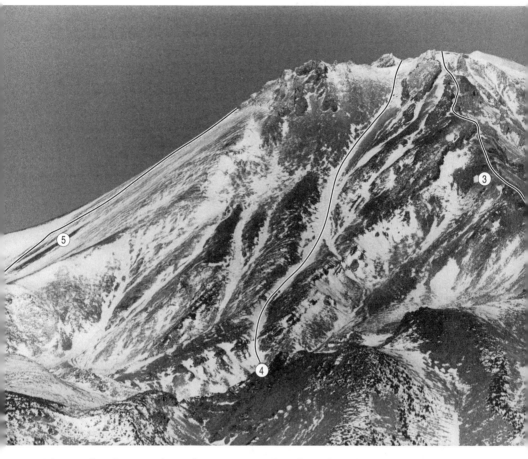

The west face of Mount Shasta showing routes 3 through 5 (Photo by Steve Porcella)

Glacier and is fairly easy. Because of its remoteness, Cascade Gulch allows an ample supply of tranquillity and wildness.

There are many variations for reaching Hidden Valley. From the Sierra Club Hut at Horse Camp, hike northwest toward the Casaval Ridge. Stay low on the southwest bulge of the ridge and traverse it heading north. The first gulch that you run into when rounding the base of Casaval Ridge is Giddy Giddy Gulch. Traverse up and across Giddy Giddy Gulch toward a tower almost directly north of you. Traverse below the west side of the tower. When you come around the tower you will see a large, gently sloping valley (Hidden Valley) in front of you and Shastina beyond. Continue across Hidden Valley, aiming directly for the low point that you will notice in the ridge between Shastina and Shasta. Once you reach this notch, Shastina is only a short scramble off to the west. Sisson Lake is slightly northeast, while the Whitney Glacier runs from southeast to northeast. Follow the ridge that runs along the south side of the Whitney Glacier and connects Shastina to Shasta. This last section is a long talus trudge and eventually tops out on the Red Banks next to Misery Hill.

Descend via the same route.

Route 6, Whitney Glacier, Class 4–5

There are several ways to reach the trailhead for the hike to the base of the Whitney Glacier. North Approach via Graham/Whitney Creek is good, but it does not get as close as North Approach via Bolam Creek. Bolam is probably the best access because it's direct and gets you closest to Whitney Glacier. Bolam requires a four-wheel-drive vehicle. North Approach via North Gate does not require four-wheel-drive but you must traverse quite a few gullies and ridges in order to reach the base of the Whitney Glacier.

This is the largest glacier in California and it offers the climber everything from long talus/moraine approaches to spectacular serac and icefall climbing. The Whitney Glacier is very active as glaciers go and because of its size it contains many of the exciting and yet dangerous aspects of a glacier. Crevasses are everywhere and are constantly appearing and disappearing. Therefore, it's a good idea to stay roped up with partners no matter where you are on the glacier. Rescues are expensive, time-consuming, and embarrassing. Seracs abound near the Shasta-Shastina saddle, so utmost care is required when negotiating this area. Because of its dynamic, technical nature and its 2-mile length, this is one of the best routes on the mountain.

Once you reach the base of the Whitney Glacier and begin climbing, stay generally in the middle of the glacier. The northeast side of Shastina is where it is the steepest. This is also an area of active rockfall. The Whitney-Bolam ridge also can be a source of rockfall, especially at the midpoint of the glacier. The most difficult and dangerous part of the route is the ice fall that lies between Shasta and Shastina. During late summer and early fall, this area becomes active with seracs toppling and shifting almost constantly. It is best to either go around to the left (east) or through the ice fall early in the morning. Be on the lookout for a large bergschrund above the ice fall which, in late summer months, spans the entire width of the glacier. If the bergschrund is present you can traverse left (east) or right (west) around it, although left is more direct to the summit. Once you have gained the saddle between Shasta and Shastina, continue eastward toward the summit.

Descend via the same route.

Route 7, Whitney-Bolam Ridge, Class 2–3

There are several ways to reach the trailhead for the hike to the Whitney-Bolam Ridge. North Approach via Graham/Whitney Creek is good, but it does not get as close as North Approach via Bolam Creek. Bolam is probably the best access because it's direct and gets you closest. Bolam requires a four-wheel-drive vehicle. North Approach via North Gate does not require four-wheel-drive but you must traverse quite a few gullies and ridges.

This ridge climb lies between the Whitney Glacier and the Bolam Glacier to the east. Although basically a long talus trudge hike during the middle to late summer, it can be a pleasant route when snow is present in the early to late spring. This route takes one to two days.

Descend via the same route.

The north-northwest face of Mount Shasta showing routes 5 through 9 and the Bolam (left) and Whitney Glaciers (right); arrow indicates east ridge to Shastina (Photo by Steve Porcella)

Route 8, Bolam Glacier, Class 3–4

The Bolam (which means "great one") Glacier can be reached from either North Approach via Bolam Creek or North Approach via North Gate.

The route goes up the center of the first glacier to the left (east) of the Whitney Glacier. There are two large bergschrunds that must be crossed, but except for these two difficulties, this route is fairly easy. Skirting the bergschrund on its eastern edge offers a more direct approach to the summit. Bolam Glacier is considered one of the easier and safer glacier routes on the mountain. In fact, many people use Bolam Glacier as their first big glacier route. Rockfall is minimal on this route and the angle is fairly gradual. Some steeper ground is encountered near the top of the route, but this section is not considered difficult.

Descend via route 7.

Route 9, Bolam Gully, Class 3

Bolam Gully can be reached from either North Approach via Bolam Creek or North Approach via North Gate.

Bolam Gully is not so much a gully as it is the next expansive and continuous snow slope directly to the east of the Bolam Glacier (route 8). On the left or eastern edge of the Bolam Glacier are two large rock outcroppings. Ascend to the left (east) of the lower one and continue up and to the east of the upper one. There are many variations to the final portion of the route. One may go either just to the right (west) of the Hotlum Headwall or stay on the rounded crest of the rocky ridge.

Descend via the same route.

Route 10, Hotlum-Bolam Ridge, Class 4

Access can be gained from North Approach via Bolam Creek or North Approach via North Gate, but the North Gate Trailhead is easiest.

This route was first climbed by Bob Rears and Jack Davidson in 1963. This is probably the safest, most popular and pleasant route on the north face of Shasta. This route takes one to two days.

From North Gate Trailhead, hike southwest around the North Gate hill. Stay to the right (west) of a large lava flow and angle toward two prominent rocky outcroppings that are almost 9,000 feet in elevation. Stay to the east of these towers and begin climbing up the ridge that divides Bolam from Hotlum Glacier. The route follows the ridge, passing a large, convoluted, rocky mass to the west. The route ascends a steep snow slab with the Hotlum Middle Icefall to the left (east). On the right are broken rock cliffs that lie above the Bolam Glacier. Once through this long snow slab, which may contain ice, a large step or shelf is gained. To the left (east) is the Upper Icefall and the Hotlum Upper Headwall. Both of these features are very impressive. Continue southwest from the step. After a while, turn southeast and climb through a large notch. The Hot Springs or fumaroles, as well as the summit, are only a short distance away.

Descend via the same route or route 7.

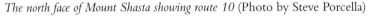

The north face of Mount Shasta showing route 10 (Photo by Steve Porcella)

Route 11, Hotlum Glacier, Class 4–5

Use the Northeast Approach via Brewer Creek.

This route was first climbed by Allen Steck and Bob Tripp in September 1963. The Hotlum (which means "steep rock") Glacier can be one of the most demanding and technically difficult routes on the mountain, taking two to three days. The difficulties are more a matter of what variations you choose rather than anything inherently difficult. In other words, the sections that make this route one of the most difficult can often be bypassed.

From the trailhead, climb up the lower northeastern slopes and head for the large eastern lobe of Hotlum Glacier. The first difficulty encountered is known as the Lower Headwall. This formation is a large rock band or cliff that contains the Lower Icefall on its north side. The Lower Headwall can be directly ascended, encountering loose rock and blue ice, or it can be bypassed by climbing to the right (north). Once past the Lower Icefall, angle southeast with the Middle Icefall on your right. The Middle Icefall contains a wide variety of good ice-climbing seracs and all the dangers inherent with these formations. Climbing farther up, bypass the Upper Icefall on your left (east) with the rocky Upper Headwall looming above it. From here, three variations may be climbed.

Descend via route 7, 9, or 10.

The northeast face of Mount Shasta showing routes 11 and 12 and the Wintun (left) and Hotlum (right) Glaciers as well as the Lower (L1), Middle (M1), and Upper (U1) Icefalls (Photo by Steve Porcella)

Route 11a, Left Chute, Class 4–5

Above the Upper Icefall described in route 11, angle left (east) toward a thin, narrow ice chute or gully. One or two bergschrunds may need to be crossed before entering the chute. This chute is steep, icy, and sustained. It gradually curves left to right, following the eastern edge of the Upper Headwall. Follow gentler snow slopes to the summit.

Route 11b, Hotlum Glacier Upper Headwall, Class 5.8

Stay on the Hotlum Glacier all the way, past the Upper Icefall described in route 11, to the highest point on the glacier. This is the apex of the glacier nestled in the large dihedral of the Upper Headwall. The climbing is four to six pitches, with the hardest climbing being Class 5.8. Tied-off pitons in loose rock are common methods used while climbing this headwall. At the top of the headwall, follow the rock and snow slopes to the summit.

Route 11c, Hotlum Headwall Ice Gully, Class 4–5

Above the Upper Icefall described in route 11, traverse right (west) toward the right (west) side of the Upper Headwall. On the right side of this wall is a prominent notch. The climbing in this notch can be mixed (rock and ice). However, most of the time it appears to be very good hard ice (late fall). This variation is steep and sustained, but very spectacular; it takes two to three days. Once past the difficulties of the gully, the route continues up and above the western portion of the Upper Headwall on less steep rock and snow slopes to the summit pinnacle beyond.

Route 12, Hotlum-Wintun Ridge/Northeast Ridge, Class 3–4

Use the Northeast Approach via Brewer Creek.

First ascent was by Norman Clyde, Oliver Kehrlein, W. Horsfall, C. S. French, C. Reid, T. Hunt, H. Sills, and Kirkwood Bourett on September 6, 1934. This is one of the easier routes on the northeast face, it takes one to two days, and it has three variations one may take.

Climb left (south) of the Lower Hotlum Icefall and the Lower Headwall cliffs. Continue up the large and expansive snowfield. Small crevasses may be present on this permanent snowfield, so be wary. Above the rocky outcrop that contains the Lower Headwall, the Middle Icefall of the Hotlum Glacier can be seen far off to the west. At this point, any of the following three variations can be climbed.

Descend via the same route or via route 7 or 9.

Route 12a, Hotlum-Wintun Ridge–Ridge Proper, Class 3–4

At that point where the rock outcropping containing the Lower Headwall ends and where the Middle Icefall of Hotlum Glacier can be accessed, the true ridge of the Hotlum-Wintun Ridge can be obtained. Traverse southeast onto the ridge and follow snow (late spring to early summer) or rock (late summer), staying on the crest of the ridge as much as possible. Staying on this ridge may involve sustained Class 4 climbing and, therefore, a rope may be advisable. The route takes one to two days.

Route 12b, Hotlum-Wintun Ridge Left Gully, Class 3–4

Between the Hotlum-Wintun Ridge–Ridge Proper Route (route 12a) and the Hotlum-Wintun Ridge Main or Right Gully Route (route 12c) lies a smaller, indiscriminate, shallow gully that leads up and to the southeast. This route stays just left (east) of a rock rib that borders the main gully (route 12c). Eventually this route joins up with route 12a and both routes continue up decreasingly steep rock and snow to the summit pinnacle. This route takes one to two days.

Route 12c, Hotlum-Wintun Ridge Main or Right Gully, Class 3–4

For this one- to two-day variation, climbers must stay in the main snowfield all the way. Near the top it gradually narrows as it passes left (east) of a rock rib. This rock rib is just to the left (east) of the Upper Headwall of the Hotlum Glacier. Past the narrow section, the route follows snow slopes and rock that lessen in steepness to the summit pinnacle.

The east face of Mount Shasta showing route 13 (Photo by Steve Porcella)

Route 13, Wintun Glacier, Class 4–5

Use the Northeast Approach via Brewer Creek.

The Wintun Glacier (named for a local Indian tribe) offers spectacular ice falls, crevasses, and some loose talus. It also catches the early morning light, providing a spectacular light show of early dawn colors. This early morning light also has the potential to loosen rock and ice, frozen the night before, creating potentially hazardous conditions. There are three variations for doing the Wintun Glacier and they all take one to two days.

Descend via same route as ascent or via routes 12, 12a, or 16.

Route 13a, Wintun Glacier, Right Side, Class 4–5

From the trailhead hike to the south to three relatively flat-topped small hills. Hike toward the highest of these three small hills. From here, traverse south toward Ash Creek, which lies in the drainage below. Attempt to maintain your elevation while angling toward the lower northernmost lobe of the Wintun Glacier. (The southeastern lobe may also be climbed but offers more difficulties because of the crevasses.) Ascend the northernmost lobe of the glacier until the upper reaches are obtained. Stay to the right (north) of a small triangular buttress of rock. Follow the main course of the snow slope as it enters some smaller rock bands. Eventually the slope backs off and the summit is a short distance away.

Route 13b, Wintun Glacier, Center, Class 4–5

Follow the directions for route 13a until the small triangular buttress is reached. Stay to the left (south) of this buttress and continue up the broad expanse of the snow slope until the summit plateau is reached. The true summit is a short distance away.

Route 13c, Wintun Glacier, Left Side, Class 4–5

The southeast tongue of the Wintun Glacier resembles the Whitney Glacier in some aspects; they are both long, serpentine, and comprised of numerous ice falls. Follow the description given for route 13a until the steep gorge of Ash Creek can be seen. As with routes 13a and 13b, traverse south but this time aim for the lower lobe of the southeastern portion of the glacier. Once this lower lobe is obtained, you can traverse farther south and follow the southern edge of the glacier to the summit plateau, or you can stay on the right (north) side of the lobe and follow that to the summit plateau. The right side of the glacier is more spectacular and indicative of true glacial alpine with some rockfall potential, while the left side (south) is more circuitous, involving more talus, but it is safer.

Route 14, Konwakiton Glacier, Class 4–5

Use the East and Southeast Approach via Clear Creek.

The Konwakiton (which means "muddy one") Glacier lies above the largest canyon on Mount Shasta. Mud Creek Canyon is without a doubt the largest feature on the mountain besides Shastina. There are two variations for climbing the Konwakiton Glacier and both avoid Mud Creek Canyon because of the inherent danger from rockfall. This route takes one to two days.

From the Clear Creek Route (route 15), traverse left under the first large rock outcropping on the left (south). You should come out above the Mud Creek Canyon and to the east of the Konwakiton Glacier. Enter onto the snowfields above Mud Creek Canyon and proceed upward. Rockfall is very dangerous on this portion of the route, especially when the early morning sun has had a chance to warm up the snow and rock above. A number of variations may be climbed at this point; snow gullies or loose rock ribs to either side may be climbed. Once on the Konwakiton Glacier, the angle decreases until the summit plateau is reached.

Descend via route 15 or 16.

Route 15, Clear Creek, Class 2–3

Use the East and Southeast Approach via Clear Creek.

This is an easy and very gradual climb, taking one day.

The route ascends primarily up the Clear Creek drainage. During late summer, this route is not recommended because most of the snow is gone, making the route a long talus trudge. Rockfall is very minimal and there are no crevasses. This is an excellent ski ascent and descent route during the winter or early spring.

Descend via the same route.

The south face of Mount Shasta showing routes 14 through 16 and Sargents Ridge (arrow), The Thumb (T), and the Konwakiton Glacier (K) (Photo by Steve Porcella)

Route 16, Wintun Ridge, Class 2–3

Use the East and Southeast Approach via Clear Creek.

This route takes one to two days.

Ascend the wide southeastern bulge of the ridge. There are many variations at this point and all are easy. Follow the rounded crest of the ridge, staying just to the left of a southern tongue of the Wintun Glacier. Eventually the summit plateau is reached and the true summit is a short distance away.

Descend via the same route.

References

Brooks, N. "Mount Shasta." *Marysville Appeal,* August 29, 1861.

Carver, Larry. "Mount Shasta—An Adventure Sample." *Summit,* May-June 1983.

Colonna, B. A. "Nine Days on the Summit of Shasta." *The Californian* 1, no. 3 (March 1880).

Cooke, Wm. Bridge. "Record Climbs of Mount Shasta." *Sierra Club Bulletin* 27 (1942).

Daily Evening Bulletin (San Francisco). September 23, 1856; October 2, 1856.

Duran, Fray Narisco. "Expedition on the Sacramento and San Joaquin Rivers in 1817." Diary edited by Charles E. Chapman. *Publications of the Academy of Pacific Coast History* vol. 2 (December 1911).

Fremont, John C. *Geographical Memoir upon Upper California. Map of California and Oregon.* Washington, D.C.: 1848.

Hall, Ansel F. "Mount Shasta." *Sierra Club Bulletin* 12 (1926).

Holsinger, Rosemary, compiler. *Shasta Indian Tales.* Illustrated by P. I. Piemme. Happy Camp, Calif.: Naturegraph Publishers, 1982.

Isaacs, A. C. "An Ascent of Mount Shasta: 1856." *California Daily Chronicle,* April 9, 1856.

Jepson, Willis Linn. "Early Botanical Ascents of Mount Shasta." *Sierra Club Bulletin* 27 (1942).

Johnson, Steve. "Mount Shasta, the Lonely Giant." *Summit,* September 1974.

Jones, Chris. *Climbing in North America.* 1976. Reprint, Seattle, Wash.: The Mountaineers Books, 1997.

King, Clarence. *Mountaineering in the Sierra Nevada.* 1872. Reprint, Lincoln, Neb.: University of Nebraska, Bison Books, 1970.

MacNeil, F. H. "Some Facts About Mount Shasta." *Mazama* 4 (December 1915).

Matthes, F. E. "Little Studies in the Yosemite Valley IV: El Capitan Moraine and Ancient Lake Yosemite." *Sierra Club Bulletin* 9 (1914).

Muir, John. "A Perilous Night on Mount Shasta's Summit." 1918. In *Mountaineering Essays.* Salt Lake City, Utah: Gibbs Smith Publisher, 1980.

———. *The Mountains of California.* 1894. Reprint, San Francisco: Sierra Club Books, 1988.

Off Belay. December 1980.

Ogden, Peter Skene. "The Peter Skene Ogden Journals." T. C. Elliot, ed. *Oregon Historical Society Quarterly* 11 (June 1910).

Pacific Railroad Reports 6 (1855.)

Pearce, E. D. "First Ascent of Shasta Butte—Interesting Narrative." *San Francisco Daily Herald,* August 28, 1854.

Powers, Stephen. "Tribes of California." *Contributions to North American Ethnology* vol. 3 (1877).

Rodgers, A. F. *Report to the Superintendent of the United States Coast Survey on the Question of a Signal or Monument for the Summit of Mount Shasta, California.* Washington, D.C.: MS, United States Coast and Geodetic Survey, 1870.

Selters, Andy, and Michael Zanger. *The Mount Shasta Book.* Berkeley, Calif.: Wilderness Press, 1989.

Sierra Club Bulletin. "Mountaineering Notes." *Sierra Club Bulletin* 20 (1932–1935).

Stewart, Charles L. "Early Ascents of Mount Shasta." *Sierra Club Bulletin* 20 (1932–1935).

Wilkins, Thurman. *Clarence King: A Biography.* Albuquerque, N.M.: University of New Mexico Press, 1988.

Yreka Union, September 16, 1856.

Index

About the Authors

STEPHEN F. PORCELLA started climbing at age nine and has nearly thirty years of experience on peaks throughout the West. His articles and photographs have been published in *The American Alpine Journal; Climbing; Rock and Ice;* and *Mountain* (Great Britain). In 1991 he and co-author Cameron Burns published a brief guide to California's fourteeners, which provided the impetus for the current volume.

He holds a doctorate in microbiology and has published numerous scholarly papers. He has taught at both the University of Montana and the University of Texas, and currently works at Rocky Mountain Laboratories (NIH) in Hamilton, Montana, where he lives with his wife, Sandy, and children, Vittoria and Angelo.

Colorado-based journalist, CAMERON "CAM" BURNS was born in Australia and spent the summers of his childhood roaming the mountains of Tasmania. In 1978 his family emigrated to the United States, where he learned technical climbing and earned a degree in architecture at the University of Colorado.

After working in the film industry in Hollywood for several years, he began writing fulltime. His articles, photographs, and fictional stories have been published in newspapers and magazines here and abroad. He served as American editor for *Mountain Magazine* (UK) and *Mountain Review* (UK) and is the author of *Colorado Ice Climber's Guide; The Maroon Bells: A Climbing Guide;* and *Kilimanjaro and Mount Kenya: A Climbing and Trekking Guide.* He is married to Ann Robertson and lives in Basalt, Colorado.

THE MOUNTAINEERS, founded in 1906, is a nonprofit outdoor activity and conservation club, whose mission is "to explore, study, preserve, and enjoy the natural beauty of the outdoors. . . . " Based in Seattle, Washington, the club is now the third-largest such organization in the United States, with 15,000 members and five branches throughout Washington State.

The Mountaineers sponsors both classes and year-round outdoor activities in the Pacific Northwest, which include hiking, mountain climbing, ski-touring, snowshoeing, bicycling, camping, kayaking and canoeing, nature study, sailing, and adventure travel. The club's conservation division supports environmental causes through educational activities, sponsoring legislation, and presenting informational programs. All club activities are led by skilled, experienced volunteers, who are dedicated to promoting safe and responsible enjoyment and preservation of the outdoors.

If you would like to participate in these organized outdoor activities or the club's programs, consider a membership in The Mountaineers. For information and an application, write or call The Mountaineers, Club Headquarters, 300 Third Avenue West, Seattle, Washington 98119; (206) 284-6310.

The Mountaineers Books, an active, nonprofit publishing program of the club, produces guidebooks, instructional texts, historical works, natural history guides, and works on environmental conservation. All books produced by The Mountaineers are aimed at fulfilling the club's mission.

Send or call for our catalog of more than 300 outdoor titles:

The Mountaineers Books
1001 SW Klickitat Way, Suite 201
Seattle, WA 98134
1-800-553-4453
e-mail: mbooks@mountaineers.org
website: www.mountaineers.org

Other titles you may enjoy from The Mountaineers:

MOUNTAINEERING: The Freedom of the Hills, 6th Edition,
The Mountaineers
The completely revised and expanded edition of the best-selling mountaineering book of all time—required reading for all climbers.

THE HIGH SIERRA: Peaks, Passes, and Trails, *R.J. Secor*
The most complete guide available, covering all known routes to approximately 570 peaks, plus permit information, safety and history.

CLIMBING IN NORTH AMERICA, *Chris Jones*
A reissue of the complete history of North American mountaineering, from the early nineteenth century through the 1970's. Brings to life the climbers and their routes, peaks, and adventures with a storytelling style and historic black-and-white photos.

SIERRA HIGH ROUTE: Traversing Timberline Country, 2nd Edition,
Steve Roper
A guide to a spectacular 195-mile route in the beautiful sub-alpine region of California's High Sierra, from Kings Canyon National Park to northern Yosemite National Park, with overviews of geographical and historical points of interest, maps, difficulty ratings, advice on safety, and more.

75 HIKES IN™ CALIFORNIA'S LASSEN PARK & MOUNT SHASTA REGIONS, *John R. Soares*
A comprehensive guide to popular hiking destinations in the Northern California Cascades. Includes day hikes and extended backpacks, recommendations on gear, safety, and etiquette, plus information on local history and camping options.

100 HIKES IN™ CALIFORNIA'S CENTRAL SIERRA & COAST RANGE, *Vicky Spring;* and **100 HIKES IN™ NORTHERN CALIFORNIA,**
John R. Soares & Marc J. Soares
Two titles in the series of fully-detailed, best-selling hiking guides.